# Gardner Cox

Gardner Cox in his studio, Ipswich Street, Boston.
Herbert Randle, photograph.

SKETCHES FROM LIFE

INTERVIEWS RECORDED AND EDITED BY

*Phoebe Barnes Driver*

WILLIAM L. BAUHAN, PUBLISHER
DUBLIN, NEW HAMPSHIRE

COPYRIGHT © 1995 by PHOEBE BARNES DRIVER

All Rights Reserved. No portion of this book may be reproduced without permission of the publisher, except by reviewers quoting brief passages in newspapers and periodicals.

Library of Congress Cataloging in Publication data:

Cox, Gardner, 1906-1988
Gardner Cox: Sketches From Life / interviews recorded and edited
by Phoebe Barnes Driver.
   p.  cm.
Includes bibliographical references and index.
ISBN 0-87233-112-1
1. Cox, Gardner, 1906-1988—Interviews.  2. Portrait painting, American.  3. Portrait painters—United States—Interviews.  I. Driver, Phoebe Barnes, 1908-  II. Title.
ND237.C78A35   1994
759.13—dc20
[B]                      94-3435
                          CIP

The excerpt from *Robert Kennedy and His Times* by Arthur M. Schlesinger, Jr. © 1978 by Arthur M. Schlesinger, Jr. Reprinted by permission of Houghton Mifflin Company. All Rights Reserved.

The sketches of Robert Frost, John Lord O'Brian, and Felix Frankfurter are courtesy of the National Portrait Gallery, Washington, D.C. James M. Byrne is from "Lawyers Painted by Gardner Cox," Harvard Law Library, Cambridge, Mass. 1984. Self-Portrait, page 2, courtesy of the National Academy of Design, New York. Photograph of the Dylan Thomas portrait is used by permission from Mrs. Winifred Stout. Photographs of Gardner Cox in his studio and Dylan Thomas portrait by Herbert Randle, Waltham, Mass.

William L. Bauhan, Inc., Publisher
Old County Road
Dublin, New Hampshire 03444

Printed in the United States of America

How very exciting the world is. How lucky I was to experience it.
How many satisfactions I have enjoyed—and enjoy—in this life.
After it, I will return to what I was (or *was not*) in 1906.

(From his note books)

—Gardner Cox

# Contents

| | | |
|---|---|---|
| Acknowledgements | | xi |
| Introduction | | xiii |
| 1. | Provincetown and Harvard | 3 |
| 2. | Commissions: Art and War | 28 |
| 3. | Hocking, Whitehead, and James Byrne | 53 |
| 4. | New York Bankers | 78 |
| 5. | Inside Washington: Acheson & O'Brian | 90 |
| 6. | Marshall and Harriman | 110 |
| 7. | Wives' Eye View—and F.F. | 127 |
| 8. | Kissinger | 148 |
| 9. | From Olympus to the Backyard | 170 |
| 10. | Changes in the Arts (I) | 185 |
| 11. | Changes in the Arts (II) | 199 |
| 12. | Kingman Brewster of Yale | 221 |
| 13. | "On Human Nature" | 239 |
| 14. | Levi of the University of Chicago | 247 |
| 15. | Wilmarth Sheldon Lewis | 261 |
| 16. | At the Harvard Fiftieth | 275 |
| Chapter Notes | | 279 |
| Chronology | | 289 |
| Sources | | 293 |
| Index | | 295 |

# List of Illustrations

| | |
|---|---|
| Gardner Cox in his studio | facing title page |
| Gardner Cox, self portrait, 1969 | 2 |
| Phyllis Byrne Cox, sketch, 1940s | 25 |
| Picking Cotton, Georgia; Squad resting, Camp Wheeler, 1944 | 30 |
| Phyllis after Poppy's birth; Kate Cox | 36 |
| Ben Cox listening, c.1946 | 37 |
| Robert Frost, sketches for portrait | 51 |
| James Byrne | 72 |
| Dean Acheson, sketches | 93 |
| John Lord O'Brian, sketches | 106 |
| General George C. Marshall, sketch for portrait | 115 |
| The Harrimans, from the sketchbook, c.1975 | 123 |
| Portrait of Dylan Thomas, 1953 | 142 |
| Felix Frankfurter, sketches; Walter Lippmann, sketch 1952 | 143 |
| Henry Kissinger, sketch for portrait, 1977; chair | 159 |
| Learned Hand, sketch for portrait | 172 |
| James Cox, 1952; "Mop and Ben at the piano", 1946 | 182 |
| James and Poppy Cox as children, 1952 | 183 |
| The Serenity of the Eggs, preliminary sketch | 207 |
| Kingman Brewster in his study, sketch for portrait, 1966 | 229 |
| Edward Levi, sketches for portrait, 1973 | 248 |
| Gardner Cox, self-portrait, 1965 | 274 |

# Acknowledgments

This book is based on the oral history done for the Archives of American Art, Smithsonian Institution. Credit for its publication goes to Gardner Cox's three children: Ben and James Cox, and Poppy Koch. Ben and James, particularly, formed a triumvirate with me to make it possible.

Sally T. Scott has been indispensable in this project. We thank her for her time and encouragement, her archivist's knowledge of G.C.'s work, her superb secretarial skills, and her enthusiastic support. As G.C.'s archivist and secretary since 1965 and close family friend, she helped organize and collect the sketches used here.

The first ten chapters were expertly typed and annotated by Elizabeth Stouffer of Arlington, Mass., the last six chapters by Pat Ciconne of Medway, Mass. I am deeply indebted to them for making sense of my spelling, in particular, and my constant revisions, and for their enthusiasm for the project throughout.

My thanks to John P. McMahon and Frederick S. Voss of the National Portrait Gallery for their generous gift of time in culling the Cox sketches, and their loan of copies for use in this book.

My gratitude goes to Hope Hare for leading me to the Dylan Thomas portrait, which is reproduced here kindness of Mrs. Winifred Stout of Foster, Rhode Island. And thanks also to Herbert P. Randle of Waltham, Mass. for his photographs of G.C.'s work and to the St. Botolph Club of Boston for use of material from the Memorial Exhibition catalogue, including the self-portrait.

I want to thank my publisher, William L. Bauhan, for his patience and his expertise and sensitivity as editor; and W.W. Keen James for his ebullient copy editing, his meticulous preparation of the index, and most of all for faithfully following orders to keep Gardner's voice.

My gratitude also goes to Sarah Forbes Bauhan for her gentle prodding to keep things on track—over and above her fine job of typesetting.

And my special thanks to Bill Driver for his interest and support throughout.

P.B.D.

*September 1994*

# Introduction

An article in the *Washington Post* of May 31, 1975, suggested that someone should do a portrait of portrait-painter Gardner Cox. Here it is. A self-portrait.

In his own words, not in paint, he has portrayed his reactions to people and life. Many of the chapters are insights, laced with anecdotes, of the prominent people he has painted: college presidents; members of the Supreme Court (at least seven); and four secretaries of state, to name a few. Also, he told me, he had been approached to paint President Kennedy. After the assassination, he was asked to do a portrait posthumously. "I've never been able to get the feeling of a person from photographs .... I tried for a year on that Kennedy thing, but it was no use. No use. So, I gave up." Later he painted Robert Kennedy, but the family didn't like it. It is now in the National Portrait Gallery in Washington.

So in the fifties, sixties and seventies, it might be said that Gardner Cox was court painter to Washington. The last, perhaps, because President Carter cut off government funds for official portraits. The Cox Kissinger portrait sneaked in under the December 30th, 1978, deadline.

His inner life, his "being down there where it really is", runs like a motif through people and events. This creates a fugue between his inner and outer life. The main account is from interviews taped by me, plus excerpts from four hours of taping for the Smithsonian.

To go back to the *Washington Post* article. It went on to say that Gardner Cox would have been a portrait-painter's dream: thick, wavy hair; bushy eyebrows above gold-rimmed spectacles; always the jaunty bow tie, and the red suspenders seen or unseen; and always the red or blue bandanna, tucked in the breast pocket of sport or dinner jacket.

He was born in Holyoke, Massachusetts, on January 22, 1906. At that time his mother and father lived in Boston; but they braved the midwinter weather to travel to Holyoke so Dr. Cox, the grandfather, a crusty, much-beloved country doctor could deliver the baby. He turned out to be their only child. His mother was Katherine Gilbert Abbott. She was a fine artist who, before her marriage, had studied at the Beaux-Arts in Paris, winning prizes there. His father was Allen Howard Cox. He was a well-known Boston architect with his own firm. After Gardner had finished Harvard and the Boston Museum School, he persuaded him to take a course in architectural design, 1929-1931, at M.I.T. (Gardner always referred to it as "Tech") and later to join his firm where he stayed for about five years. He already was building a name for himself as a portrait-painter, so he left in 1936—he was already 30—to make painting his full-time career. One can see that he came by his artistic talents very naturally, both genetically and environmentally. When he was five, his parents moved to Cambridge. They bought a lovely old house at 88 Garden Street, which was to be home to him the rest of his life. He was very much a Massachusetts Cantabrigian.

Socially, he was a witty, genial, sophisticated man, with a unique talent for friendship with both men and women. He was a member of many of the elite men's clubs in both Boston and New York, the Tavern in Boston and the Century in New York, to name two. And he was a member of both the National Institute of Arts and Letters and the American Academy of Arts and Sciences, the latter, a rare honor for painters.

He was very fond of his two sons. In the summer he loved to play golf with them on the beautiful, nine-hole golf course in North Haven, Maine. The first and fifth holes pass each other on a ridge overlooking the Camden hills across Penobscot Bay. Deliberate, and sometimes irritatingly slow, he could easily be identified against the skyline by his incipient Tweedledum silhouette, his floppy-brimmed, white duck hat, and his reverse stance. Gardner was a lefty. I played golf with him just once. It was a disaster. On the second hole, I felt faint and staggered off the fairway to lie down before I collapsed. Gardner was stunned. He didn't know what to do. So he sat down beside me, like a faithful dog or horse beside a fallen master, and waited for me to recover. Fortunately, it was late in the afternoon, so no golfers came past. Only one of our good friends, who was walking her dogs, stumbled on this bizarre tableau; and, I may add, she never let us forget it.

And for years he had three season tickets to the Harvard football games. He and his sons always sat on the fifty-yard line, on the Yale side, way up under the roof of the arcade.

As an artist, he spent many hours alone, just reading and thinking. He would say, "You know Phoeb, [To Gardner, I was usually 'Phoeb.'] something is always going on outside my window. A bird may fly across, a streak of color. Or a tree may suddenly have dropped her leaves or taken on the first surprise of snow."

He left a series of notebooks written over a period of time and occasionally cited here, as, for example, his wonderful "tiger's eye" insight into painting at the opening of chapter 10. The notebooks reveal him as something of a poet and a philosopher, and it was in these quiet hours that much of his painting took form. "I do a lot of painting in my head before I put brush to canvas." This was part of what Gardner called his "fly on the wall" technique—"a preliminary act of sustained observation" according to the Boston critic Robert Taylor, who notes that Gardner's initial step in creating a portrait was to study the subject interacting with the environment." * Gardner often refers to this "fly on the wall" approach in these interviews.

No one was allowed to invade his inner sanctum. Although how can one be sure? He was a very compartmentalized man. Fire doors sealed off sections of him.

This book is his account of his journey through life as an artist and a man, a selective account—much of it of his own choosing.

"But no private stuff, Phoeb. No private stuff. I don't care for myself, but I don't want to hurt anyone I'm close to."

Once I thought I might sneak in an insight. I asked him what influence women had had in his life.

"OOOO oo oo," he chuckled. "I just heard a twig snap. I just heard a little twig." That was that, and we both laughed the question aside.

How did it happen that I became the quasi Boswell of Gardner Cox? It started with the Smithsonian Institution and a man named Robert Brown. He was and is the head of their Boston office of the Archives of American Art. Mr. Brown had started interviewing Gardner as part of a program to tape oral histories of men and women prominent in the field of art. These tapes were to be transcribed, edited, and then microfiched for the National Archives. After two sessions, Gardner balked. He said he would continue only if his friend, Phoebe Barnes, did

---

* Robert Taylor's essay in Gardner Cox Memorial Exhibition catalogue, St. Botolph Club, Boston, 1988.

the interviews. I was interviewed by Mr. Brown and given the job.
Why me?

In the first place, Gardner and I had been friends for years. Usually, we saw each other in the summers at North Haven, Maine, at picnics, cocktail parties, summer get-togethers, that sort of thing. We shared a love of the natural Maine landscape and seascape; and also a passion for explaining the Meaning of Life. "E. O. Wilson says that we are not genetically composed to understand God, Phoeb." This while sharing a brilliant sunset over the Camden hills. Our friendship was the kind in which we picked up exactly where we left off, no matter how long the interval between meetings.

In the second place, Gardner knew I had done a lot of work with a tape recorder. I had just finished an oral history of a family we both knew, which was to be privately printed; and he knew I was an intermittent volunteer working at the Radcliffe archives. Our first session took place in North Haven, Maine in July of 1977; our last at my house in Chestnut Hill, Massachusetts, February 6, 1980. Half of the time, we would meet at my place; and half of the time at his Boston studio on Ipswich Street. This last was a great privilege, because for almost two years I was close to his work. These were the years of the Kissinger portrait and its rejection. These were the years of his painting President Brewster of Yale and President Levi of the University of Chicago. And, of course, I never missed an exhibition, no matter where it was. I remember flying down to Washington alone for the day, when he was exhibiting at the Corcoran Gallery. It was a wonderful two years that I was privileged to work so closely with this remarkable man.

We made a pact that everything was to be done very professionally. Friendship was to be put on hold. There were two rules: One, that I was to be paid my regular charge for oral history. (The Smithsonian had refused to subsidize us, although they were eager for the results.) The second rule was that it was to be strictly business and by God! it was. Not at any time in those two years did we so much as share a glass of sherry or a sandwich. Gardner would arrive at my house, we'd gossip a bit, and then get right down to work. The subject had been planned ahead. We both had done our homework. He, to think ahead and jog his memory with notes; and I to get background information at the Boston Athenæum. When we finished taping, he would put on his hat and coat and off he'd go. This would happen in reverse when I went to his studio. But it was not *all* serious business. It couldn't be with him.

He had a wonderful sense of the ridiculous and we wasted a lot of time chuckling and laughing at absurdities. Gardner was a very funny man.

The first ten tapes—there were eighteen—were checked and annotated and put in a loose-leaf notebook. Gardner's dialogue was transcribed complete with pauses, hesitations and guffaws. Most of these have been left alone—to retain the sense of his own voice. (The series of dots . . . in the printed text do not indicate omissions—as is usual—but pauses in his conversation.) There were three copies; one for Gardner, one for the Smithsonian archives, and one for me.

At this point, just as the manuscript was finished, my husband died. It was six months before I got back to Gardner, suggesting that he O.K. the remaining tapes, so that they could be finally edited and typed. He wanted nothing more to do with it. He just didn't want to go back to the project. The impetus in him was dead.

"But what will I do with all the material?"

"Forget it, Phoeb. Forget it. I don't care what you do with it. Burn it, if you want."

I did forget it. Completely. Well almost completely. I guess that's what you do with rejection unless you let it haunt you.

Our friendship eventually resumed where we left off, almost as it was before. Not quite. We had shared too many laughs and confidences to resume completely the pick-up-where-we-left-off earlier rapport. I had been a widow for six years. The pieces had shifted. I saw Gardner very little the last eight years of his life. (He died in 1988.) First, he would call every month or so. "How are you, Phoeb. Is everything all right?" Then, it was every six months. And finally, not at all.

It's a wonder I didn't throw the tapes out with the junk when I remarried, eight years later, and sold my condominium. Everything had lain dormant for eight long years. I had my copy, which I had almost forgotten, too; Gardner's was found by his son in his studio after he had died. The Smithsonian copy has never been found.

His real friends understand that once a friend of Gardner's, unless something awful happened, it was for life. Even now, he is very close through all these tapes and all these pages. Even now, he is a friend I miss.

# Gardner Cox

Gardner Cox, Self-portrait, 1969.
Herbert Randle, photograph.

# I

# Provincetown and Harvard

*Looking back at your life as a painter, let's begin with your college years at Harvard. Were you painting at that time?*

G.C.   Yes, I was painting in the summers. At the end of my freshman year I went down to New York to the Art Students League. And I went to . . . Rockport, yes, Rockport under Hibbard. Aldro T. Hibbard,[1] who was having great success as a landscape painter at that time. In my opinion, he was a good enough teacher—down in the studio on Bearskin Neck. I painted there all summer—two summers.

*Were you doing landscapes?*

G.C.   Those were landscapes, yup. The one summer in New York was anatomy under Bridgman,[2] a very celebrated drawing teacher who they all thought he was going to be Michelangelo, but who had no sense of color at all, so he had to settle for drawing. He was extremely good at it. As a matter of fact he taught us in a very mannered way. Muscles were all bulging, a lot of exaggeration here and there, but worth my spending a lot of time in New York. Before that of course, I'd been painting and drawing for a long time . . . I started this stuff, you know, a long time before I went to Provincetown. I went down to study under Hawthorne. Of course I wasn't very good. It didn't amount to much, but I did it. And then again in the summers from the time I was seventeen on.

*Where did you live in Provincetown when you were seventeen?*

G.C.   I lived in a boardinghouse and ate at the Gray Inn, and I lived with three other men.

*Did they become artists?*

G.C.   Alfred Easton Poor[3] became a very well known architect in New York, still is. And a fellow named John Taylor,[4] who was at Yale and never became well known. He was a very nice man and professional painter. Ended up being a teacher. And the other was . . . uh—a teacher of botany at Stanford University. I suppose he was in his early thirties, and he stayed on and started the Dennis House Players. We all lived together—at least one summer we lived together, and we joined into the nightlife of Provincetown, which was very different from what it is now . . . much more exciting and much more fun.

*In what way?*

G.C.   Oh . . . Mary Heaton Vorse[5] was sort of the Mrs. August Belmont of Provincetown and she had all kinds of people come to stay with her. Eugene O'Neill was a great friend of hers. At that time, he was working out on the dunes. He had a little cottage out near Race Point, and he'd write out there. He'd come in and he was an old, old friend of Mary Heaton Vorse. He was married to Irene, Oona's mother, then. He was around, and Frank Shay,[6] who started the Provincetown Playhouse, was around, and a little newspaperman named Barry, and O'Neill would get angry at him . . . get jealous for no reason possible. He would go off with O'Neill's wife, Irene. They'd go blueberry picking, and one day they came back to the Vorses' and Irene went upstairs, and O'Neill went after her . . . and *Smack! Smack!* She came down with a mouse on her eye as big as an apple.

A lot of things happened around there. I liked O'Neill. A very charming man. I was about seventeen or eighteen years old at that time. Provincetown was . . . sort of the Newport of Greenwich Village. Anyone who could get on a flatcar or had enough money to make it would come to Provincetown. It was very crowded. At night it seemed quiet, very quiet, but there was quite a lot of life going on. People would have parties and everybody would come. And people would see people on the street and say, come on, and they'd go, and sometimes it was very good fun. They weren't necessarily big either. They varied. Sometimes they were quite wild and then sometimes they were very funny. Peter Hunt,[7] the man who painted those decorative hearts and flowers on furniture and so on, was there. He had a little gallery and he was a very entertaining fellow. He was gay—definitely gay—and . . . he was a great fellow for charades. I can remember having charades at the Vorses' house. I can remember Peter coming in with a bunch of celery hanging down in front—as Adam. [*Chuckling*] Of course he had his drawers on, but it was all in good fun. He wasn't fooling around with any of us at all, and they accepted him. Oh, countless funny things happened there.

*Who did you study under?*

G.C.    I studied under Charles W. Hawthorne.[8] He started Provincetown. He went down and started painting classes in the late nineties, I guess. At the turn of the century. I don't know exactly when it was. In those days painters . . . very good painters . . . were . . . rather housebroken, and he was quite elegant, well dressed. He had a large class. Quite a famous class. The best summer class in the country at that time, as far as I know. And he operated out of New York. He was from Maine originally, I think, but he went down there and became a very successful man. He was a member of the National Institute of Arts and Letters, and a member of the Century Club—a gentleman. Artists tried to be gentlemen instead of bohemian in those days, but they were by natural temperament bohemians sometimes. He would have this large class and they would go out and paint. They'd paint all week. They'd paint outdoors and there was also a big studio. You could work in the big studio if it was a bad day. You'd do still lifes or a model. Not a nude model. On bad days the model would pose. I'm not sure she wouldn't pose on good days, but the main thing was they were working outside. They worked all along the docks . . . all around the town, and, when I was there, they weren't the only artists working there. Some other people would come along too: George Elmer Brown[9] and a man called Hopkins[10] and a few others at that time. So, when you'd go around the town, you'd find people painting all over the place. Oh, there'd be women with hats with veils around them—you know—couldn't keep a hat on. There'd be young ones and old ones . . . all different ages working away . . . set their easels up. It was nice, very nice. It was congenial in a competitive way without thinking of it in that way.

People would paint in the morning and afternoon, all day long—everybody. And, uh . . . on Saturday morning they'd go up to the studio. There was a great rack in the studio about eighteen, nineteen, twenty feet long, two sides, the kind you see people using now to carry plate glass. And this rack would be loaded both sides with pictures on little shelves like an easel shelf. Then we'd all get in there and sit around. It was kind of like little bleachers. It was a big studio. Before then, the monitors had got the first bunch of pictures up, and there'd be say twelve pictures on the rack by one person. And . . . uh . . . you'd be waiting there, and at about two minutes of ten you'd hear this dog—a great big collie—a very beautiful collie . . . come in and bark. This was Hawthorne's dog; and then Hawthorne would come in. Hawthorne was a big man. He'd have on white flannel trousers and sneakers or white shoes, and a nice tweed coat and loose white shirt and a necktie. As I say, he was rather elegantly dressed. Very respectably dressed, as we thought fitting for painters in those days. He might have been a businessman. That was the tone of the times. And then he criticized the pictures. He'd have a pointer and he'd say what he thought was good about them, what he thought was bad about them, and give general suggestions of what they might do to make them better. He was a great colorist. You could call it a theory. He disregarded lines. Lines were just when two different colors came together opposed to one another. Think of it that way.

So people all worked with putty knives and palette knives. A great deal was done with the putty knife. This was not a requirement, but, essentially, the idea of the whole course was to go there and loosen up on your color. And a lot of teachers of painting came there in the summer to free themselves a little bit. They'd get away from any finickerly stuff. They just put the tones down and some of their pictures were quite lovely as a result of this. French impressionists had done this in the past, but they tried to put in all the colors they could. They put purples and maroons and oranges in the shadows.

*Did that influence your painting?*

G.C.   Yes, it certainly did for a while; and probably I've never lost some of it. I see people who are still doing it and it's a little overdone. It was self-conscious the way some people did it. Hawthorne did it very well. His things were really very joyous. He'd say . . . and he had a funny little sibilance in his speech—he often referred to "jooshy color." He'd say, "this is very jooshy." And his color was "jooshy." It was a very fortunate effect he had there. I've got a couple of his things. He had very good what we call "taste" today. He was a masculine man . . . and his work was tenderly done. He was really damn good. His pictures still do well. And once a week he'd have a demonstration, painting with a putty knife and so on, with a model. A very typical model would be one with a straw hat on so her face would be partly in shadow... and a white shirt or a blue shirt, reflecting the light upward. He'd do one of these demonstrations a week and, at the end of the summer, we'd draw lots for them. On good days we'd stand around or sit on the ground and he'd paint on some dock and we'd watch him.

*Were you down there two summers?*

G.C.    At least.

*And then you went to Rockport?*

G.C.    I went to Rockport after my sophomore year.

*Wasn't that a tremendous contrast to Provincetown?*

G.C.    Yes, a contrast. Hibbard did some very good landscapes at that time. He came from somewhere around Boston. He wasn't an extraordinarily cultivated fellow. He hadn't gone to Harvard after high school and that kind of business, but he went to the Museum School and started to paint very well. He was very talented. He painted very much like Willard Metcalf,[11] who was really a little bit better. But he was damn near as good as Metcalf when he started off as a freshman. He won the highest prize in the Boston Museum School. He was the fair-haired boy around there. The Boston Guild thought he was the greatest guy in the guild. And... uh... some of his earlier pictures still hold up and are excellent now.

*Was living in Rockport the same as Provincetown?*

G.C.    No. It was not at all the same. That was one of the reasons, at least a partial reason, it was a good place to go, because it wasn't quite as distracting. Provincetown got quite distracting after awhile. You could really tear around a lot at night. It became a life in itself.

*Before we leave Provincetown, have you got one incident that stands out in your memory?*

G.C.    Well... I've got a number. I'm trying to think of one that jumps to my mind. I used to go back in the fall sometimes, because I had a girl there—Mrs. Vorses' daughter, Ellen. That's why I was around the Vorses' so much. Ellen and her older brother, Heaton Vorse, we were all friends, and so was John Taylor a friend of theirs. Taylor liked Ellen, too; so we were both around quite a lot. I came back to see her in the fall. This was before I went to college . . . and . . . uh . . . Frank Shay would get drunk once in awhile. I remember one of those times when they had an opening which he directed at the Playhouse. They had been working up this thing and rehearsing and then had the opening night. It was singularized by Frank Shay getting drunk and crashing through the scenery behind the scenes. He was just walking through woodland scenes [*Laughing*], you know, ripping the canvas apart. Oh, it was terrible! *rrippp*! That was Frank Shay absolutely smashing everything to pieces. [*Much laughter*] He did this once in a long while. Not often. And he had a wife named Fern and a little baby.

I was sitting around the Vorses' one night, and O'Neill was there, and Mrs. Vorse and Ellen, I guess. I suppose Heaton, too. And suddenly, up the path came Fern Shay with the baby in her arms. And she was panting, and she said that Frank was drunk and he was raising hell and smashing everything. He had bounced the baby off the wall a couple of times, then picked it up and just forward passed it, and she'd picked it up and run up the street with it. Yes, he'd picked the baby up and plugged it against the wall, and she'd caught it on the rebound, kind of, and took off up the street. Mrs. Vorse rushed down to Shay's house, but I didn't. O'Neill was a calm fellow about this kind of stuff; so I went down with him. Mrs. Vorse was a very spirited and courageous woman. A great person . . . she really was a great personality. She took off at a great run . . . went down very fast. But we walked down the street, the regular main street . . . Commercial Street . . . so crowded these days—we walked down. I suppose it was a hundred yards away. We got there and Shay had passed out. Before he passed out Mrs. Vorse, to shock him into some kind of sensibility, rushed up to him—some other people were there, other neighbors—and stuck up her chin and said, "Hit me!" And he came up with an uppercut that lifted her off the floor and laid her out flat. [*Great laughter*] Absolutely flat! And then he passed out. It didn't get through to him at all. It was just a chin sticking out and he let her have it. [*Laughter*]

*Was she out when you got there?*

G.C.   Yeah. Sure. Sure. She wasn't badly injured; but when we came in she was out. So was Shay. Fern Shay was a painter and what he'd done was he'd gone out—and put his foot through every one of her pictures. He'd taken an iron stove absolutely apart. He'd got it all apart with ashes all around, and he'd upset the bookcases; he ... it was a real mess. He's done a really heroic job. This was a tremendous piece of work of its kind [*Laughing*] O'Neill, who'd gone to Princeton, came out and said, "Typical of a Harvard man." And he knew I was going to Harvard. He was amused ... but not shocked. They kind of admired Shay's performance. [*Laughing*] There were only two things that he had not been able to smash ... and the other people who had been witness before we got there, of course they were trying to keep him from doing this, but he was throwing them off like Mrs. Vorse. He was a tall, wiry guy—and crazed with drink, of course. One of the things left was a little framed pledge not to drink. They said he'd taken it off the wall and he'd jumped up and down on it [*Much laughter through all this*] and hadn't been able to smash it. He tried it again—and again. He'd— uh ... he'd taken the stove apart, but he couldn't smash this thing. Then the other was a plate of soup with not a drop spilled out of it ... resting on the *upturned* bookcase. I remember those two things particularly. But all of Fern's pictures ... a disaster. That was one incident; but there were a great many others.

*What happened to him?*

G.C. Oh, he died eventually; but he started the Provincetown Playhouse and he was very much respected by everybody.

*Did Fern stick with him?*

G.C. I don't know how long; but she didn't leave him on account of that. They were quite understanding about that kind of stuff. Probably quite rightly. Of course, O'Neill's wife left him. That was Oona's mother. She was a very pretty woman; but he was very jealous, unreasonably jealous.

*How about O'Neill? Did he drink at that time?*

G.C. Oh yes. Oh yes, but not like Shay. He'd drink now and then, but I never saw him drunk. I mean he wasn't drunk when I was around. He'd go on periodic drunks. He'd come to town to Mrs. Vorse's. Mrs. Vorse was a lady. She was born a lady, so to speak, with a genteel upbringing. Her father was a professor at Amherst or something like that. And she married a man named Vorse. She was a women's-lib type.

She had all kinds of children and had had all kinds of affairs. She was a plain, gaunt woman, but she had a lot of charm and a lovely voice and manner. And she was mixed up in all kinds of labor disputes and she'd been to jail as a result. She was the leading person in that town when I was there. Very much so. She had a very nice old house. It was very free and easy around it, you know.

*What happened to Ellen?*

G.C.  Ellen's married to somebody. I haven't seen her for fifty-five years. We broke up when I went to college and kind of got running around.

*Were you painting when you were in college?*

G.C.  Yes. I was painting right along, although I frittered my life away in college.

*What did you major in?*

G.C.  I majored in English. I did the regular things in my freshman year, you know and then I concentrated on English. I took fine arts courses too, and a couple of courses in drawing. I did those to draw and, also, they were a great help to me, because you had to have three C's and a D in order to keep off probation. I could always get high marks in the drawing classes with no trouble at all, so I only had to get another C or D. I really wasted a lot of time in college, but I had an awful lot of fun. But I never was in any danger of getting into trouble academically, because I had those two drawing courses. Most of the time, actually, I did pretty well.

*Where did you live?*

G.C.  I lived in Gore Hall my freshman year and then moved . . . to a house at 59 Plympton Street which has since been torn down. It was where the Fly Club lawn is now. I lived there for two years. Then I resigned at the end of my junior year to paint. Actually it was a rather fruitless year. I lived at home; but I really hung around college a lot and I had so much fun. It was almost like still being there without going to classes.

*Were you able to paint at home?*

G.C.  I painted around but it wasn't a good year.

*Did you go back to Harvard and get your degree?*

G.C.   No. I left in perfect standing. I wasn't fired or anything. I just resigned. In fact, what happened was I completed my field of concentration in three years, and then the last year I was to take all the courses you had to take, like German. I took German the first year and hated it. I'm not good about that kind of thing and I didn't pass it. Didn't try to, really. And ... uh ... there was Philosophy and there was going to be a science course. They were just requirements and I didn't want to do them. I thought I'd do better if I got out and painted. But, as I've said, that year didn't amount to much. I just fooled around and had a good time, but still drew for the *Lampoon*.

*You were on the* Lampoon *?*

G.C.   Yeah ... oh yes. I was kind of a star on the *Lampoon*. After all, I'd been painting and drawing for a long time. So, I had done a whole lot of stuff by the time I got to college. Quite a lot ...

*Had you ever done anything humorous before you went to the* Lampoon?

G.C.   Oh, I think so. I did things for the paper and things. Sure. Sure. I'd been drawing a lot all my life. I did a whole lot of covers for the *Lampoon*. I did many. I did many. They were pretty good, some of them. I've got a big pile of 'em. I meant at one time to put them in a frame ... a lot of 'em ... about ten or twelve of them in a big frame, to put up in the house for decoration, but I never did it.

*Didn't you enjoy working for the* Lampoon? *I think "Lampy" riding backwards in full armor is wonderful.*

G.C.   I'd never noticed that until you pointed it out to me. I never heard anybody mention it before. *Lampoon* had a fifteen-hundred-dollar prize ... which was a big prize in those days, four or five thousand dollars today at least. They didn't give it very often. And I got it. I finally used it to go abroad with, to travel around. I went to Washington. It lasted me quite a long time. So I did a lot of those covers. I continued to do them the year I was out, you see.

*Were your mother and father supportive of that year off?*

G.C.   They couldn't help it. I don't think they thought much of it; but there was nothing much they could do about it. The next year, which would have been my first year out of college, I went to the Museum School. I realized it wasn't working, this fooling around, so to get more discipline I went to the Museum School, into the intermediary year. I skipped all the first year where they do cast-drawing . . . warming them up. I'd done all that, and so I went into one of the portrait classes. And . . . after a while I did pretty well there.

*This is the first time you've mentioned portraits. Was this the first time you really worked on them?*

G.C.  No. I'd done drawing of people lots. I did a whole series for the *Lampoon* of portraits of professors, series in which they'd have their picture and a poem at the bottom of the page. Kittredge[12] I did, and Lowes,[13] a number of them.

*Have you got any of them?*

G.C.  Kittredge—and—in a portfolio someplace. And then I'd drawn people down in Provincetown. It was all around me at home, you know—I did my mother and my father, things like that. The first commission, the first time I painted for money . . . was down at West Chop . . . one of the Dalton girls. Little Fratty Dalton? Kay Dalton's younger sister. She was a cute little kid and they wanted a drawing of her. I did this one of her the summer before I went to college. I had been in Provincetown, and I went down to West Chop after Labor Day or something like that.

*There was an early period when you did a lot of children. Did this lead you into it?*

G.C.  No. The one that really led me into it was . . . well, I'll go back a little bit here. I went to the Museum School and then I'd go to M.I.T. as a special student (which you could do then) in the afternoons and evenings. They went to classes at Tech in the morning and they'd do their design, their architecture, every afternoon and evening. They worked every night, you know. And . . . when I was at Tech, I ran into Dick White,[14] who was a sculptor in town at that time. He was sharing a studio with Joe Coletti.[15] I'd known him in college some, and we'd been friends. We'd have lunch together. He was a very good friend of mine who I haven't seen for a long time. A feller I picked right up with. I saw a lot of him in those days, and they wanted me to do little Peter White. So I took a crack at Peter White, and they tell me now it is terrible. [*Laughing*] We all thought it was good at the time. They thought it was great and it looked pretty good, as I remember it. Ellie Lamont[16] saw it... she was very fond of Neilly,[17] you know... and that next summer I went up to North Haven and did little Lansing Lamont. That's when I really began doing kids. And I got a lot of them to do and some of them were pretty good before I got through.

*Which one of the Lamont children did you do?*

G.C.   I did Lansing. I went down to New York to do Teddy and failed. I did little Ellie[18] ... young Ellie ... at the end of that first summer. She came down and I did her in Cambridge ... in my house.

*When did you do my son-in-law, Johnny Caner?*

G.C.   I did him that first summer in North Haven.

*How were they done?*

G.C.   In pastels. They were all done in pastels. I did a man or two at that time, and I went up to Worcester to do one of the Wheeler children.

*How much did you get for them?*

G.C.   Probably a hundred dollars ... I think I started off at a hundred fifty, then got up to around three hundred, something like that.

*When did you sort of work into adults?*

G.C.   Right along there.. I think I did one of Mr. Nichols who was a neighbor—Arthur Boylston Nichols Sr.,[19] a very nice man. I got an empty store with a big front window not far from my family's house, and ... uh ... I made it into a studio, and did him there. I can do a lot better now, but it was quite good. I'm sure they've still got it.

*Was it done in oils?*

G.C.   Yes. Oh, I'd been painting in oils a long time, you see. After a while I did some children in oils, after I started doing them in pastels. They weren't fuzzy pastels. I never relied on this caking stuff. Caking drops off if it's jarred and you lose half the stuff. Mine were quite permanent pastels.

*Did you enjoy the kids while you were working on them?*

G.C.   Oh yes. Oh sure. . . . Peter White was really very young . . . a baby almost. I had a very quick memory, a pretty strong visual memory, and I was young. Then I had ways of doing it. I'd do parts and put them together. I'd do a little piece of an eye, a nose, an ear, then I'd do a little piece of another part; and then I'd put these together. I did a lot of them all over the place. I went to Rochester, New York, for one.

*Didn't you have a hard time with your grandson, Danny, getting him to stay still?*

G.C.   He was a little too young. Now he's two and a half . . . he's about ready. Well, I didn't want to get typed doing children, so I did a great big picture of my father . . . I remember I had a show at the old Junior League building on Arlington Street, and I took in this huge picture. And I think I used . . . yes, I put in Johnny Caner's picture . . . even though he was cross-eyed. He *was* cross-eyed, you know. He was definitely cross-eyed.

*Well, I know he is in the picture. Did you get a degree from the Museum School?*

G.C.   No degrees anywhere. Never got a degree except from high school. You don't get degrees from the Museum School. They'll write you a certificate; but I didn't want to go through their fourth year. There really wasn't any need for me to do it. In the summers at that time, I went straight to Tech all the time. I did four years of design in two and a half years by going always in the summer. All through the year. There were a lot of special students. John Churchill was a special student, and Nat Saltonstall was a special student. Phil Graves came later as a special student. They took in people like that who'd gone to college somewhere else and then just came into design. They didn't get degrees.

*Was that your first association with Nat Saltonstall?[20]*

G.C.   No. I knew him in college. He was in the Spee[21] as a matter of fact. That's where I got to know him. My . . . uh . . . closest friend in college was Joe Wheelwright. But he got fired and went out west.

*Fired? For what?*

G.C.   Falling in love with Nancy Hale. Nancy Hale ran him out of college because he couldn't do any work. He was a very bright fellow, you know ... uh ... as bright as he could be, in fact. You had to have those two C's and a D and that was it. If you got below and stayed below more than one time ... out you went. That was it. He got fired his freshman year and, of course, came back. They gave you a second chance and then he did all right until he ran into Nancy Hale. And he and ... uh ... Nancy Hale and Aggie Murchie and some other guy—I can't remember who it was now—they had kind of a little foursome. They used to go into the studio I've got now, I think. You know the second one ... downstairs. I think her father, old Phil Hale,[22] had that studio then. I think that's the one they went into and moused around. Nobody did very much, you know, in those days. It was pretty innocent. And Joe was madly in love with her. He used to write poems to her. I remember one of them ... "Leaves whirling" ... and then the last line ... "Oh, Nancy, if only you would charge my soul with only the love that you can give." [*Laughing*]

I used to say "Some day you're going to laugh your head off about this."

"God!" he went, "*WRRRRO!*" [*Laughing*]

I used to make it awfully hard for him. I really did.

I told you about Eaton[23] making it hard for him? About "Gabriel"? I found out they had names for one another. Aggie Murchie was "Miss Lollipop", or something ... and Wheelwright was "Gabriel." And Eaton found this out. He didn't find it out from me, though. I certainly wouldn't have hesitated to tell him because we were riding Joe about this. It was awfully pure ... the purest kind of love. And I remember Eaton was rather coarse and said, "Hello, Gabriel. How's your horn?"

And Wheelwright went, "*Sssssss.*"

They were in the club and he didn't want to hit him in the club. [*Much laughter*] I thought it was pretty awful myself. We were all pure then. Pretty holy stuff it was, you know, that kind of love. So he ... uh ... didn't think of anything carnal. But he got two C's and an E. And out he went. He couldn't get the guy to up the E to a D minus. [*Laughter*] So then ... Nat and I became close friends ... special friends.

*Didn't you paint Fred Eaton just recently?*

G.C. About three years ago.

*And hasn't he been after you to paint Justine?*[24]

G.C. Yes. He even sent me a check for a thousand dollars, this winter, as a gentle prod. Of course, I haven't cashed it. I haven't torn it up or anything. Just there in a little file someplace. I'll try to do it sometime. I don't know whether I can or not. I'm feeling all right, but I'm not sure how sharp I am on this stuff. The picture of Bailey Aldrich[25] is going along now, but I should have done it quicker. Yet it may come out very well indeed. We have a lot of fun talking. He's turned out to be quite different from what I knew of him. We sing and he's got a very good and ribald sense of humor. He usually sings towards the end of the sitting. He knows a lot of old songs and I chime in. And I hum a little piece and he takes it right up. And altogether we have a good time, probably too much fun. Talk too much. We both talk quite a lot. He doesn't seem all that busy . . . at least he doesn't seem to mind coming a lot. It's a very good pose.

*To go back to your career. What was your father's architectural firm?*

G.C.   Putnam and Cox. He was the Cox and Mr. Putnam was William E. Putnam, who had gone to M.I.T. with him. Mr. Putnam had been to Harvard first. He was a track star and he was a great tennis player. He used to play with Mrs. Shurcliff[26] and they used to win a lot of things together. His father was a banker in Boston and he was one of the Putnam family . . . a very nice fellow. He had admired my father at Tech and he was the one who asked him to come back from Beaux-Arts—about the year nineteen hundred, something like that . . . that's where he met my mother . . . and Mr. Putnam said he'd pay his way back. My father was a very good student at Tech and he did very well at the Beaux-Arts. He was a very good designer. He had a good sense of proportion indeed. An artist. And Putnam had this great faith in him and offered to pay his way back if he would go into the Boston Athenaeum competition which was a nationwide competition . . . the biggest that had been in the country for quite a while. McKim, Mead and White wanted to do it and Carrère and Hastings and all of them . . . Cass Gilbert . . . the lot.

*What is the date on this?*

G.C.   About 1902. And they were right in there . . . all these big offices. Guy Lowell . . . all the big architects[27] all over the place. They were going to move the Athenaeum . . . pull up stakes and put it where the Ritz is now.

*Was the Athenaeum where it is now?*

G.C.   Oh, yes; but they figured for various reasons they didn't have enough room... they needed to expand and so on. And they were going to get the land... (the land where the Ritz is now), which you can see was the prime spot in the town on which to build. So my father came back and got himself a room down on State Street... and working all alone he did the whole thing himself. Putnam didn't work on it at all. Everything himself. Rendered it and... most firms had one main designer, and they'd have a renderer rendering it, and another man do certain drawings. But my father did the whole damn thing himself.

This led eventually to a move among the trustees... Rose Nichols and Amy Lowell being two of them. Rose Nichols was a great mover in this. She had been a friend of my father's. And... uh... they persuaded people not to move on it. Actually I think they were right, now as I look back on it. It's a lovely old building and so on. And so, it was never built... which he accepted at the time without thinking very much of it. He told me he felt he'd win another competition. He was very confident. But, if it had been built, it would have altered his whole career, my bringing-up and everything else. Then he'd have had the building under his belt, and he would have been like Charles Platt or Cass Gilbert... who was a cousin of my mother's... a big shot in those days. He was well able to compete with them as an artist and this competition put him on the map all right. Then he and Putnam went into partnership. He did pretty well. He did a lot of things and he was very imaginative... uh... did a lot of work... but the firm never sank out of sight or dissolved during the Depression when a great many firms foundered.

*What did he build?*

G.C.   Oh, they built a lot of things. He did a great many of the buildings at Mount Holyoke College, for example. The big buildings there. And he did a wonderful library... the Frost library at Amherst. He did a lot of things at Amherst College. But the library is a beauty. It's a lovely building. Then he did the Unitarian building next to the State House... just an eclectic building. Then he did Carver Street, that little complex of brick buildings, since torn down. He did a great many other things. He did a lot of houses, but... uh... he didn't do any skyscrapers. He was a succesful architect and he taught at the Tech for a while when he came back... as a designer; and he used to be on the committee for Rhodes scholarships. He was very respected among architects. And then he went into partnership with Putnam, and Putnam was a very nice man who turned out to be rather a lame duck, architecturally.

*Your mother had been painting at the Beaux-Arts. Did she continue her painting after she was married?*

G.C. Well, she had me. She was quite temperamental and never really exhibited again. She was quite old when she got married... about thirty-eight. She was older than my father but she seemed a lot younger than she was. When she died she had the figure of a girl. She was seventy; but she didn't seem old to us at all. In fact, she seemed young.

*Have you any of her paintings?*

G.C. Oh, there are some around the house. Sure... some of them. She was a very gifted woman. She won the... uh... bronze medal in the International Exposition in France in 1903, or whenever it was. That was a big thing. She got a diploma for it. This for a young woman was pretty good.

*Gardner, don't you think it's extraordinary how many artists and writers come from families who are artists and writers?*

G.C. Well, my family had lots of that. My mother's sister... I believe there were ten children in my mother's family and there was a twenty year span between her oldest sister and her... Aunt Dora. A first-class character. She was a very good sculptress. She's the one who went to Europe and was so seasick and never came back. She went over to England as a young woman and got so seasick on the way over that she lived there until she was eighty-eight and never came home. Some doctor... some damn fool doctor... told her it would kill her. [*Laughing*] And she believed it. And... uh... she had a very elegant life in England. She never married and... I imagine they didn't think anything of it in those days... she lived with a woman named Marian Ferguson for years and years. Marian Ferguson was the daughter of Queen Victoria's doctor. Apparently, they had quite a life with a sort of a —not a salon... but they had quite a lot of people around. And my aunt was a sculptress... quite a successful one. She did a bust of Octavia Hill[28]... in London. It was apparently a very good thing. She was a talented woman. Then my mother's cousin was Cass Gilbert. He was president of the American Academy of Arts and so forth. So, there's quite a lot of that kind of thing in my family.

*And your father's side? Were your father's family talented?*

G.C.   No, not beyond my father. My father's father was a doctor in Holyoke and he was sort of an eccentric . . . very much a character. I was very proud of him. He . . . uh . . . he collected a library . . . a library good enough so he had a library card made. And he played the violin. He was an unusual man. He had some artistic leanings all right. He played the violin in his office, and when people came in he wouldn't stop playing. That kind of stuff. I was just old enough to remember him when he died. I think I was six when he died. And I remember the church at his funeral was just jammed with people and out into the street. He was a very beloved doctor, not just of the rich. He took care of a lot of poor people . . . a lot of people for nothing. He was a gruff man . . . I think a saddish man. He had a melancholy streak in him. He was a big man and he did all kinds of kindly things. He took things into his own hands. And he had a horse and his horse was named "Dinah." He'd drive around and Dinah'd know what to do, you know. He'd drop off and go over a fence and Dinah would keep going around the block. He took care of the mill hands among other people.

One day he went into this mill hand's hovel . . . a little place . . . to deliver his wife of a child. And there the wife was . . . there was no furniture . . . she was lying on grass or hay, so to speak . . . very very poor, having this child. It was very run down indeed and . . . uh . . . he delivered the child and then in the door came the husband . . . drunk. And . . . uh . . . my grandfather was so sore that he beat this bird up and knocked the hell out of him. He beat him up and went out . . . came back and took care of the woman later on. And he didn't see the husband again. A year later a nice-looking young feller came up to him in the street . . . a strong, big, nice fellow . . . and he said, "I want to shake your hand." he said. "I was the fellow you beat up. And I've never touched a drop of liquor since." That's nice, you know. He'd straightened that fellow out.

There's lots of things like that about him. There was a lawyer who was giving some old widow a hard time and he went to the lawyer's office and . . . uh . . . told him not to do this. The lawyer said something and [*Laughing*] he picked the lawyer up—he picked the lawyer up and hugged him like a bear until he fainted. Then he dropped him to the floor and went out and the lawyer straightened everything out. [*Laughing*]

Then there was a priest . . . a priest . . . there are a lot more of these stories but these are the three I remember. Well, my grandfather was taking care of this very poor family and they didn't have any money to buy medicine with. So he gave them twenty-five dollars for medicine for this sick woman... or child... or whatever it was. He gave them money to get medicine. He came back in a couple of days and said, "How's it working out? Have you given her the medicine?" And they said, "No we gave the money to the priest." And he said, "Which priest?" And they told him which priest got the money. And he went [*Laughing*] all over town looking for this guy and he finally found him and grabbed him by the shirtfront and said [*Much laughter*] "You get the money back where it belongs in an hour... within an hour... or I'll knock the stuffing out of you." And the priest slunk off, and they got the money back and the medicine, and everything was all right. People liked this, you know.

*Was your father an only child?*

G.C.  No. No. He had... I had an uncle who was rather like my grandfather. Uncle Stanley. He was a doctor. My father had two brothers and a sister. He was the oldest. And there's another story I remember. This hypochondriac my father knew well came in and my grandfather went on playing the violin. He kept on playing and after a while... he played for a long time, something like fifteen or twenty minutes. And this feller finally said, "Aren't you going to do anything for me, Doctor?" And my grandfather said, "What's the matter with you?" And he said, "I've got a terrible cold." And my grandfather said, "I've been playing for fifteen minutes and I haven't heard a sneeze out of you yet." "*Rrrrrrr... Owwowwoww.*" And the guy never came back again.

So, he wasn't very artistic... he was educated. He came from Vermont and went out to Michigan to study medicine after the Civil War and then came back and settled down outside of Holyoke, Massachusetts. All the big mills were there.

*Were they Slater mills?*

G.C.  They were Skinner mills. Oh, he took care of the Skinners. My father was a great friend of theirs, of course. The Skinners were the big ones. No. Whiting. There were some Whitings. The Slater mills were in Webster.

*To go back to your career as an architect, how many years were you in your father's firm?*

G.C.   It was ... uh ... about five, until '36.

*Did Nat Saltonstall go in with you?*

G.C.   We went in there together and a another fellow from the Tech. He wasn't a partner ... that feller went in as a draftsman and we went in as draftsmen too, as a matter of fact. Nat and I went right along there ... and then I left. Nat stayed there. It became Saltonstall and Morton eventually. He stayed there and then my father died and Mr. Putnam got out. They were mixed up with Linc Boyden[29] and Cecil Wylde[30] and Mr. Putnam ... a lot of 'em ... sort of a combination, who were independent using the same offices. Then Nat and Oliver Morton[31] carried on. Morton had been in the firm a very long time. My father had picked him up out of ... at Andover. He was a wonderful fellow and he was a very very able man. He became partner with Nat, and then they both died and the firm went; but it lasted a very very long time.

*Didn't you do the Frederic Winthrop house in Ipswich while you were there?*

G.C.   We altered the house, we didn't build it. Yes, I did that. Nat had nothing to do with it. We'd take different jobs, of course. I was the one in charge of that one. Oliver Morton and I did that. They had this great big old house down there ... a great big old house that old man Winthrop had. I don't know whether it had been in the family for a long time, but certainly the old man had it. Well, I tell you it was a very gloomy house. It was a great big, awfully gloomy place. Very heavy ... dark. When Fred married Angela[32] we went down to do it over. It was my job, but Morton and I did it. Morton was a very experienced fellow indeed so we did it together. Yes, I did a lot about that house, but I had lots behind me helping out with certain practical details. Oh, we made a very nice house out of that. It's very cheerful and nice now. We broke up the inside of it. It hasn't changed much outside. Changed some. We had a good landscape man come in ... Cheney ... he did a lot of stuff. It turned into a very cheerful house.

*Then, didn't you do Dick and Neilly White's house in Cohasset?*

G.C.   Yes, that was the first one. Yes, I did that house.

*You didn't get your round room?*

G.C.   God! How we fought over that one! It wasn't a round room. It was one room above the other. I had a little unit with a bedroom upstairs and then a little spiral staircase. Just a little iron thing you could go around like they have in lighthouses ... they're stock things. And I put it in the corner so it wouldn't take up any room. The bedroom upstairs and a little dressing room downstairs ... a little living room, too ... a study. A living place where you could dress and have a fireplace. The children out in the other part of the house ... and they'd have it all to themselves. Big windows looking out from the bedroom, and downstairs, a little terrace. It was a hell of a good thing, I thought, and I couldn't wait to go down and tell them about it. [*Chuckling*] I remember Morton saying, "When you get through with them, there won't be a shred of that thing left." He was correct ... correct. They said, what were they going to do when they got old? Would they go down a circular staircase at eighty? Oh, no! [*Laughing*]

Neilly was very stubborn, I thought. She and I both thought the other was stubborn. Neilly really was fond of me. She's fond of me now; but she was tough as hell. She spread word about me that I was absolutely impossible to work with, got angry, roaring like a bull, and she couldn't sleep at night and all that kind of stuff. White and I never had any trouble, but Neilly and I got into a terrible jam about this thing. My father would say, "Don't let them push you around." So I went down there like somebody coming out in football, ready to kill everybody. I'd meet them head-on saying "That's nonsense what are you thinking of," and of course it made them mad. [*Laughing*] I learned a lot on that job. I noticed when the others in the firm went down they were very tactful. I never did any of that kind of stuff again.

And there was the fight about the terrace. Neilly had a friend, Peggy Porter's older sister ... what was her name? Isabelle. Isabelle Porter. She was a landscape architect and very nice. She wanted to put a little terrace outside the house about four feet ... three and a half feet wide. No good for anything. Nothing. It should have been a terrace about twenty-five feet wide. It would have been just perfect for the house. Be a nice place where you could get out and move around a little bit. No. She wasn't going to have it. There was going to be a stone parapet so it really was going to cramp you right in. In every way it was obviously lousy. Platt was very good about that ... Geoff's father. Always had an ample terrace. You can hardly overdo it; but Isabelle was sticking to this and, of course, Neilly was backing her up ... just on principle. Neilly would back her up on anything, no matter what, just because I wasn't for it. [*Laughing*] I can remember presenting reasons and

Isabelle wanted examples. One example: one of the Platt houses with a generous ample terrace, . . . the evidence was tightening around Isabelle . . . the reasons were getting hard to brush off. She could see she was getting in atight spot. She said, "Well, even if it's better, I don't want it." [*Laughing*] And . . . and . . . Neilly agreeing with her. It made me very angry.

*What other houses did you build?*

G.C.   We did the Doug Byerses'[33] house in Andover. We did a house out in Weston and we did some . . . we did a nightclub and some part of Copley Square. There were some more. The first job I ever did, if you want to know [*laughing*], was a little alteration to Neilly and Dick's house up in North Haven. You know the gin mill . . . the red house?

*I lived there two summers.*

G.C.   Well, then you know it has the main part and then there's a little thing that shoots out towards the road . . . rather low where the kitchen is. And you know above the kitchen there are a couple of rooms where the dormer windows are? Well, I put in the room upstairs with the dormer windows. First job I did. [*Laughing*] That's absolutely *the* first. The first.

*Where did you stay when you were up there?*

G.C.   I stayed with them. I was very close to them for a long time. I used to go down to Cohasset . . . Giff Stewart[34] and I. And then I got married and they were down there . . . uh . . . Giff went off to Framingham and it just kind of . . . I used to see them once in a while. Now I don't see them much at all.

*When did Phyllis come into your life?*

G.C.   I was a great friend of Dick Scott's . . . killed in World War II . . . and he was a great friend of hers and I heard about her. And I met her . . . I met her at a dance at Ronald Lyman's house . . . uh . . . several years before I married her. And . . . uh . . . I put a soda siphon on her—which intrigued her, apparently.

*How did you happen to do that?*

G.C.   Well, we got into an argument and I picked the soda siphon up and just put it on her. [*Chuckling*] I wasn't really angry. It was kind of comical. She got . . . she got quite vehement about something so I put the soda thing on her and she thought it was very funny. And it was funny in its way. I never thought much about it again but she reminded me of this. And the next time was at . . . Jean Sears's. My mother had died. It was about a month or so later . . . and Jean said, "Do you want to come?" And I did. Phyllis was a great friend of Jean's; Jean Sears was about her best friend. They were very good friends . . . yeah . . . old friends. It was a fancy-dress thing and I went to that. And then I . . . I was kind of taken by her. She was beautiful . . . beautiful . . . and I was struck by her. They were all going skiing in Jaffrey, New Hampshire. She was sort of Charlie Pierson's girl. He was kind of the leader of the group . . . of the skiers, I mean. And she said, "Why don't you come along?"

And I said, "Well, maybe I will."

And then I didn't think much about it. I didn't think I'd go, maybe. And I was working late at the office one evening, two or three nights later, and I went to get a picture out of the newspaper and in the paper it said . . . I don't know whether it was in the social news or something . . . I suddenly saw my name. This group was going to Jaffrey. So I thought, what the hell, as long as I'm listed down there I'll go. So I went. And that's where it started up, and about a year later we were married.

*Didn't she come from New York? Did you go down there to see her?*

G.C.     Not much. I went down and painted in Greenwich that spring.

*What year are you talking about?*

G.C.     About 1936 . . . no, we're talking about 1937. Well, I was painting McAlpin . . . Ronnie McAlpin . . . Molly McAlpin's children. Molly McAlpin was President Angell's[35] daughter. McAlpin was related to the Rockefellers somehow. I painted their two kids and they were pretty good. I remember her. I don't remember him at all. And Phyllis came down to see me in Greenwich. She came up to Boston a couple of times. I didn't go down to New York. She used to come up to see the Scotts and Jean and that sort of thing. Then she'd come up and go skiing. Bill Wister and she and I went along one time . . . at least we met at Mt. Washington and we had a good time. She's a lot of fun you know.

Then . . . uh . . . then we went abroad in the spring. I was going over to do a picture of Angela Forbes Winthrop in Saint-Brieuc, France. And

Sketch of Phyllis Byrne Cox from the early 1940s.

we went over together on the . . . uh . . . I think it was the *Champlain*. And we went around England together for a while. Things were beginning to heat up a little bit. Then she took off with Ian Fleming and I went over to Saint-Brieuc to paint. I was going to meet her in Paris. She went over to Berkeley Castle with Ken Pendar.[36] And she'd known Ian someplace or other. Anyway, somehow she was going over to the Continent with Ian to meet Ivor Bryce, and they were going to Salzburg or something like that, and I was going to meet her in Paris. And I got this message saying she was going with these creatures and I was upset, you know. Then I got this telegram from Nancy, France, saying, "I'll meet you in Paris." She'd had a fight with Fleming. [*Laughing*]

*Wasn't that long before he wrote James Bond books?*

G.C.   Yes. He was a kind of correspondent . . . a journalist then. He got so mad at her. He tried to get into her room the first night they got there. She went over with him to Calais where they met Ivor Bryce, who subsequently married her sister, Sheila. Ivor Bryce. He was a bad one He was known in England as "Burglar Bryce." He's very well born, but he couldn't go back to England. They had to meet him across the Channel. He's over here somewhere now. And he was a real charmer. He was very faun-like. Quite attractive . . . certainly to women . . . very elegant. But every place he was he was kind of like a germ, that feller. He was bad. He really was.

*Did his marriage to Sheila Byrne last?*

G.C.   Nooo. He was kind of like a germ.

*What did Phyllis fight with Fleming about?*

G.C.   Oh, I don't know. He had tried to get into her room the night before and she sensed this and got a bureau up against the door. She didn't want any part of him and he didn't like that at all. He got after her. He finally got so low that his final remark was, "I think you've got negro blood in you." [*Laughing*] "I think you've got negro blood in you." She had kind of curly hair and dark eyes. Anyway he was so desperate to find something to hurt her with, he'd flung this out.

*Did Phyllis's family object to her travelling around Europe with you? In 1937 that was pretty free thinking.*

G.C.   They didn't have anything to do with that at all. She wasn't so young, you know. By that time she was twenty-eight. After all, she'd been around quite a lot. We travelled around for a while. Went over to Kitzbühl . . . Paris for a few days; and then, of course, we went to Salzburg and so on. I was going down to Italy and she was going back. So I went down to Italy and then finally I ran out of money and came home. That was the fall. The next time I saw her I visited her in Bar Harbor and that's when we got engaged. We were married about a month later.

# 2

# Commissions: Art and War

*Gardner, you have indicated at one time or another that there was a certain mystical quality in your thinking, at the end of the war.*

G.C.  I considered it a time . . . and I suppose it was in a sense . . . what you'd call a religious experience . . . of that nature, which was a whole new thing to me. I felt rather . . . large feelings. It's hard for me to describe it. I felt very well.

*Thank you. Now would be a good time to talk about your experiences in World War II.*

G.C.  Well, I went into the war as a . . . let's see, I was thirty-five years old . . . thirty-six years old when I went in. And I went in directly commissioned as a camouflage officer in the Army Air Corps. In those days they were trying to get people in the services quickly in various areas where they could use them, and the Air Corps sent out a notice saying they wanted camouflage officers. They wanted people who had been theatrical designers, architects, landscape architects, painters, et cetera . . . that kind of person to become commissioned directly in the Army Air Corps to do that kind of work. We were to go to California Tech in Pasadena . . . Cal Tech . . . and study all the techniques of camouflage and so on for several months, and then we were to go out and serve wherever they thought we were needed. We all went out to the Jefferson Barracks outside St. Louis, and I remember Ham Robb,[1] an architect, and John Lavalle,[2] who was a painter, from around here. And we went out there together. There were about thirty or forty . . . fifty . . . people of that sort. Don Oenslager[3] was one of them, and Jo Mielziner,[4] the stage designer, was another, and they had a lot of landscape architects, too. They had some very able people and . . . uh

... we just frittered away our time out in the Jefferson Barracks. They didn't know what to do with us. There never was any basic training. I didn't even know how to salute correctly. So we were quickly put to beautifying the base. Little drawings improving the chapel, and they landscaped around the chapel... one thing or another of that kind. Just waiting. This engineer officer turned up... a major... and we were all told to assemble to meet him at the post theater, where he addressed us. We were all looking forward to going to Cal Tech; first to go to Fort Belvoir for a little basic training, but Cal Tech was the main place to go. And this major said, "You're all being changed. You're not going to be in the Air Corps. You're going to be in the Engineers and you're going to be sent right off on a task force abroad."

Without any education at all except for two weeks at Fort Belvoir. And this chilled this group. I know one fellow rushed off to the telephone and called his wife up in California, saying, God! he was going to be shipped overseas immediately and he didn't want to go that fast. So we were indeed changed to the Engineers. We took off our little wings and put on castles. The last thing we wanted was to be Engineers in any form. You know, artists don't go for Engineers in a big way. They like their friends around, but slide rules and figuring out stuff like that is not particularly simpatico. It was quite funny. Cal Tech was out and we were sent to Fort Belvoir on the outskirts of Washington, eighty miles outside of Richmond.

There were funny things that happened about that. There was a major, an awfully nice fellow who had been head of the park commission in Richmond. He had three or four friends, also nice guys, who were landscape architects and had been mixed up with him in Richmond. This Ammon was a major so he had a lot of clout, so he got his friends together and got them in the first batch to go to Belvoir... there were about twelve of them. They thought this was going to be great because they'd get home weekends, and afterwards they'd be put in some base nearby in the United States, for a while at least. They weren't crazy to be sent out of the country, so he got them into the first assignment so they could go down to Richmond on the way. This burned everybody up, because it was supposed to be first come, first served. Ham Robb, Lavalle and I... and Tommy Laughlin[5]... were the very first ones out there in St. Louis, and we should have been the first ones to go. We were in the second bunch and we arrived at Belvoir just as Ammon and his group received their orders. They thought it was

Picking cotton in Georgia.
G.C.'s sketch of a family outing in the cottonfields, Christmas, 1944

Squad resting, Camp Wheeler, 1944

going to be Andrews Air base, near Washington, but their faces were a foot long. What they'd got were orders to go immediately to Fort Dix and embark. [*Laughing*] Which they did. And they went to England and never came back for I don't know how many years. If we'd been in that first bunch, we'd've been shot over, too, without any military training. It was just funny because everything went wrong for them. They were just shot right out . . . right off . . . without even a chance to say goodbye to their wives. They were a very dismal group. [*Laughing*] And we came, and I was assigned . . . and so were Robb and Mielziner . . . several others . . . Graham Erskine, John Erskine's[6] son, who was a very nice fellow and an architect . . . we were all together and were sent to Miami Beach for six weeks of basic army training. How to, you know, command troops, how to have 'em march and maneuver and all that kind of thing. Meanwhile, as I say, Ammon and his gang were happily across the Atlantic [*Laughing*] while we were in Miami swimming all the time. Then we were assigned to this battalion in Richmond. [*Still laughing*] I don't know where they were.

*If you were in the engineer corps, what was your job at this point?*

G.C. Camouflage. You see, this is one of the inter-service rivalries. Engineers: Their function is to take care of camouflage . . . always has been, and they were damned if they were going to let the Air Corps have it. So we were taken out of the Air Corps and trained under the Engineers as camouflage officers and then sent back to the Air Force as engineers to train the air people in camouflage. So then we went to the Richmond air base in this camouflage battalion . . . 1066 . . . something like that, I don't remember. A little West Pointer was in command of it. His nickname at West Point had been "Little Jeff." He was a little bit of a guy . . . eager . . . but he didn't like his assignment any more than . . . well, we didn't mind this assignment, but it was a very low man on the totem pole for a West Pointer to be running that outfit. It was composed, as nearly as they could make it, of people who had been mixed up in the arts, so it wasn't a very military outfit, from a West Pointer's point of view. He did the best he could to shape us up and we did all right. We were there quite a while. We went there directly from Miami on orders, and then we were . . . uh . . . given ten days' leave by this colonel, the head of the battalion. So we all went home to our various homes. It was the summer that Phyllis had a house at Nahant, and I went there. We had a very good time and so on, and when I came back at the end of ten days they were all standing around the common room and were kind of giggling when I came in. I had been appointed commanding officer of the headquarters company, and also the engineer property officer of the base. That meant that I was responsible for every piece of engineering equipment on the base. They were giggling because they had lost a sixteen-ton trailer and I was responsible. They had taken it off on some kind of a little maneuver and it just got lost. Nobody knew where it was. There was an air force regiment . . . a regiment in support of the air force . . . the Twenty-first Engineer Regiment . . . which was going over to aid the air force in Africa. That's about two thousand men . . . a helluva lot of people . . . and they had been equipped with . . . uh . . . you know . . . sixteen-ton trailers and every kind of engineering equipment that came into the base to get that bunch off. And that went from compasses to little dividers to other graphic tools and, as I say, sixteen-ton trailers. A steam engine came in and I had to sign for it. If I didn't sign for it I was to blame. It was tough as hell on me. I had a couple of assistants, enlisted men, and I worked with the property officer of the regiment, a fellow named Farwell. He had a couple of assistants, lieutenants, with him. Between us we outfitted that regiment that was getting ready to go abroad. There were vouchers and memorandum slips . . . all kinds of paper work to this thing. And we lost that sixteen-ton trailer. They had taken it into a swamp and nobody knew where it was. And I was supposed to find it, and if I didn't . . . I wasn't afraid of the enemy anymore. I was only afraid . . . that the army would put me in the cooler [*Laughing*] for negligence. We finally found the damn trailer in the Virginia swamps like a queer, elemental, huge animal. It was there and nobody could move it. [*Laughing*] Oh God! That's the kind of thing that happened. I remember finally the regiment got off. We were all up all night helping them. There was kind of a barn they had—a shed—those little army shacks, with papers all over the place. Check off: short, one trailer; short, one compass. Everybody racing all around. Where was the compass? Finally Farwell says, "If you're short of anything, I'll just write back to you and say we've lost it in battle. Then you can record that and you'll be in the clear."

At the very end of this thing I said to Farwell, "What did you do before the war?" He was with the engineering regiment, and he had been a poet! His assistant had been a commercial artist, [*Laughing*] and there was the other guy who had been a teacher of English . . . and I was a painter! The engineers would have loved the stuff we were doing, you know. The most beautiful equipment. The equipment was superb. There were thousands of items . . . four, five, six hundred items [*Laughter*]: tweezers, trenching tools, everything you could think of that wasn't a gun.

But this was a bad period. [*Laughter*] This was bad. I was running a company. There were company complaints here and there. A fellow would be bullied by a sergeant or something like that. There is a very nice touching thing here. A man came to me, a young enlisted feller in my company who was having a terrible time. He was in basic training. He hated the army and was miserable and so on. He wanted to talk to me and he told me that the only way he could get through the day . . . he would get up a little early in his barracks. And he would open his locker and he had in his locker a picture by Cézanne . . . a reproduction. And he said, "I look at that and drink it in, and that's the only way I get through the day."

And this sergeant had found him looking at it and started to kid him and to give him a hard time generally. He was really a nice fellow, but he was giving this kid a hard time. I got the sergeant in, you know and I was in a position to straighten him out. That kind of thing was going on too, and the drilling went on and the other stuff. So I had a very busy time for a while.

Ham Robb was the executive officer. He had his own troubles himself. [*Laughter*] We got to be friends. We got to be great friends. We were together for about a year one way or another. Oh, we had funny times there. You see I used to go to town and try to find a place for Phyllis and the children to live. It was terribly hard to find a place, and Ham, he was looking around, too. We'd get Saturday afternoons off in general for that purpose. I happened to go by a house, and some people were sitting on the porch, and I just said to 'em, "By any chance, is there anything to rent around here?"

I'd been going around just seeing people and asking them in the street. And they said, "You can rent this house next week."

And by golly, it was a very nice little house . . . a very nice little house . . . with some nice people moving out for a while. Ham couldn't get anything, kept looking, and couldn't get anything. He just had bad luck and I had this extraordinary luck. So Phyllis came down with Ben and Kate, and I came back and spent every night there. Ham still couldn't find anything, and his first wife . . . I can't think of her name at the moment... Ruth... came to live with us. They lived there in the back room. They had a big, mahogany headboard as high as that picture there... a huge thing... big, double bed. And I remember him coming home one night. He'd had this day off... I don't know whether it was Saturday or Sunday ... and he'd gone around looking ... looking around... and no luck. He came back and he was disgruntled. He could get good and disgruntled. He came back this night, said goodnight, and went into the back room ... took off his shoes and flung himself down on the bed. And there was the most terrible crash! [*Laughter*] Then there was dead silence. We rushed down the hall and opened the door. Ham had flung himself down on the bed, and the headboard had come loose and come down and flattened the two of them. [*Great laughter*] The end of a perfect day! Everything had gone wrong that could. No hits, no runs, no anything!

*Wasn't it very social in Richmond during the war? Didn't a lot of men bring their wives down?*

G.C.   Some, but they were scattered around pretty much. Richmond was awfully crowded with the base and military activity. We saw Ham a lot and we saw two or three officers quite a lot, and the Robbs had some friends outside Richmond named Robinson and we used to go out there once in a while. Yes, we had a pretty good time, really, except I was so damn busy trying to keep track of all this engineering equipment. Just trying to keep one jump ahead of the sheriff.

*Did Phyllis spend a lot of time alone in Cambridge during the war?*

G.C.   No ... uh ... I was never out of the country, you see. After Richmond I went out to Utah, then down to southern California and then to Georgia. I was training all the time. We were training officers. At least I particularly was. No. Most of us were training officers. Some were taken out and put into intelligence later towards the end of things.

*Were you still in camouflage?*

G.C.   Oh, yeah. I was ... uh ... training Air Corps troops in camouflage ... uh ... in booby traps and fire-fighting. We'd do demonstrations and so on. I enjoyed that quite a lot before I got through. I knew it cold by that time. That stuff I did all right. Phyllis came out to Utah. She came every place I went to. There never was a long, long period when we were apart.

*Was Ben around then?*

G.C.   Yes, he was around. He certainly was around. He was awfully amusing. He was born in '39, so he must have been four or five. Kate was two and a half or three. James was born in 1943, during the war. I was kind of depressed after a while in the army. Then, I got to Utah and I felt this . . . this . . . great sense of proportion come over me and I read *Varieties of Religious Experience* . . . by William James. And an article by Harry Emerson Fosdick[7] sort of set me off; then came James, because I was thinking about these things. I . . . felt very good. Later I volunteered to be a combat artist. You'd go up and sort of fly around and make sketches afterwards. But that fell through just before the war was over. That was the only gesture of that kind I made. I tell you the war wasn't prolonged at all by my actions, but I don't think it was one second shorter because of me. [*Chuckling*]

*Afterwards did you go back to 88 Garden Street and set up in Cambridge from there?*

G.C.   Well, I'd had a studio on Chestnut Street in Boston before the war and I went back there. Two or three years later I moved up to 30 Ipswich Street where my studio is now.

*Did this new effulgence go into your portrait painting?*

G.C.   Yeah, it went into everything. That was a very good period indeed, for a couple of years . . . two or three years. Then a little less good. It varied back and forth and so on. That was a very important moment.

*Has it recurred during your life?*

G.C.   Off and on. Off and on. Not quite the same particular thing . . . but some. That was a very strong moment.

*Since for most of your life 88 Garden Street has been your home, let's take time out to go into its history. Were you born there?*

G.C.   No, no. I was born in Holyoke, Massachusetts.

*When did your father buy the house?*

G.C.   He bought it when I was about five. I think we moved in when I was six.

G.C.'s sketch of Phyllis an hour after Poppy's birth, (*above*) July 1946 and sketch of Kate at the washbasin (*below*) drawn about the same time.

Ben Cox listening to a story, c. 1946

*How old is it?*

G.C.   It was built the same year that University Hall was built, in 1810 ... the same year ... '10 or '11. The last person who owned it had been Asa Gray.[8] Then Harvard owned it. They were going to destroy it because Gray's collection was in it and they thought it was a firetrap ... which it is. Was and is. And they were going to destroy it. It was in the middle of the Botanical Gardens, and my father, an architect, bought it for ten thousand dollars, I think, and just moved it across the street. Subsequently Harvard put up a big brick building where it had stood to house Gray's collection. You haven't been in the house, have you?

*Never.*

G.C.   The so-called playroom, which was also a dining room, was a big room, somewhat bigger than this. It had been Gray's study and he had that filled with cupboards around it ... very, very lovely cupboards, as a matter of fact, and he put in little shelves he could put his dried plants on. Hundreds and hundreds of 'em all around. My father left a whole lot of those ... some upstairs ... they're still in there.

*Was that wing a part of the original house or did your father add it on?*

G.C.   No. The house is an old Georgian house with four rooms downstairs and four rooms upstairs. A very good thing. And it has this wing and I think the wing has been on for a long time. My father didn't put it on. Who did, I don't know. I went there when I was about six years old.

*Are all your childhood memories in that house?*

G.C.   Pretty much. I was born in Holyoke because my grandfather was a doctor there and I was taken up there to be delivered by him. My parents lived in Boston. I came right back with them again and I can remember a little bit of Brimmer Street and Acorn Street.

*You married Phyllis Byrne of New York, didn't you?*

G.C.   Yes.

*What year were you married?*

G.C.   Nineteen thirty-seven.

*Had your mother died?*

G.C.     Yup. She'd died a year or so before.

*After you were married, did you move right into the house?*

G.C.     Yeah. After my mother died, my father and I lived there together. And after I married, he lived on with us for several years. It worked out very well. We had this ... uh ... it's quite a big house and he had his little area he went to. There'd be some passing back and forth, but he was a very easy person to have around. Then he remarried and moved out.

*Didn't Phyllis's sister, Helen, marry Walter Lippmann?*

G.C.     Just before I married Phyllis. Helen had been married to Ham Armstrong, Hamilton Armstrong,[9] who was for years editor of *Foreign Affairs* ... who built up that magazine. A very nice man, too.

*When the Lippmanns stayed with you in Cambridge, where did he do his writing for his column?*

G.C.     They never stayed very long, but when he was there he tried different places to work.

*I suppose I'm trying to lead you up to that wonderful story you've told me about the morning France fell in 1940.*

G.C.     Oh, yes. That time. We were going up to North Haven that summer and were starting quite early, actually. We were going to take the children up there in the morning and France was falling ... was falling any minute. Walter Lippmann[10] was up in Northeast Harbor, and he came down with Helen to get to Washington. They didn't have any TV then so he couldn't learn much up in Maine, so they stopped over with us. The night they arrived, France fell. The next morning Walter got up ... uh ... he had to write something. Big moment. And the family were getting ready to get into the car—a couple of cars ... two children, Phyllis, myself and the cook, Lena; and Mary Spencer, who did the washing and other things, too. And they were lugging things up and down stairs. There was a choreman named Floyd. He was helping. Now I have to revert to what the cook told me, who had an extraordinary recall of events and what people said.

Walter came down trying to write in the dining room. Everyone was going by the door carrying trunks and making noises and so on. And Helen was very nervous about this; said Walter had to have absolute quiet. And Lena said she remembered coming down the hall ... the hall of the house that goes from front to back . . . and Mr. Lippmann came out of the dining room and just ran into her. He didn't even say he was sorry. She was surprised because he was a very polite man. Just bounced off her and went down the hall looking kind of wild. Helen grabbed him and got him out to . . . they took him out to the studio which is at the rear of the house. It's joined to the house by a little passageway . . . a glass passageway which you go out through to the street. They put him in the studio which abuts the street, and he started to work there. Well, my father was also in the house then and he was sort of hovering around here and there, not mixing much with it, and Floyd was helping. Floyd looked just like Alfred E. Smith.[11] Almost exactly. Extremely good description of him. An extraordinary resemblance. Floyd was a choreman and was . . . uh . . . a free-and-easy type. He was helping lug things around and my father saw him and said, *sotto voce*, "Don't make any noise, Floyd. Mr. Lippmann is working." Floyd nodded his head.

Then a few minutes later, Floyd apparently ran into Helen, and Helen said, "Don't make any noise, Floyd. Mr. Lippmann is working."

I think I saw him and said, "Take it easy, Floyd."

Then maybe Phyllis saw him. In each case he nodded his head. And then he went into the kitchen and my father whispered to him again, "Don't make a noise, Floyd. Mr. Lippmann is writing."

And Floyd shouted, *"God damn it! I'm not making any noise!"*

And he went out and took the kitchen door which was very near the studio, and slammed it so it shook the whole house. He went through the passageway that led to the studio and the street, and slammed both those doors so that it shook Lippmann and everything else. [*Laughing*] And all the time he was shouting, *"God damn it! I'm not making any noise!"*

And then he took off on his bicycle and ran into a hurdy-gurdy man about a block away and gave him a dollar and said, "Go play in front of that house there."

Which he did. [*Much laughter*] And everybody rushed out of the house and gave the hurdy-gurdy man five dollars and told him to beat it.

*Was Mr. Lippmann as brilliant a conversationalist as he was a journalist?*

G.C.   He was very good about . . . very generous about giving. If it was a question he thought was intelligent... or really interested him, he was quite good about it. He liked ladies. I don't mean in a rakish way, but they stimulated him. A pretty woman could get things out of him... could get a good response, but to anyone who was anxious to know, he'd give. He was a very distinguished journalist, of course, but he didn't philosophize. He was rather a shy fellow. He'd come into a room... and, if the conversation sort of died, he wasn't good at small talk. But he was sensitive to certain things. He could get upset. He could get quite upset. Noise bothered him terribly. In Washington, he had an absolutely soundproof room. Couldn't hear a thing. That's why it was such a terrible thing that happened the morning France fell. [*Chuckling*]

*What about that famous editorial he wrote against the Jews?*

G.C.   The best I can say about that is that I'm not sure which one you are referring to. He said that Hitler wasn't all wrong? Something like that? I think that's the one. Really, all I know about it I got from Frankfurter[12] while I was painting him. Frankfurter had been a friend of his, but he fell out badly with him. They never patched it up. Frankfurter had kept the whole file of their correspondence, you know, and he went right to it about him with me. I told him I was Walter's brother-in-law before he embarked on this thing... after he got started. I just wanted him to know this. The articles... remember they had something about saying there was something to be said for Hitler's treatment of the Jews. This was, of course, before we knew how bad it was, but Lippmann hadn't condemned him right off. He had dispassionate views, and he didn't like fusses. He minded falling out with Frankfurter very much and tried to make up with him; but Frankfurter wouldn't make up. So they broke up.

*Didn't he disagree with Acheson?*

G.C.   I don't know what it was about, but they fell out, too. He fell out a lot. He fell out with people not because he was abrasive with them, but, like many Washington friendships, ideologies clash and they change a lot. Thick as thieves one minute and then... out. And, of course, he was a newspaperman. He kept to his views... wrote things that made people mad. He made the Lamonts mad at him. He used to go up to North Haven and stay with them and so on, and he liked them and they liked him very much. Then came the time when the Morgans got in trouble with that attorney general . . . what's his name . . . Piscora? Pecora?[13] A perfectly good man; but he attacked all the banks. They got Mr. Morgan[14] with a midget on his lap. Walter was perfectly objective about it and it burned them up. He was pretty cool this way. Pretty cool and objective.

When I came up for the Institute of Arts and Letters, of which he was a member, he never said a word for me, because, he said . . . I was told . . . he couldn't speak for me because I was his brother-in-law. He could have said something if he'd wanted to. I'm rather glad he didn't, but he might have. He kept himself awfully out of it.

But to get back to Frankfurter: the person he really didn't like . . . the person well up there . . . was Justice Douglas.[15] God! He disliked Douglas. He made no bones about it at all. He said, "Look at that face! Look at that face. Did you ever see such a cruel mouth in your life?" He hated him.

*Did he disagree with his decisions on the bench?*

G.C.   I don't know. He never told me the details of why he didn't like him. I guess Justice Douglas was a very difficult fellow. Very quick and bright, but he got in very wrong with Frankfurter. Frankfurter didn't like the way he left his wife, to begin with. That was just one thing— just one thing. Chemically, it was all wrong. I don't think he liked Chief Justice Warren, particularly; but nothing like that. He was critical of people, but he was awfully warm and I liked him very much. I got on very well with him.

*Did you paint him while he was on the Supreme Court?*

G.C.   Right. I painted him about 1960 and he'd been on the court for a long time . . . had gone on with Roosevelt. I started drawing him . . . one of the early times I was drawing people ahead of time . . . in . . . uh . . . his house in Georgetown. He had a long thin room . . . I suppose thirty feet by ten feet . . . something like that . . . with a fireplace in it. It was his study or he worked in the garden. He had a cold, so I went down and drew him in this room and made a lot of sketches of him first. He had a fire, and it was so hot there I ended by wearing no underclothes. Drew him that way. I just put on shirt and trousers without any underclothes. Drew him that way and still I was boiling. [*Chuckling*] But he was a very entertaining man. I had a lot of fun with him and became a friend of his.

*Did you stay in his house?*

G.C.   No. No, but I did a lot of drawings of him there.

*Did you sketch him in court?*

G.C.   Oh, yeah. You could just see the top of his head he was so small. So, when I was there, he always got up and asked a lot of questions, giving me a chance to sketch him. And I remember one thing that he said I liked very much about an attitude he liked, admired. He quoted Carlyle[16] an example of this attitude which he said he aspired to. Carlyle went off and spent an evening with a young painter whose name now escapes me. His paintings never got anywhere... he never made a name for himself, but Carlyle said of that evening, "We walked and talked all night long agreeing in all things, excepting only opinion." I think that's fine. "In all things, excepting only opinion."

*We're getting a little ahead of ourselves. Let's go back to an earlier portrait. When did you first paint Robert Frost?*[17]

G.C.   I painted him in... uh... I think in '54. I'd have to check on this, but I think it was '54. And I painted him again about three or four years later, several years before he died. The first time was for the St. Botolph Club, as a gift, actually. Dave McCord[18] got me to do it and I was glad to do it. Frost had been a member there for a long time and he was a great force there. That was the first one. And then I did a second one for Middlebury College. I've forgotten who the man was who commissioned it, possibly someone connected with the college. He commissioned it and paid for it himself to give to the college. For the Frost Library... the Frost Room of Poetry in the library... and it's there now. It turned out quite well. It won the popularity prize at the Boston Arts Festival and was reproduced in *Time* magazine. Then I did one for the Amherst library at the same time, the big, dark one you saw in the Corcoran Gallery exhibition in Washington. It was a compositional sketch for the Middlebury one, but different in handling, different in paint texture and different in colors. It wasn't right and I rejected it... put it aside. Three or four years later I learned something from Lily Saarinen.[19] She was doing a bust of... me, I think; and she walked round and round the head. In painting you have a tendency to think of a head as a flat thing. I'd forgotten that faces are always going away from you; from the bridge of the nose back. This opened my eyes to a point. I recalled something about planes that had to do with the Frost thing ... the one that wasn't good enough; so, I made up two or three wallops ... strokes ... on the Frost portrait I had put aside and it made it very good indeed. It ended up being better than the Middlebury. Better than the first one of its type.

*Did this change your painting technique?*

G.C.   No. It's just this happens all the time. You get accustomed to looking at a thing a certain way and then, pretty soon, you stop thinking about it. Then suddenly you realize you've become aware of something you'd kind of forgotten ... or you'd ceased paying enough attention to.

*Did you stay with Frost while you were painting him?*

G.C.   No. The first time he used to come into the studio. Well, he did in both cases. It was very easy to get people to bring him in. All Phyllis's friends and my friends' wives were only too anxious to bring him in and take him away. Adelaide Marquand[20] used to come and get him; Phyllis would bring him or take him away; once in a while, there were one or two others. Adelaide Marquand nearly froze him to death on Storrow Drive. She ran out of gas, one bad February night, and they sat there for hours. [*Chuckling*] He was nearly eighty, too old to take that kind of stuff.

*Where did you do the preliminary sketches?*

G.C.   In his case, I did them right here in the studio. I didn't follow him around, at least not the one for the St. Botolph Club. The second time, I went up to Amherst. He wanted me to see him in action up there. So, I went up one evening ... went up in the afternoon ... and we had dinner together in just a regular trolley-car lunch place ... a diner it was. Then we went over to a fraternity house, where we met with a group of students. We spent the night at the Lord Jeffrey Inn and went to see the president of Amherst the next morning. Cole,[21] I think his name was. The fraternity house consisted, apparently of the brightest undergraduates. It was the intellectual fraternity house. Actually, it was a building designed by my father, a very good one too. A very attractive building. The boys were all clustered around this living room. It was very informal: sitting on the floor, sitting in chairs, any old thing. And ... uh ... he started off and dominated the conversation entirely. He rambled around about many subjects. He liked to speculate. He speculated constantly. This was the second time I was getting ready to paint him ... the one for Middlebury and now this one for Amherst, and he used to speculate with me. I have many examples of this but I'll stick to the one at the fraternity house. Incidentally, the reason they gave for wanting his portrait for the Frost Library ... the argument for it ... was that this was only the second library named after a poet. The other one was the Pushkin Library.

Well, he'd told me before there was a theme he liked to follow: Don't bother about degrees. Go out and do what you want to do ... after reflection, of course; but feel free to make changes. The first time I'd painted him he'd talked about this a little, and to illustrate the point, he said, "You know what the Bible says, 'Quit ye like men.'" I don't know exactly what it means. I haven't been much for the Bible, but I got it all right. He tried it on the boys in some kind of connection that was appropriate. They didn't get it. Not one of them. Thirty-five or forty of 'em and not one of them got it. It struck me as odd, because in our generation ... mine ... even as biblically unread as I was, I got it. So he went on talking away ... and I think it kind of irritated him ... and in about half an hour, he worked it in again. And this time he worked it in with an anecdote he'd told me before. It was about some feller who'd tried for a Ph.D., and he really didn't like it. He didn't enjoy what he was doing. Frost asked him, "What would you really like to do?"

And the feller said, "I'd like to go down to Peru and raise chinchillas."

Frost said, "Why don't you?"

And the fellow did and he was very successful at this. And then Frost for the second time said to the boys, "You know what the Bible says? 'Quit ye like men.'" Nobody got it the second time around. [*Laughing*] So he stopped everything to explain it. I don't remember much about the rest of the conversation. They asked him questions, about things. He was quick-witted. He had answers ready. One time, suddenly there was silence and he started speculating. He said, "You gotta be rich now. You gotta be rich to be president."

There had been Roosevelt, and Averell Harriman was trying for it. He mentioned Willkie.[22] Then this feller spoke up and said, "You wouldn't want a bum for president, would you?"

Frost snapped back at him, "You mean like Abraham Lincoln?" This got a big laugh.

Next day, in his office, President Cole asked Frost to come down and ... uh ... speak to a large group of alumni in Palm Beach or Miami.

They were having some kind of convocation and he knew that Frost used to go around there someplace in the winter. Frost said he'd like to, but he didn't want anyone else speaking... nobody else barking around there at all... if he were going to do it. The president said he thought this could be arranged. No, he didn't want nobody else. [*Chuckling*] It was naked... naked... self-advancement. He didn't make any bones about it at all. [*Laughing*] He wanted to be number one and he didn't want any number twos. Just one feller speaking, and that was going to be him.

He made lots of little jokes. He liked to make little twists of words. They made a lot of him up at Amherst, you know; and the night we went to the fraternity house he said, "I'm suffering from me-sickness, but I really like it." [*Laughing*] That was typical of him: "I'm suffering from me-sickness and I really like it."

*Was he as kind as he looked?*

G.C.   No. Everybody knows about that now. No, he could be quite mean. I remember the very first time that kind of thing came up... long before I painted him... when I was a very young man just out of college. I revered him, you know, and my father was a great admirer of his works and so on. He was granite... he looked patriarchal and kindly and you expected great compassion and understanding out of him. I remember this one night after dinner at the St. Botolph Club. We were sitting around... young fellers and other people... and he was talking. And there was some woman poet he picked on and he really gave her quite a going-over in rather a vicious way. I can remember it was quite a shock to me. It was unnecessary. It was *not* compassionate. It was *not* tolerant. It was *not* kindly. It was just small-time stuff. It was scornful, snidely scornful. I've forgotten what he said about her, but it denigrated her plenty. It was not Lincolnian at all. I remember noticing it and being disappointed in him. And then it turned up a few times, of course, in my painting him it turned up. He was so rugged-looking, you know, but he was extremely sensitive and touchy. It didn't show too much with me because people in my position when you go to work on them, they naturally don't put their worst foot forward if they can help it. It comes out, of course, now and then, but they don't try to put it out. If they were drunks, they'd be sober for that week, at least. I've never painted drunks. But people don't parade their weaknesses when they are being painted, but they come out, of course. It didn't come out with

Frost much. He was extremely sensitive.

*Sensitive of what you were thinking; or to what people said to him?*

G.C.   Do you want an example? The way he reacted was the way he treated a man I had painted named Joseph Deering. An awfully nice man from Saco, Maine . . . Biddeford . . . Saco. Deering was a sort of . . . a Booth Tarkington character of the third generation of people who had been prominent in this small town. They'd gone to Yale . . . been educated and gone back. He was a very nice fellow; he was the last of his line and he'd asked me to paint his portrait because there'd be no more Deerings to attend to the bank, the library, the children's home, and so on. And there was a great collection of Americana that I didn't know about at that time, in the great old Victorian house that his father had . . . in a great vault. It was just priceless. One of the very famous collections in the country . . . the early Jesuit papers and so on. Deering was a great big . . . he's still alive I think . . . big, Tarkingtonian type. A good nice man and he . . . uh . . . greatly admired Robert Frost. Frost didn't want people . . . I never brought people in to see him while he was being painted and he didn't want me to. I didn't make anything of him in that way. I didn't pay off favors by saying, "Come on and drop in and get a lock of his hair."

But when Deering called me up about something and didn't know what I was doing, I said to myself, "By God, I'll let Deering in whether he likes it or not." Deering really did have great respect for him. I knew it would mean a lot to him. So Deering turned up. He came in and he was rather abashed. He wasn't normally an abashed fellow at all, and I'll digress here a little. He went back to his Yale reunion when I was painting him . . . probably one of the thirtieth reunions . . . and Walter Paepcke[23] was in his class. They were all going down to Savin Rock, or wherever they go, and Paepcke said he was too busy to go. And my friend just picked him up and carried him onto the bus. Paepcke was desperately trying to get off the bus and catch a plane or something, and Deering, who was a big fellow, kept him there. So you see he was not an abashed type, but he was kind of abashed by Frost. Frost was polite enough to him; but then Deering made a big mistake. He didn't quite know what to say and he said, "When you write, do you have some feeling how it's going to impress people?"

And Frost froze up on him. "You philistine! Of course not." (Communicated by *manner*, not words.) And he was kind of rough on him. It was unnecessary and I can remember not liking that. And that was an example. He should have sensed this fellow's quality. It was very insensitive. As a matter of fact, he had his eye on people plenty when he made up things. No doubt about that.

*Do you really think he did?*

G.C.    He certainly did when he made his jokes and stuff like that. "Quit ye like men" brought in twice and so on. No, he wasn't spontaneous like that, but I think he was when he wrote. Of course, he wasn't self-conscious when he wrote. Then he was kind of mean about Dave McCord. I think he liked McCord, but he could be mean about anybody. He thought that Dave was kind of an old lady, that he had been with his mother too long. He kind of put him down, not badly; but I didn't like it because I knew how much Dave thought of him. He wasn't kindly. You wouldn't have done it and I wouldn't have done it. He was not being bitchy or nasty, but he was not returning in kind. I was a little surprised by all that stuff written about him later, but not totally surprised. I'd seen enough to realize there was something there.

*Did he have a sense of humor?*

G.C.    Oh, yes. He had a good sense of humor. Sure . . . oh sure.

*Did he ever mention his early life?*

G.C.    Yeah. The very first day I saw him. I went to pick him up and drove him into the studio. He had a little house on Brewster Street in Cambridge. The first trip there I picked him up there to take him in—and he talked about himself. He talked about an incident that happened to him in California when he was a boy . . . a small boy. When he was twelve . . . or younger . . . some carpenters had been working on the roof of their house. And he had a little sister. And one of the carpenters in some way insulted his sister, or he said something Frost thought he shouldn't have when she was around. He may have said "shit," or some other dirty word. And . . . uh . . . it apparently infuriated him, and he took a hammer and threw it at the guy. And he was very pleased with the fact he did this. It was very courageous and he took the trouble to tell me that . . . I suppose to give me the impression of something about him. This was one of his heroic acts. Nothing had led up to it particularly. It was just an example of how intrepid he was as a kid. It was just amusing that he told me.

*Did you have a true friendship with him?*

G.C.   No. I'm sure he liked me, I liked him. I was very flattered to do him, but I didn't see him a lot. Every time he saw me he was glad to see me, and he liked the portraits very much. He died, of course, not long after I painted the second one. No. I couldn't say I became an intimate friend of his at all, but I knew him pretty well at the time.

*Did he have a good marriage?*

G.C.   I don't know. I don't know. You've read about it. He had a very tempestuous one, apparently. The only time he ever referred to his wife... he only referred to her once... he said, "My wife is a very serious woman." And then, to illustrate it, he said that when he first made a success after years of poverty... just scraping along... she didn't like it. He said it was because she thought that maybe it would corrupt him. He wouldn't be quite as good as he had been. There's another thing. I don't want to say he was such a liar as they claim he was... or found out he was, as they now know he was. I didn't know this then and I believed everything he said. But that may have been one of his little things. Another one I'm pretty sure of was when he told me that when he came back from England... when he got off the boat... he had only fifty cents to his name. Three children and a wife and that's all. But, of course, he was met by his publisher at the dock. That might have been true and it might not have been true, as I look back on it. He didn't have much, no doubt about that, but he claimed he had only fifty cents.

*Would he tell things that weren't true because he thought they were true?*

G.C.   This is something I don't know. I didn't know him well enough to tell. These things that I'm saying now, if you were listening one hundred years from now... these are the things he said to me, and I have no reason to believe they weren't true except now I know he stretched things a bit. That was the only time he mentioned his wife. He mentioned a daughter. He said very little about his son. He spoke about his early life some; his father some. His wife was a very bright person, apparently; but that was the only time he mentioned her.

Another thing he said, "I'm always speculating. I'm always speculating. My mind is always surprising me." And he said, "When my mind stops surprising me, I'll die."

Now when I quoted this to his friends... and this is an exact quote to me ... they said, "W-e-l-l, you know, that's probably not quite true. [*Chuckling*] That's what he thought was true when he said it, but his mind doesn't surprise him all that much all the time." [*Laughing*] Maybe he was stretching it a bit.

Then he had ideas on education. He said, "To hell with degrees! A.B.'s, M.A.'s, the Ph.D.'s: They don't mean a thing. All there is to education is hanging around until you catch on." I like that ... I like that. And I've told that to many people. It was typical of him, and as far as I know he never said that to anyone else.

Another thing that was typical of him were his views on religion. He said he believed his religion was ... his faith was "believing the future in," instead of believing in the future. Again it was typical of him and that's how he felt. It's not a bad description of faith. There's a lot more, but these are the things that spring to my mind.

He had a lot of little sayings. He'd say ... and this was the first day I was driving him in, too ... he was talking about his writing habits—when he had a hard time getting time to write because he had so much to do. And he said about his hours of writing, "Some I seized like a man; some I stole like a thief; and some were dropped in my little tin cup." That's a nice little quote. I've never heard that any place else. And then he ... uh ... he liked to take things and turn them around and twist them and give them different meanings. Even when he gave me his book and said, "This is my life. Everything I've done." Again, he must have been stretching it because it was a small book, not a big one. [*Chuckling*] But I later got a big one and he autographed it for me. He put in, "To Gardner Cox for making so much of me." Which is very typical. This was after the picture was over and people had taken him in and out of the studio and made much of him in that way. You could take it in a lot of ways: so much of him; or so *much* of him. It meant what the people had done ... very endearing ... typical. And I'm sure he thought about that before he wrote it. He didn't sit down and knock it off. He took it home and thought about it, I'm sure, and I'm flattered that he did.

But there's one little thing on the mean side, if you call it mean. Every Christmas he would ... he'd send out little cards that he'd written something on and had printed. It would be some little thing he'd send people and I would have liked to have got one, naturally. I believe I said that to him and he said, "I'll send you one." And Kay Morrison, who worked for him, said she'd see that I got one ... he was going to send

G.C.'s studies for portrait of Robert Frost, 1960s

me one anyway. But he never did. It might be that he just thought, "Oh, to hell with him!" And it might have been a little quirk in his mind, because he was very friendly with me. Our relationship was a very pleasant one. But I would have liked it and it would have been a very easy thing to do. If I did this, it wouldn't mean anything, but it meant something with this guy and he could do it very easily.

And I remember I spoke at the St. Botolph Club, one time. I spoke and Charlie Wyzanski[24] spoke, and I was nervous. Frost saw me later and said, "You were kind of scared, weren't you?"

And I said, "Yes, I was."

He said, "Wyzanski wasn't scared."

And I said, "No, he wasn't."

*Did you ever know of Charlie Wyzanski being scared of speaking anywhere?*

G.C.   No. No. And there's another story worth putting in. Later I painted Tooey Kinsolving,[25] then rector of St. James's in New York. He'd been a great friend of Frost up at Amherst . . . the first church he had was there. He was an awfully nice man, as you know. And . . . uh . . . when he was at Trinity in Boston, he had his first son at the Phillips House. When they told him in the waiting room that the kid was born, he was racing down the corridor to see his first son. It may have been his firstborn. At any rate, it was his first son. And a nurse came out and grabbed him and said, "Robert Frost is in there and he'd like to speak to you."

This happened just as he was tearing down to see his kid. Kinsolving told me this. So he thought, he's an old man and the baby can wait a few minutes. So he went in and told Frost he had this son. Frost immediately began to speculate. He said, "I suppose he thinks he's here to see what's owed him, to find out what he's entitled to in enjoyment. I suppose he's thinking that, when all he's here for is to see if he amounts to anything."

Kinsolving told me this and he said . . . it was the time of the liberals and Roosevelt, the beginning of '33, '34, '35, and Frost said, "It used to be 'I'm holier than thou' but," he said, "now it's 'I'm tenderer than thou.' " [*Laughter*]

# 3

# Hocking, Whitehead, and James Byrne

*Before Frost, what were some of your earlier portraits—wasn't there one of Hocking?*

G.C.   Ernest Hocking, a lovely fellow... William Ernest Hocking.[1] And he wrote a very famous book in his day called, *The Meaning of God in Human Experience*. He was a philosopher... not a very well known professor at Harvard. He wasn't, you know, one of the great ones like James and so on, but he was a very good one in his day. And he wrote and wrote. I think he was in the Academy of Arts and Letters. He certainly was in the Institute of Arts and Letters, which the average professor doesn't get into, you know. Galbraith[2] and Schlesinger[3] and such... but they don't have too many. And... uh... but now he's forgotten, of course.

*Who were you painting him for?*

G.C.   For the family. Painting for the family. The thing about him was... he was one of the early people who promoted me, you might say. He wasn't the first, but he and his wife... uh... uh... they thought I had a lot on the ball. I did him, and my mother did a picture of him. He was very fond of my mother. In those days, you know, nobody ever did anything about this stuff, but I just knew he was fond of her. He was very fond of his wife. He was a *very* nice man. He was a very good man and... uh... he was married to Agnes Boyle O'Reilly... old John Boyle O'Reilly's daughter. She was a poetess and she was a character from way back. And she adored him. They made quite a pair. They started Shady Hill School... she did, you know, with people like May Sarton. In the very beginning it was an open-air school... finally developed into what it is now. And... uh... I did him when my mother was doing him. And I did a better one than she did. She was floundering around on it and having a tough time as people do sometimes, and I got a . . . pretty good one. It felt like him and so on. It was a big picture, very lively, and it was very charming. Wasn't the best piece of painting in the world, but . . . at my age, it made a great impression on him and his wife. He's the one who got me to do Whitehead[4] very quickly after that. And, after that, Ralph Barton Perry.[5] Those came right from his influence, almost directly. He wasn't the only one, as I say. He didn't discover me, so to speak, if you call it that, but . . . uh . . . he was a great encourager and his wife was, and they both respected very much what I could do and they promoted me. Then I painted him again when he was ninety and he was still very hearty . . . I say hearty . . . he was red-faced. He was a lovely person. Big man . . . kindly . . . philosophic . . . lovely laugh. Very . . . like a charming minister. Of course I talked to him about many things. When my mother died, I went up to their farm in Madison, New Hampshire, and tried to paint his wife. My father went up there, too. They still have that farm. They called it "Back Acres" . . . a good name for it . . . obviously a joke name, but they had worked on it and built it up to what it is now, a kind of family compound. The whole family still lives there . . . and his son, who had been in my class, who I knew since a boy, Richard Hocking. He was also a professor of philosophy at Harvard . . . a very nice, spiritual fellow. They all lived up there and I did him a second time when he was ninety up there. I can't do justice to him at all, so there are just little anecdotes.

I was up there painting him on his ninetieth birthday, and I remember he got up and said . . . He made a little toast in wine. It was a very undrinking family, but just this much . . . a very very pure family . . . very nice . . . and he got up and said, "Well now, age is just relative. The world goes around the sun once a year. "Here," he said, "that's ninety years. If I'd been born on Jupiter, where it takes thirty years to go 'round, I'd be only three years old." [*Chuckling*] He had another in the middle . . . some planet, I can't remember its name . . . I think went around in ten years, something like that. Anyway, the big one was Jupiter. Only three years old. [*Chuckling*].

His wife told me an interesting story about him. She was very dramatic and very devoted . . . very lively . . . very poetic. And she said when they were first married . . . they must have gone through all kinds of stuff about what their religious beliefs would be after they got married. She was brought up a Catholic and stopped being a Catholic.

And I think John Boyle O'Reilly had probably stopped being a Catholic. He was quite a boy in his way, you know. And ... uh ... I can't remember the details, but they struggled with themselves. Went to different ministers in different places ... they *really* worked at it. People don't do that today that much. I don't think they did then, for that matter, but they had very great consciences. When they got married they went out to California ... he was working away on these ideas he had. He'd gone to Harvard at the Ph.D. level ... post-graduate level as an older man ... worked before. He'd been poor and everyone took him in because he had a very lovely quality about him ... very distinguished ... lovely quality. Finally he got it all together and made this speech ... talk ... lecture. He thought he had a breakthrough, you know. This was everything he felt and thought in this direction. And at the end of it they went back, and she said they lay in bed ... they went to bed and lay there. And she said, "I knew he wasn't asleep and he knew I wasn't asleep," and neither of them said anything. Finally, he said, "They didn't understand a word."

And she said, "No, they didn't."

And this meant he hadn't got it across. Nobody got it. It was very depressing. He was an instructor out there, so he just kept on. And then a little later ... a year or so later ... he came out with a book. He had got it in book form. And that was ... that was *The Meaning of God in Human Experience*, which was a famous book in its time. It was the greatest thing he did, I guess. Maybe I'm wrong saying it was the best he ever did, but it was the first. It put him on the map. Then he got offers. When the book came out, he was still in California where nobody had understood him. He got offers from Yale, Harvard, and Princeton. He went to Yale ... and subsequently to Harvard. But this great thing happened. It was very thrilling. You think of academic life not having its drama, but this ... I remember this story very much ... how they lay in bed and neither dared speak.

I could go on about him for a long time, but I guess it's not very important. But he was a very distinguished man in his day, and he was so pure. Whitehead liked him, though Whitehead liked people who had devil in them, and there wasn't much devil in Ernest Hocking. He was a little too square and pure. He wasn't all that pure, come to think of it. One time we were talking about ... love and so on, and I said, "Where do you rate ... where do you rate physical love?"

I thought he was going to say ... well, not very important. He was ninety. He said, "Very important, indeed."

I was very pleased when he said that [*Chuckling*], because he was so pure and Mrs. Hocking was so pure that when they came to Cambridge first... I was very young and I became a friend of their son's... we were brought together... and they... uh... had a canary. Two canaries. So they married them. They had a marriage ceremony with the children around. They gave them the works. [*Chuckling*] They didn't want any illegitimate canaries around there. They got married [*Laughing*] before witnesses... all the children, so I didn't know what I was going to get when I asked that question all those years later.

*How about Alfred North Whitehead?*

G.C.    Before we get into Whitehead... for a second... if I was a writer I could probably take Hocking and make a lovely picture of him. I feel rather badly not to be able to do justice to people as nice as this. The same with Whitehead. I wish I'd written down more about Whitehead, because I can't remember anything particularly about him. I remember some things but they aren't really of great significance. And they certainly aren't anything very deep. But there's enough to talk about.

*Did you ever study under him, yourself?*

G.C.    He lectured to one course I was in, a couple of times, and I'd seen him around.

*Did he influence you?*

G.C.    Not that way. He influenced me in some ways. Not intellectually in college. I saw him at people's houses occasionally—but ... uh ... the thing about him was that he... everybody interested him. If they were boring, he'd be interested how boring they were. Didn't make any difference what they were, he was interested in what they were as an example of the human race; so he was never bored with anybody as far as I could make out. And... uh... he loved change. In the Saturday Club, Lucien Price[6] once said this about him. They were all taking about... Cassandra-ing... after the atomic bomb had gone off... and all the implications were how tough it was going to be. And he said, "Oh, I love change. I love change."

It was that kind of thing. The point was, everybody was *woe-woeing* it and sweating it out and feeling terrible, and so on, and he was just, "I love it. I love it."

Whitehead had the most benign look on his face and he was the most philosophic philosopher I can ever imagine except possibly Hocking. Whitehead was famous when I started to paint him. I had been at a party where he had been, at the Copley Greenes'.[7] They had two daughters, Joy and Francesca, and they lived in Cambridge. And they gave a little party in their house... not much of a house... a small house, and had the victrola playing and they gave a little supper. I suppose there were about fifteen girls and seventeen boys... maybe smaller than that. It was small. Just a little Cambridge party. And Whitehead was a great friend of Copley Greene's, so after dinner... before the dancing began... they separated. We went into Mr. Greene's study with Whitehead... the boys did. And he was so charming and so interesting ... brought them out so... they never went out to dance at all. Say dinner had been probably about seven... something like that... and then at half-past eight he went on until half-past eleven or twelve o'clock, and the boys didn't leave. He didn't know he was doing this and... I remember he would be interested in their point of view...elicit questions. They would ask him things that were on their minds... He had this quavering little voice... extremely articulate... and he ruined the party. The girls all sat around in the other room... had the victrola on... and nobody came in. They danced with themselves, I guess, in the end. So, when I started to paint him, I remember saying to her, "Do you remember that party?"

And she said, "Oh, yes. That was the party that 'Alfie' ruined." [*Laughing*] "Alfie" ruined the party. It was the most terrible thing, but he had no idea of it.

*Was his technique in talking to the boys different from Frost's?*

G.C.    Yes. Well, not entirely, but he had a whole different manner about him. Same kind of thing. But he was very interesting in eliciting their point of view. He was more... uh... Frost was *telling* them a little bit more and he was *learning* from them. I think that's what made his particular charm. Here was this very distinguished fellow who was only too interested if anybody interested him to hear what they had to say. And that was a great incentive for people to give. That's the reason they didn't leave the room, come to think of it. He had more of that than Frost. Oh, yeah, I would say so. This is a judgment I never tried to make. I never thought of it before that way. But this is the way it must've been, because he was this terrific sounding-board. I think that's a very good description of it. He was learning and Frost was telling. I imagine that's an extremely attractive quality which he was totally unaware of. It just spun out of his natural interest. And another thing I liked about him, of course, he never answered letters . . . never . . . never! He wouldn't even answer a telegram. Nothing. He wrote a great deal to Bertrand Russell[8] about *Principia Mathematica* . . . I think it was . . . which I never read a page of. Couldn't, I don't think. But he couldn't write a letter. His wife did it all.

*No comment.* [*Chuckle*]*

G.C. And she did help him in all kinds of ways. She adored him. He lived to be old, and I remember, they had a son, North Whitehead,[9] who's a nice fellow . . . older than I was, a good deal. He just told me something that interested me . . . interested me. During the First World War he was stationed in Africa, for some reason, with some troops. There he was and . . . uh . . . it was hot, of course, . . . very . . . in the summer . . . and they had a lot of trouble with the sentries leaving their posts. And . . . uh . . . they were frightened and he didn't know what to do about this. Suddenly he thought, put their overcoats on. And he put their overcoats on in this sweltering weather. They put them on and they were all right. They had been walking in these little shorts and a little shirt in the night . . . exposed like this in this sweltering weather against the black jungle . . . black African stuff . . . and as soon as they put the overcoats on 'em they felt protected. They did all right then. They were sweating blood, but they didn't want to take them off.

The thing I greatly regret about Whitehead was that we got on well . . . oh yes . . . yes . . . I gotta say this. He liked people with a little devil in 'em and . . . uh . . . and so did she. I remember an incident he told me that I thought was awful funny. They thought it was terribly funny. They had this young man . . . I guess he was an artist . . . who they'd befriended and they took him to the country with them and . . . he . . . he drank. They had to protect him from this. They wanted like anything to help him and get him going. There was a very rich tycoon who lived in a nearby town . . . city. They thought it would be great if they could get him together with this painter who would paint his portrait or go and do something that would start him off. Well, they watched the painter the day the tycoon was coming to dinner and, by George, around four o'clock . . . five o'clock . . . he was missing. Just as they'd figured, he'd gone down to the pub. So he came back and they

---

* G.C. never wrote a letter if he could possibly help it—and then it would be a labor of days.

SKETCHES FROM LIFE 59

had this dinner, and there was the tycoon and there was the fellow and there was Whitehead at one end of the table and Mrs. Whitehead at the other. And this painter was plastered, when he got himself to the table, and he made faces at the tycoon all through the meal. [*Laughing*] He was squiggling his eyes and twisting his mouth [*Mumble, mumble while G.C. makes illustrative faces*] and they sat there and they were nearly dying of laughter. Didn't shock 'em or upset 'em or anything, but they had a terrible time and the tycoon was frightfully uncomfortable. They didn't try to stop this guy or anything, they just let him go. And they both thought that was wonderful. They didn't like the tycoon much. It was an example of both of them. Their problem was to keep from laughing, not to do anything about it. They got through this hideous evening still laughing and nothing came of it, of course. The tycoon couldn't get away fast enough. Whitehead had a lovely sense of humor. A ridiculous sense of humor.

But the thing I feel very bad about is, he offered me his friendship. He used to ask me to come over after dinner for coffee . . . things like that . . . and I was a little shy with him. I was too immature and I didn't want to go over after dinner and drink coffee. And I didn't do it. I didn't take advantage of that thing, which I so greatly regret. Other people would have taken advantage of it, but I was a little shy. I liked him very much.

*What was your painting technique at that time?*

G.C.   I was doing what you call alla prima.* Later on I went and studied . . . before the war . . . at a thing called the Painters Workshop, made up of Frank Stern and myself and George Holt . . . two or three others and some Fogg people. Waldo Forbes[10] used to come in and show us some things now and then. This was not long before the war . . . pretty close to the war. Everybody used the alla prima technique pretty much up to then. Sargent[11] and all those earlier people did.

*What is the alla prima technique?*

G.C.   Canvas and oil paint. Then in the Painters Workshop we started things like tempera painting and the Venetian technique . . . mixed techniques . . . of egg emulsions and oils which I did after the war. I learned it before the war, but I guess I didn't really do any portraits in it until after the war. I do both now. One time I'll do one, and one time I'll do another. The ones you've seen . . . most of them . . . the one of Kissinger was certainly alla prima . . . just oil paint. The one I'm doing

---

* Technically, doing a portrait at first sitting.

of Judge Bailey Aldrich... which is going pretty well... that's got some egg emulsion in it. I go back and forth. So, my techniques haven't changed except for the experiments I've done... lots of experiments at different times... tricks I've learned myself, or made up. I haven't been any technical virtuoso. I've invented some little ways for my satisfaction and I've experimented a good deal, but these early portraits were just putting it on.

The Whitehead one was a pretty good one. It's in Emerson Hall now, in the Philosophy Department.

*Did you do it for Harvard?*

G.C.   Yes. I did it for Harvard. And Hocking engineered that absolutely. It's a little raw. I looked at it about three years ago. I got the cheeks a little too pink, but it's pretty good. It's pretty good of him. And it's got a nice expression. He had a sweet kind of look on his face. There's one of Ralph Perry up there, too.

*Did you do preliminary sketches of them the way you do now?*

G.C.   No. No. I don't think I even drew along with it much. I may have drawn... I'd draw somebody sometimes first. One drawing. Certainly I didn't do them the way I do now.

*When did you start doing those preliminary sketches?*

G.C.   I certainly was doing it by 1961. I may have done it before —the late fifties. I don't think with Acheson I did it very much. They used to come in and I'd draw them and paint them and that kind of thing, but I didn't hang around their offices until about Frankfurter's time. I did it in his house a number of times. I would say it was in the late fifties.

*Did Whitehead talk to you while you painted him?*

G.C.   Oh, yes. I painted him in his apartment up there in that... there's a big apartment house on the Charles River opposite the stadium. A whole cluster of them... I forget the names of them now. That's the last stop before Mt. Auburn, they say. People... widows ... still go there. They live there and the next place they go is Mt. Auburn Cemetery. Oh, there's quite a lot of them there. It's a very respectable place. The Whiteheads were living in one of those and I did him right there. So she was around and he was around. They were both around. I remember that room. And the thing was, the whole room was black, almost shiny black ... wood anyway, you know. Of course all books ... white china and so forth ... very attractive. Actually very cheerful.

*All the woodwork was black? Had you ever seen a black room before?*

G.C.   Oh, yes. Yes, it's very good. People look awfully well in a dark room when some light comes into it. They look wonderful against it, you know. If it was all black it would be bad, but you see, the point is with the books ... so all the books are counter-colors and the mantelpiece was black, and black on the walls ... dark neutral ... so everything counted. The china on the mantelpiece was little spots of light. It was great with the sun coming into it. Very cheerful coloring. All the furnishings and the rug very bright. Did you ever go into the Signet?[12]

*Never.*

G.C.   Well, that had a room which was a lovely room in that way. Long room in it. And ... uh ... two mantelpieces. It's a long room but not quite as wide as this one, I guess, and goes back about as long as this house. Two mantelpieces, and they were black. Very nice mantelpieces. And they were black and the room was all dark ... dark brown, very deep dark brown. And again, the books were very nice ... very cozy. And when they'd have meetings ... dinners ... or anything like that, all the people in a room like that looked great, like the Oak Room at the Plaza, because their faces looked bright pink and light against the background. And their shirt fronts all contrasted. All the people looked great and you didn't notice the room at all that way. It was much more cheerful than when they got it all light and the people kind of dark against the light. But a while ago they got this idea that ... uh ... the old Spee Club had the same thing. They had a wonderful old, great big, dark room in it and everybody looked fine in it. It was very comfortable and ... uh ... very attractive. When the place burned down they built the new building and did the same thing they did at the Signet. A young architect came and painted it all light to make it gay, you know. The boys were ... all these dead, brown faces around, just melting into it. Nowhere nearly as attractive. If you've ever been to the Plaza, that's a good example of it ... or the big room in the Harvard Club in New York. You wouldn't want it in a house, maybe. In Whitehead's case it was books ... mostly books. They made the color.

*I'm afraid we must move on. When did you paint your father-in-law, James Byrne?*[13]

G.C.   I painted him before the war.

*Did you paint him in New York?*

G.C.   No. No, I painted him up in Bar Harbor in the summer. I had a studio up there that used to be a studio down in a place called The Fields, I think. It was a very good one . . . a very old-fashioned studio. I suppose people had painted in the past there, and I rented it for the summer. He used to go down and I painted him there.

*Was this on the Byrne place?*

G.C.   No, no. It was down in the town. At least, I would say in the town. It was down a little lane with several other houses. It was near the sea and . . . there were fields . . . there were fields . . . part of a small town. I think Herman Kaiser lives in it now.

*Wasn't Mr. Byrne a colorful man?*

G.C.   Yes, he was. He was a very able corporation lawyer . . . and he was a liberal. He had a tremendous voice. In his day in New York he was one of the best in the city. Quite a corporation lawyer. As Judge Hand said, he'd put everything but the kitchen sink into a case . . . wasn't exactly selective. He'd get it all together so every fact in the world was in there. [*Chuckling*] I never told the family this. They all revere him. Actually, Phyllis is pretty objective about this, but if you attack him, they get pretty excited.

*Did he come from a family of lawyers?*

G.C.   No. Phyllis says he's potato-Irish. Her grandfather was potato-Irish. He came over in the potato famine and nobody ever knows how . . . Phyllis's father was brought up in Springfield. Mr. Byrne married pretty late. He was over fifty when she was born . . . yes, he married quite late and lived to be eighty-six and was very vigorous practically up to the end. Yeah, very much. But how his father got up to Springfield, I don't know, because his father came over at the same time when so many Irish got stuck in South Boston or East Boston and starved or lived in squalor. Her grandfather missed all that. He . . . got to Springfield somehow when he got off the boat and became postmaster there. He . . . uh . . . he had quite a responsible position and . . . uh

... he was an unusual fellow. Apparently he became a non-Catholic. He was one of these rebels.

*Was Mr. Byrne non-Catholic?*

G.C.    No. Mr. Byrne was a Catholic. The old man ... the grandfather ... bucked it. I don't know whether he became a non-, come to think of it, but he was rebellious, apparently, and he must have been quite intelligent. He had quite intelligent children. Mr. Byrne went to Harvard, of course, and came down and tutored. And he was a great friend of the Lowells and started the Signet. He was a very distinguished fellow.

*Did he go to the Harvard Law School?*

G.C.    Oh, sure. He endowed a chair there. He endowed the chair that Frankfurter had.

*Did he earn his way through college?*

G.C.    Yes. I'm sure he did by tutoring. Not the Lowells. They were friends ... lifelong friends. Yeah. He was the first Catholic member of the Harvard Corporation ... Mr. Byrne was. He was on the Corporation a number of years and then he went off. He ... uh ... he was a very able fellow. But he did, apparently, when it came to those cases ... he would pile everything in. He was a very hard worker ... he'd just get everything in.

*Who did he marry? Who was Phyllis's mother?*

G.C.    He married ... uh ... Phyllis's mother's name was ... uh ... Macgregor, and she came from Indiana. She came from a good family, so to speak and ... uh ... she certainly came from a better family than Mr. Byrne did. Mr. Byrne didn't come from any family at all, but she took them all on. [*Chuckling*] She was a very beautiful woman and she was the most gifted woman in decorating a house ... that kind of thing ... that I ever saw in my life. She could make elegance and warmth— she'd beat anything I ever saw. She had such taste she could mix up all things together so they all went ... whether they had anything to do with each other at all. Hooked rugs and French furniture and all kinds of rugs ... and it was never stuffy at all ... or oppressive. It was very cozy.

*Was she intellectual?*

G.C.    She was very bright. She had to be bright to do that. The house in Bar Harbor is really the loveliest there . . . most attractive. I'd say *the*. She did that whole house . . . she got the curtains and everything . . . that whole house of furniture . . . in one afternoon in . . . uh . . . London at an interior decorator's. It couldn't have been all the rugs, but she did get all the curtains for all over the house, and she had only one curtain wrong, about one-half . . . about six inches. You can't be stupid and do that. She wasn't intellectual in a sense of . . . uh . . . a Whitehead, but she was very intelligent and she was a very attractive woman. She was a beauty. She looked very much like Phyllis. All of them got their looks . . . the old man looked all right . . . but her four daughters and son got their looks from her.

*Were the rest of the girls as good-looking as Phyllis?*

G.C.  Oh, yeah. I think Beatrice was a great beauty . . . her two sisters, Beatrice and Sheila. Sheila was the great beauty. Beatrice and Sheila were apparently . . . I've heard it again and again . . . not from the family . . . other people . . . how beautiful they were. When they came out in New York they were the belles of the place. Sheila was breathtaking . . . Irish beauty . . . but she was elegant, very elegant. Very elegant-looking.

*You said Sheila married Ivor Bryce. Who did Beatrice marry?*

G.C.  Beatrice died. I'm afraid she killed herself. She was twenty-three and supposed to be the most attractive of the lot. They all loved her. But she got some . . . I think she got ill. She had cancer or something or other. There's a little mystery about this, but she and Sheila were great belles. Even now you hear about them. Phyllis was kind of a belle too. She was awfully pretty, you know, but she wasn't any prettier than they were. Beatrice wasn't quite as beautiful, but she was the most attractive of the lot. She had all kinds of beaux. Siegfried Sassoon, the English poet, tried to marry her for a long time, but she wouldn't have him. They were quite glamorous.

*Where did Helen, Walter Lippmann's wife, come in?*

G.C.  She was the oldest. She married Ham Armstrong when she was about twenty. Helen was spunky. I think at eighteen she went over and became an ambulance driver in the First World War. Very spunky for a young girl. Against all kinds of advice and so on. She was awfully young when she did it.

*Mr. Byrne was a Democrat, wasn't he?*

G.C.   Yeah. Yeah.

*Wasn't he involved in New York politics?*

G.C.   Yes. He got involved as a ... as ... as ... he never had an office, but he was one of the regents of New York state .. but that's not a political office. It's one of the educational appointments. He had a tremendous speaking voice. He was a frail ... rather slender fellow, but he had a voice like a ... he had an organ. God! You could hear him for miles. They didn't have an address system in those days so they'd wheel out Mr. Byrne. [*Laughing*] Mr. Byrne could sit in the middle of Times Square and you could hear him from one end to another *roaring* it out!

*Did he back any particular political candidates?*

G.C.   I don't remember much of that. He was a great friend of all the boys ... Charlie Burlingham and all those fellows ... intimate friends of his. He was mixed up in politics but he never held an office that I knew of. He was president of the American Bar Association and member of the Harvard Corporation. He resigned from that after five or six years. Yes, he was very able. He was very able. When I painted him I had a yelling contest with him.

*You mean in the studio while you were painting him?*

G.C.   I knew he could make a lot of noise ... not by screaming or stretching, that's the point. He just talked. He just talked. He didn't have to get up and bellow. He could bellow without trying if he wanted to. And ... uh ... we had ... in the studio ... And I said, "Let's try it out."

So I got up and yelled just as loud as I could ... I was up on my toes *screaming* at the top of my voice. My throat was sore, you know. Everything I had.

And when it was his turn he just went, "*Nnnno!*" and the windows rattled. [*Laughing*] God! The whole place. It was a great performance ... a terrible racket.

*Didn't that make his face alive to paint?*

G.C.   Oh, his face was lively enough. He was a ... oh yes .. he was a very amusing fellow. I liked him, but ... he was ... I had reservations.

He was kind of a bully. He was difficult. Some people loved him; some people didn't like him at all, I guess. But a lot of people swore by him. He was very much like Phyllis in that . . . he was much more controlled, of course . . . but he got irritated with things and didn't know what was irritating him. He'd sit and have the window open behind him and he'd have a draft on his neck and he'd bawl out the first person who came in the door, you know. He didn't know enough to shut the window. [*Chuckling*]

*Was he hard on Phyllis?*

G.C.   Oh, yes. He was hard on everybody. He was kind of scared of Phyllis. She'd give it to him back. He didn't like scenes. He didn't mind making the scene, but he didn't like someone making one on him. Oh, he said some awful things! He'd say mean things to her . . . hurting things. And again, he didn't mean it too much. He just meant it at the moment. She's very like him, except as a man he was much more controlled. Of course, as a lawyer, he didn't blow his top when he shouldn't. He was very careful. He picked his shots, you know. Around his house he could give it to his family all right, but he couldn't give it to her. He was very chary about giving it to Phyllis. He told her mother that somehow she could get him very upset. [*Chuckling*]

*How about Mrs. Byrne's maid, Marie Louise?*

G.C.   Well, Marie Louise was Mrs. Byrne's sort of companion . . . companion to the whole family. She was . . . uh . . . General Dorio's cousin. She was an educated . . . lovely person and . . . uh . . . she knew the family inside out, and they loved her. She was the factotum of the family. You asked if Mr. Byrne gave Phyllis a hard time. Well, this is the kind of thing he did. He stopped, but he did in the beginning. This sort of thing I'm going to describe discouraged him . . . quite a little bit.

He brought back to the house one summer morning . . . he came back with President Lowell[14] and Bishop Lawrence.[15] And they went down to this big, elegant living room . . . quite a big house . . . and done in Mrs. Byrne's way . . . beautiful. And there was Phyllis in her nightgown playing the piano. Mr. Byrne addressed himself to her and told her very sharp to get out . . . it was disreputable that she should be around there in her nightgown. He gave her quite a going over, apparently. It was out of place . . . and then, as Marie Louise described it, "Miss Phyllis rose and answered him." And that's when he wished he hadn't started it. I think she ran out of the room. Anyway, "she rose and answered him." That was the end of that. He could take it too, because he took this. Anyway, he didn't do it again. He didn't do any of that stuff again.

I put down a number of things about him I enjoyed. One of them was he'd always say, *"Rustic Vorwage!"*

That was, "Courage forward," I believe. So I used to call him "Rustic." Not to his face. And I know one time, listening to him on the telephone at Sutton Place . . . at the Sutton Place house . . . they lived there about twenty years . . . a long time. I heard this conversation in the winter. I heard this conversation between Mr. Byrne and the janitor. Mr. Byrne said, "I'm cold."

There'd be a mumble at the janitor's end.

Then he said, "I don't propose being dealt with in this manner."

Mumble at the other end.

Then he said . . . just free gratis he said, "I don't like you. I never liked you."

I always liked that: "I don't like you. I never liked you." [*Laughing*] So, the fellow put the heat up.

And the other was a little story he told me about the Roosevelts. Theodore. I don't know how intimate he was. He was an acquaintance anyway . . . a friend. The Byrneses had a house in Oyster Bay which Mrs. Byrne did. A wonderful house, apparently . . . a beautiful house. I've seen photographs of that. She used to like to take houses and . . . and fix them all up. She loved to do it. Then, after a while, she'd sell them and get out and go to another . . . she'd do another one. She liked to do them. They had a number. They had one on Fifth Avenue, one in Planting Fields . . . the one in Oyster Bay. When they were in the Oyster Bay house, Mr. Byrne was going out one day on the train from New York and he and Mr. Roosevelt sat together . . . talking . . . and . . . uh . . . Mr. Byrne told me this. They got talking about church. And . . . uh . . . Mr. Byrne said . . . it turned out that Roosevelt went to church every Sunday. And Mr. Byrne, making conversation, said, "I suppose if you keep right along going like that, you get to like it." And he said, "Roosevelt struck the end of his seat and said, *I deny it!*" [*Laughing*] Nice little gentleman story.

Mr. Byrne had a very good sense of humor. He knew how funny that was. He was perfectly unaware of the fact that he got excited and there were all kinds of stories about him in his office. He'd throw a cigar in the wastebasket. Of course it flamed up . . . caught on fire . . . and he pressed all the buttons on his desk that he could and the whole office came in. He got them all in there and said, "Who did this?"

Nobody, of course, would answer up.

And he said, "Somebody's going to get fired for this."

Somebody finally had the nerve to say, "Why did you throw your cigar in the wastepaper basket?"

And he said . . . that would have stopped most people, but it didn't stop him. He said, "Why wasn't the wastepaper basket empty?"

So I guess he fired somebody and then he'd take them back right the next day. There was one fellow he, apparently, fired all the time. He'd fire Brown again and again. Brown would get fired on a Friday and then wouldn't turn up on Monday. Mr. Byrne would come in having forgotten all about this and say, "Where's Brown?"

And they'd say, "You fired him on Friday."

And he'd say, "Brown knows perfectly well I can't get on without him. [*Laughing*] Get him on the phone."

So Brown would have another day's vacation and he'd come in on Tuesday and go on again until he got fired another Friday. This happened again and again on Brown. And Brown liked him. Some people didn't, apparently . . . here and there. But this is the kind of thing that happened. This was the way it was.

One time he went to the theater . . . when he was about eighty-four and . . . uh . . . I hadn't been married long . . about a year. We were down in New York and Phyllis said, "You'd better be prompt. He likes to be prompt." So we were prompt. We got dressed up and went to this affair and sat in about the second row. We got there a little early. We were supposed to get there about half-past eight and we got there at twenty past. And . . . uh . . . about five minutes after we got there, a man and his wife came down and they sat beyond us. The man sat next to Mr. Byrne . . . then I came . . . then Phyllis came. No. I guess Phyllis was between us. Me, Phyllis, Mr. Byrne, this couple. The man sitting next to Mr. Byrne. The man suddenly sneezed. Mr. Byrne whipped out his handkerchief and held it between him and the man like a screen, looked over the top of it and glared. Glared at him over the top of the handkerchief. The fellow was kind of embarrassed . . . very embarrassed . . . with this fellow hunched over away from him, and holding this thing up . . . . The fellow sneezed again a couple of times . . . he couldn't help it because he'd started off, you know . . . all the time Mr. Byrne would look over the top of the handkerchief . . . glare at him over the top. Finally the guy got up and moved, and his wife sat next to Mr. Byrne. And then he put the handkerchief away in his pocket and he forgot all about it. That was all taken care of.

Mr. Byrne had pneumonia thirteen times. He was very susceptible to it. Any time anyone sneezed anywhere around him, he would do everything he could to get away or put something between them to break it up. [*Laughing*] But he didn't hesitate a minute on this one, and I'm sure the guy never forgot it. Mr. Byrne had rather angry, red, blue eyes when he got sore. You could just see them ... this evil ... this fierce look coming across from the top of the handkerchief.

Well, we sat there and everything quieted down. Half-past eight came and the theater began to fill up; and twenty-five minutes to nine came ... twenty minutes of nine ... and they began to clap. Mr. Byrne, I could see, was clapping. [*G.C. clapping*] We were all clapping. It would die down and then it would start again. They'd clap. Then Mr. Byrne would be clapping longer than anyone else. [*G.C. still clapping*] When it died down, he was still going. [*Clap, clap*] And then suddenly his voice rang out ... I told you he had a tremendous voice ... power ... without any straining ... and he said, "*This is outrrraageous! In my day this wouldn't have been tolerated for oooone minute. Begin!*"

The clapping swelled with a great swelling and above the noise you could hear him shouting, "*This is outrrraageous! Begin!*" And then they would die down. Quiet. Then it would start again, and again he'd go off. Again the same stuff. Those were the words. "*In my day this wouldn't have been tolerated for oooone minute.*" [*Laughing*]

It reached a crescendo and the people behind me leaned over and said, "Is this 'Hellzapoppin'?"[16] They thought they were in the wrong theater. They thought ... they thought he was a "plant." The rest of the people didn't realize he wasn't a plant, so they went on and the clapping would go up in the air, and each time his voice would go rising up and rising above it. By God, it was extraordinary! The galleries were going wild. It was pandemonium. It would quiet down. Of course, they'd get tired clapping. It got to be almost nine o'clock without anything happening. And he kept on doing it. "*Begin! Let the play commence. Begin! Begin!*" Then, "*Outrageous!*" Then again, "*In my day this wouldn't have been tolerated for ooone moment!*"

Galleries whistling. People loved it. They loved it. [*Laughing*] There was this old gent in a tuxedo and he ... they didn't know what was going on. He wasn't straining or anything. He was just sittin' there. And then, of course, the manager came down . . . tearing down with the assistant manager behind him. Very officious little fellow. He rushed up and looked over down the line and said, "What's going on here?"

And this is what Mr. Byrne was really waiting for. He rose and looked at this fellow . . . the whole house was quiet and said, *"You miserable swindler! How dare you mulct the public in this manner?"*

The guy didn't know . . . [*Laughing*]

He said, *"You miserable swindler!"*

And the guy went, *"Woowoowoo,"* and scuttled up the aisle. And he came out and wiped the stage up with himself. He apologized all over the place. He apologized humbly to everybody. What had happened was, the play had been put on the radio and they were going to be three-quarters of an hour late. He explained this . . . then Mr. Byrne got a standing ovation . . . standing ovation. That manager never forgot that night to his last day . . . his last breath. It was a great performance. Then Mr. Byrne sat down. The fellow who was coughing wasn't sitting next to him anymore, and he enjoyed the play thoroughly . . . totally relaxed . . . enjoying every minute of it. We got out afterwards and . . . uh . . . we went back to the car and he said, "You know, there's something to always remember. Don't ever get excited when things bother you."

He'd forgotten about it! This kind of a thing would have most men shaking for a couple of days . . . just to have got up and done it. Nothing to it. [*Laughing*] I couldn't believe my ears when he said, "You know, I never get excited." [*Much laughter*] He'd had the theater going wild.

*Didn't he save the manager's hide by keeping the audience in a good humor?*

G.C.  Oh . . . oh sure. I'm sure they remember it far better than they do the play. Phyllis was funny because she kind of liked it, you know. She . . . you know . . . it amused her but she was also kind of embarrassed by it. She was looking at him kind of shifty like this. She was glowering a little bit, but she was also kind of enjoying it. It's a good story, but it requires a lot of yelling.

I said to him once, "Did anyone ever take a crack at you? A punch at you?"

And he said, "Why no. No. Nobody ever did."

And I began to figure out why they didn't was because he always used words like, "Mulct the public." The guy didn't know what he meant. [*Laughing*] He knew what "miserable swindler" meant all right. I quote him exactly. It was wonderful. You can really get "miserable swindler" out of your face with a lot of rip. The guy cowered. But "mulct" he didn't quite know what to do with.

His idea of fun was to . . . He was like a squire with a gun under his arm going out stalking, trying to shoot a rabbit just before supper . . . something like that. He'd . . . on the way home . . . he'd get into a bus and if some guy had a pipe in his mouth . . . that's what he was looking for . . . he'd go and take it out because it was forbidden on the bus. And then he'd give it back to him. And he'd get taxi drivers. If any taxi driver kind of edged an old lady or something, Mr. Byrne would rush out with his umbrella and stop the thing if he could get there fast enough. Then he'd go over to the taxi driver and say, "You . . ." What was the word he would use? . . . oh, "You contemptible scoundrel!" That's it. "You contemptible scoundrel!"

And the fellow in the taxi wouldn't know what to do. If he'd said, "You son of a bitch!" the cab driver would have got out and hit him, but you don't get out if someone calls you a contemptible scoundrel. You're stunned. [*Laughing*] He'd use this Elizabethan English on them all the time, so he got away scot-free. [*Laughing*] They thought he was a nut, I suppose. He didn't look like a nut. He was quite impressive. Then he'd go and put that umbrella up and . . . he wasn't run over . . . and he'd feel pretty good and he'd go home. But if he saw anything like that he'd get right into it. He was a character. Very much so.

I remember I painted a man named Lee McCanliss.[17] He'd been a lawyer in New York and he was a young man when Mr. Byrne was in his prime. Mr. Byrne, as I say, was president of the American Bar Association and was very active in it and had a whole big wing built, a whole new building, I think, built right next to the old one. He was very active. He did a lot for it. That's where my picture of him went.

*You painted it for the Bar Association?*

G.C.    Yup. It was a gift, I think. And McCanliss as a young feller was in the library looking some stuff up one day, when Mr. Byrne, who was then prime in the office as a lawyer . . . he came in and . . . uh . . . he had some case and he got the books out . . . he got a whole lot of books out . . . and he looked up the places where he thought he wanted to refer to. He worked all morning stacking and putting slips of paper in, so he could see where they were in each book. He had them all on this table. And he went out . . . to lunch . . . and McCanliss went right on working

James M. Byrne, G.C.'s father-in-law, oil portrait, 1938

there through the day. He spent all day working apparently. At any rate, he was there when Mr. Byrne came back. I guess even McCanliss must have gone out for a few minutes or he might have stopped the feller ... An overzealous worker had taken all those books and put them back in the bookcase. Mr. McCanliss said that when Mr. Byrne came back ... he said, "It was one of the great scenes of my life!" [*Much laughter*] He will never forget it.

*Was the Byrne portrait a success?*

G.C.   Yes. It was pretty good. That was a narrow one. He was a slender ... very slender fellow ... quite slender ... and it had a kind of angry comical look on it. It was a long thin one, so you might almost say it was three-quarters, but it wasn't. It was a long picture. His head was life-size or bigger. I've got a photograph of it somewhere.

*Did Mrs. Byrne die before he did?*

G.C.   No, no. He died first. He had a butler named Saunders and Saunders was very fond of him. I ... uh ... I got to like Saunders, but he was the kind of fellow ... kind of butler who would, if you were late for meals—which I often was—he would whip out his watch as you came to the dining room. Saunders would whip it out and just look at it and give you the message. [*Chuckling*] I got to like him, but I didn't pay much attention to him. It wasn't a very formal household. There wasn't much said about it, but he ... uh ... but he was a male servant, so to speak. He kind of valeted Mr. Byrne. He did a lot of things like that, and Mr. Byrne, as he got older, didn't like to have this supervision. He hadn't had supervision before ... but Saunders began seeing that he didn't run off and get run over. He tried to get away ... sneak off ... and he succeeded. He'd suddenly turn up in Cambridge. You see, they were living in New York, and he evaded Saunders in some way or other ... they didn't have planes in those days ... he'd get down to Grand Central Station, take a taxi from the Back Bay Station when he got into Boston, and turn up at our house. He was very fond of Phyllis. He was very fond of Phyllis indeed. Sheila needed help the most and got into more trouble, so maybe he liked Sheila best. Phyllis could handle herself a little bit more, but he liked her. He liked her and he came often. He'd turn up and then we'd get these calls from Saunders. "Where is he?"

"He's here."

And then we'd say, "Will you spend the night?" Phyllis would urge him to stay.

"No, not at all." And he'd take the ten o'clock train back.

I remember meeting him at the Back Bay Station once. It was raining and there was an incident like the janitor's. This big black man was pushing and getting his suitcase and stuff. Mr. Byrne said to me, "I don't like him. I don't like him."

Very personal. It was comical. [*Laughing*] The black person paid no mind that he heard, but he got it all right.

And my father liked Mr. Byrne. You see, Ben was the oldest son and we didn't name him after either grandfather or junior or anything. We called him just Ben, which is a family name . . . way back in my family. He was the first boy in the whole family. Sheila had girls, Helen had girls, and Jimmy had girls; so then this gent appeared. And Ben was—his head was just sort of going back and forth. He didn't know nothin', eyes not focused . . . nothing . . . in his playpen. And my father went by the door just enough so he stopped to look and listen. And Mr. Byrne was staring at Ben in his pen. And he said, "Your name should have been . . ." my father heard him say to Ben who didn't know nothin' [*Laughing*] "Your name should have been James Byrne Cox." [*Much laughter*]

He wasn't sick long. He just died. I was down in Virginia and I came up.

Mrs. Byrne surrounded him with this great visual distinction. I don't exaggerate it at all. Everybody knew this . . . felt this. He was surrounded with this distinguished ambiance. She was a genius. He, himself, in his own room, if he could get away with it . . . he'd just have an orange crate and a naked light bulb hanging, and have some books. He had a lot of books. And he was happy. He couldn't see what was going on around him at all. He had this singleness of approach to things. He wasn't trying to show off or anything like that at all. You can see some of Phyllis in him. She goes direct for something and she's not aware . . . just as he wasn't aware if he got excited.

*Did you and she go up to Bar Harbor in the summer and stay with them?*

G.C.   I think we did once. I think we did just one summer. We did one summer.

*Did it work out?*

G.C.   It worked out all right. Yes, it worked out fine. We had a lot of fun, you know, at times in the past. Oh, yes. Oh, sure. She had a lot of friends. There was Susie Scott and all of them. She had a lot of friends there. Many of them have died by this time, but she was very popular there. I think we went one summer there and I think the next summer we went to North Haven and got the Lewises' farm. Then I think the war came on.

*How did you happen to go to North Haven?*

G.C.   Well, I first went to North Haven to do Neilly White's... to do Ellie Lamont's Lansing. That's how I happened to originally, and I liked it. I liked it. And Phyllis was a great friend of Austin's.[18] She knew Austin very well... very well, long before I knew her... so she went there often and traveled to Europe one time with Austin and his mother. She used to go to Europe a good deal. So she'd been to North Haven and I'd been to North Haven, and I liked it much better than I did Bar Harbor, and she did really, too. She never liked that kind of stuff too much. What she liked was Cambridge. And she's often said at times, and said at the beginning... why she married me was on account of the house. She loved the house. She came when my father and I were living there and I asked her to come. She came for lunch and she fell in love with the house right then. She didn't marry me just for the house, of course, but she loved it. She liked that kind of thing. Her mother was a little too elegant for her; but the mother was so good it wasn't oppressive. I didn't mind it. It didn't make me feel bad. So she was willing to go to North Haven, too. And Helen Platt[19] was there... Prissy,[20] and so forth.

*Where did you stay in North Haven before you bought the house?*

G.C.   We stayed at Dudley Lewis's farm. We stayed there the summer Willkie was elected... or rather he won the Republican nomination. It was 1940, and then we went to... uh... I think the war came along after that... along there pretty quick. We may have gone two summers to North Haven before the war, but certainly not more than two. And after the war... during the war she went to Nahant with the children ... we had two... then they followed me... came down to Richmond, I told you. And... uh... after the war we went to Northeast Harbor. That's where she and Jimmy were brought up when they were young ... Northeast. They'd been brought up all their lives on Mount Desert Island in the summer and Northeast had been the first part of it. So we went back up there and took a cottage in the . . . uh . . . Harborside Inn right after Poppy was born. We spent a summer there and we began to think of buying there, but we couldn't get anything. We couldn't get what we wanted. We went to look at a house in the middle of Northeast Harbor someplace with a field around it. Kind of a tow-headed field that reminded you of North Haven a little bit. And I liked that. We both thought it was pretty nice. It was better than anything else. We neither of us liked the . . . Northeast Harbor was a little too much like Brookline, you know. Brookline's all right but not . . . you know. . . We have the same taste along that line very much. Always have. But this house, to get to the guest room, you had to walk through the master bathroom! [*Chuckling*] It was really a terrible job. And just at that point we went over to North Haven for Labor Day . . . to stay with Prissy and Pen.[21] We went down to the Platts' Fish House and they were . . . you know, Helen was a bridesmaid for her and old friends . . . best friends . . . and I liked Geoff. In fact, we had been very good friends long before that. Before the war we were friends, in fact. I tried to persuade him to come to Northeast, but he wanted to stay where he was. And we had such fun at that Fish House, and the way of life and so forth . . . I got up in the morning and got old Mr. Barnes to rent us the house.

*Old Mr. Barnes?*

G.C.    Doctor . . . Doctor . . . uh . . . it wasn't Barnes. Jesus! I know the name perfectly well! Anyhow, he owned this house his grandfather had . . . *Banks!* Captain Banks.

*Banks? Isn't he the one that owned Lea's[22] house across the thoroughfare?*

G.C.    That's right. He had the one that Lea-lea's in when he sold this one to me. He was living across the thoroughfare in that house. He had the two. He rented it to us a couple of years, then he sold it to us. But I got it that first morning. That was quite a triumph because people said he wouldn't let anyone have it and he's a sour son of a bitch and you'll get nowhere with him. I went in and I got it right away from him. We rented it right away. He was feeling good or something and we got it. And we've lived in it right along.

*Is it true you had a wonderful time in those first years up there?*

G.C.    Yeah. We had a lot of fun. For two or three years there it was just the greatest fun in the world. Then we quieted down a little bit, you know. Harry Worrall and John Worrall were so funny. John was a terribly funny guy when he set out to be. I think Maisie's discouraged him doing it because he wouldn't mind making a damn fool of himself. He didn't make a damn fool of himself. He was just very funny. The Maine stories. It was just spontaneous fun. Pen was awful good at it. He would disappear . . . I remember one time down at Bodines' . . . he disappeared and suddenly he turned up and he didn't have anything on at all except . . . I suppose he did have his shorts on, maybe . . . he must have had them on, but you couldn't tell because he was all covered with seaweed. He looked like John the Baptist. Seaweed was coming down here and kind of hanging off him. Otherwise, he was naked. He just suddenly appeared. And then, suddenly, Harry Worrall would take up a broom and pretend it was a double bass. By God, he could be awfully funny! Thump . . . thump . . . thump. We laughed our heads off. Everybody did. We had a great deal of fun after the war . . . a great deal. We had for a long time. Then . . . uh . . . oh . . . people got quieter, and John Worrall wasn't there so much. We got quieter. We couldn't keep it up, I guess.

# 4

# New York Bankers

G.C. I did Thomas W. Lamont[1] twice. Once for J.P. Morgan Company, when he was chairman of the board. And one for Exeter.

*Was he president of the board of trustees at Phillips Exeter Academy? What year did you paint him?*

G.C. About 1946 or '47. The Exeter one wasn't at all bad, in some ways, but I think they didn't like it. They took it down and I don't know where it is. Then I did one of him at the same time ... I did one of him at the same time which Austin got. A head ... a study, which was really a very good one. And Austin took it down to Philadelphia and it burnt. Burnt up and I had no photograph of it or anything like that. It was sort of shocking ... I never had a picture burn.

*Was it a fire in Austin's house?*

G.C. Yes. It was a very unpleasant feeling, that burning, because it was a sort of part of me. That was a good one and no record of it at all. And I ... and I ... it was a very good study indeed. It was better than the final thing. Then I did him again in New York. The ones I've mentioned were done in North Haven, Maine, and then another one I did in New York in the fall. He was getting older then. He was getting frail rather rapidly. And I ... uh ... did one in the fall in their townhouse there in New York. And it was ... it was, I think, a good one. It was a very honest picture indeed and he looked like a ... he looked like a ... fine old Scottish minister ... an old Scottish minister and he looked very distinguished and almost ascetic. Much more so than when he was plumper ... when he was younger. When he was younger ... when he was in the height of his prime ... Hopkinson[2] did him for the Harvard Club, and he was a sleek, plump banker, so to speak. Nowhere near as good to do as he was later on. And he . . . uh . . . he . . . his instinct, I remember, was very good about that because the picture made him look old, but it made him look all those things I say . . . and he wanted to be painted as he was . . . didn't want a rejuvenation job.

*Was the New York one for the bank?*

G.C.   It was for the bank and it made him look like the very distinguished old man he was. Tommy Lamont[3] was worried about it because he looked so old, but he looked like he did look. And . . . uh —his father didn't want any of this touching-up stuff. Tommy got a photograph he wanted me to reproduce it from . . . sweeten it up and so on . . . but his father, quite rightly, didn't want anything like that at all. No, he didn't want anything like that. I don't go into that and I couldn't do it, but Tommy wanted me to try . . . take a young photograph, that was the idea . . . of doing the picture from that. It was quite distinguished of Mr. Lamont not to want to do this, I think. But not him. So in the end the bank didn't get it and his son-in-law,[4] who was then head of the Atheneum in Hartford, had it down there; and Charlie said . . . and this is boasting to beat the band, of course . . . but he said that it was in a room with a Rembrandt and it stood up quite well. It was of an old man and it looked quite well. It was an honest picture, and now Charlie's son's got it. He was a very elegant man and a dandy. He had that quality right along. I'm sure you remember it. And he was a charming man. He talked a great deal while I painted him. He told me that all his life he got up looking forward to the dawning day's work. He liked to go to work. Incidentally, he wrote a charming book, called *My Boyhood in the Parsonage*, describing it. I liked that. He had this big house in North Haven . . . in Maine . . . and one time he said, "I'm serving seventy-five meals a day in this place."

And he regretted the coming of the income tax . . . how it would cut him down. Frederick Lewis Allen, who wrote *Only Yesterday,* was in North Haven while I was painting him. He was writing another book, and at that time he was collecting material about old J.P. Morgan the First, and he came to interview Mr. Lamont.

*Was this at North Haven?*

G.C.   Yes. This was all in North Haven. He interviewed Mr. Lamont and . . . uh . . . Mr. Lamont said several things. He said that old J.P. Morgan was the most courteous, polite fellow he'd ever known. Gentle

...sweet...charming fellow. Allen couldn't believe this. Afterwards he said to me, "It doesn't seem right to me. His memory is glossing it over." At any rate that's what he said about Morgan. Completely reversed the general impression of him that I'd heard, saying he was a very very very polite man...and considerate.

And then he gave an example of Mr. Morgan's humor which kind of interested me. He said that he had a partner named Russell Leffingwell[5] ...one of the Philadelphia partners, and Mr. Morgan ran into the Leffingwell's daughter and a friend on a street in Paris...in the summer. And he asked them were they having a good time and so on. And they said they were having a good time. But the daughter had one complaint, and that was that her old man was being rather stingy to them. "Oh, is he?" said Mr. Morgan. Then...this is the humor...he took out a check and wrote it out for ten thousand dollars, unsigned...and gave it to her and said, "Go home and tell your father to sign this." This was his idea of a great joke on Mr. Leffingwell. It struck me as an expensive joke.

*There's another similar story that his daughter tells. Apparently the Leffingwells had this lovely old house on Long Island, very simple, but very adequate and rather small. Old Mr. Morgan came for a meal or for the night one time and he said to Mr. Leffingwell, "When are you going to move into your big house?" And Mr. Leffingwell replied, "This is my big house."*

G.C. That's along the same line, all right. That's an example of Mr. Morgan's humor. It wasn't all that funny to us, but it was funny because Mr. Lamont thought it was funny.

And then he also said...and again this interested me simply because I don't deal in figures like this. Once in a while somebody would be a little late for a directors meeting. It was a weekly meeting at the bank. Perhaps somebody wouldn't be there. To make them realize it wasn't just an ordinary meeting, Mr. Morgan had a lot of twenty-dollar gold pieces made, and every time a director came to a meeting he got a twenty dollar gold piece. In gold. This gave it a little something. And this interested me, not being my scale of living. Just a little something of significance to the directors...like the gold star one gets in Sunday school.

*Didn't your brother-in-law, Walter Lippmann visit the Lamonts in North Haven quite a lot?*

G.C.  He did. But then they fell out. When I first used to go up there, he was up there quite often. At least he was up there a couple of times certainly. Mr. Lamont sort of liked Fay Lippmann, Walter's first wife ... and he liked him and they all got on very well. They liked Walter very much. I know that. Then that business when Ferdinand Pecora was investigating the ... uh ... banking business. And the time that Morgan appeared before the investigating committee in Washington and they put the midget in his lap. We all remember that. At that time, Walter did not in any way go to their aid. He reported it just like it was, so to speak. Obviously he kept the integrity of the press about the thing ... nothing to do with friendship whatsoever. And .. uh ... this was greatly resented. I don't think he and Mr. Lamont ever got together again after that. But while I was painting him, this was never brought up, of course. It would have embarrassed me and it would have embarrassed Mr. Lamont. He was a very courteous man. A gentle, quiet man and a mild one on the surface—sort of being-the-minister's-son stuff.

One time we were talking... and here I'm vague. It was either about German reparations or the debts that were owed us from the First War. We weren't getting quite enough back; and then he got very tough indeed. I remember at that time people were thinking maybe we ought to go a little easy on the Germans because they were having a hard time and everything. Not at all, as far as he was concerned. They'd hired the money, and that was all there was to it. It was very tough and, from a liberal's point of view, it was quite uncompassionate. Yet he wasn't a coarse, ruthless type at all. But when it came to that kind of thing ... there wasn't any nonsense at all. That just interested me because he had that steel in him.

*And he knew what he was talking about, because he did work on the postwar Dawes and Young[6] plans on German reparations.*

G.C.  Oh, I'm glad you said that. That's it. It had to do with reparations. I couldn't remember which it was. I knew it was one of the two. It was the German reparations. People wanted to let up on them a little bit, but his instinct was not to let up. Not out of revenge, but just because they owed the money.

Another thing he told me about ... uh ... he described a man ... some financier in New York who got into bad trouble ... I don't know what kind of trouble, but he needed help. And Mr. Lamont came to his aid.

He got a group together and they had what they called a "rescue party." They bailed this guy out or they got him out of trouble somehow or other. He'd come to Mr. Lamont in terrible shape and because of Mr. Lamont's efforts through this rescue party . . . organizing it and so on . . . they bailed this fellow out and got him on his feet again. And Mr. Lamont said to me, "You know, he never forgave me. He never forgave me." This had so hurt his pride. And Mr. Lamont said this is *not* an unusual reaction. You get a man down as much as that . . . this is a very proud type of man. Not a pleasant type, as I would take it. His pride was so excessive on that particular thing I could understand it, as a matter of fact, but it was rather interesting to hear it said.

And I remember one time I asked him . . . as I was thinking about this gentle, quiet man, put it that way . . . and I said it was my idea of a nightmare to be President of the United States. "Would you like to be President?" I said.

He got a kind of a little foxy smile on his face and said, "I wouldn't refuse it if they offered it to me."

And I thought . . . anyway, I raised my hat to him. He'd like to have been; I'd never seen anyone who'd like to have been before. This made a great impression on me at the time. He'd like to be. Yes he would. If they asked him, he would take it. But with all this gentleness . . . with all this quietness . . he gave me one of the biggest putdowns I ever got. It came out of the fact that I used to work on the portrait back in my studio in North Haven. I'd take it back and forth while it was being done.

*Was that the studio you have now up there?*

G.C.    No. That was before it was built. I worked down in the Fish House then. I had a room upstairs there. I'd take the picture back there and work on it. And . . . say . . . I was supposed to be at the Lamonts at ten o'clock in the morning, I'd work on until half-past ten or quarter to eleven and then go up. He'd only pose a half an hour or a much shorter time than he ordinarily would have. I thought it was good for me to do it that way and I thought it was good for him, too. I did this several days. And then one day I was down at the Fish House working on him and Phyllis came down and said that . . . uh . . . the butler, Metcalf [Earl Metcalf, the Lamonts' legendary butler] was on the phone and that Mr. Lamont was very upset and I had better get up there just as fast as I could. I got the picture and went up there as fast as I could. He was all dressed and all waiting, and he was sore all right. He didn't show it particularly. Before he had a chance to say much ... I guess before he said anything ... I just went in and said I was terribly sorry. I had no idea. It turned out he wanted to ... he liked to go out on the *Royal Gorge* and toot around the bay in this motorboat launch, and he'd not been able to go for three days on account of me. You see, he could have gone out if he knew I was going to be late. And I didn't know this, so I wiped the ground up with myself. I said I had no idea of this. If I'd had any idea I wouldn't have done this. I'm terribly sorry. And I was sorry. I mean an old man who didn't have too many years to live ... or days to live. And these were to be cut down on him. I was genuinely sorry. I meant it and I apologized. And I said, "I apologize."

And he said, " 'I'm sorry.' That's not good enough, [*Laughing*] I can't accept it."

And there was absolutely nothing to say. I didn't say anything. I think I just said, "Oh." And then I began to pack my stuff up, put the brushes and the paints in the box. I was going home. We were all through.

And he said, "Oh, no." He watched me do this and he said, "There's no need of that. I just wanted to tell you how I felt. And now it's all over. We won't speak of it anymore."

So we never did. I unpacked my things and we got going and never mentioned it again. That night I went to dinner there ... Phyllis and I went to dinner there and ... uh ... I witnessed his will along with John Marquand.[7] We both signed the thing.

*Was John Marquand staying at Sky Farm?*

G.C. Yes. He and Adelaide were staying there. Then after that I went down to New York and painted Lamont there. And ... uh ... he never mentioned that again.

*Was that the same year?*

G.C. Yup. He was beginning to get old then. He'd sit out on the lawn at Sky Farm with a shawl wrapped around him in the late afternoon. He'd just sit there and look at those Camden hills. And you just see the whole man. A nice picture. There he was, you know ... he was doing quite a lot, but he was beginning to fail. I went down to visit him in New York and he dressed up ... Again, he was elegant.

*Was this the same portrait?*

G.C.     No, no. The one I did in the summer at North Haven went to Exeter. And the sketch for it went to Austin. And then I did another for the bank, which is the one I've said was the best one . . . the one I did in the fall in New York . . . the one where he looked old, but he was quite grand looking old.

One time when I was doing it . . . he would nod now and then . . . I was up in this room at about the third floor of the big New York house . . . and one day he kind of nodded down and I spoke to him and he didn't answer. And I thought he was dead. I didn't know. Here's this fellow who's got a special nurse and he's got a butler . . . the whole outfit about two floors below . . . and he wasn't answering me and I didn't know what to do. I went to get the phone . . . I started to move to get somebody because I'd been *yelling* at him. And I guess I gave another yell and he popped his eyes open. Then the butler came up . . . that's it, he came up . . . I guess I got hold of somebody. He came up and Mr. Lamont came to. I didn't say anything about this to him. He was all right. And he said, "What was he doing here?" [*Chuckling*] Obviously he realized he had done something.

*How old do you suppose he was at that time?*

G.C.     I don't know how old he'd got to be. He died a little later in that year. Obviously, he was in his late seventies. [*Chuckling*] On that score you and I have about seven, eight years to go.

*I have his dates here: 1870-1948. He died when he was seventy-eight.*

G.C.     I'm glad to know how old he was when he died. This would be the year he died. I'm sure I went and did it in the fall . . . about December.

*In thinking it over, I don't want to have these sketches of the people you painted . . . these verbal portraits . . . isolated from you as a painter at the time you were painting them. When you painted Mr. Lamont, you were still on the sort of mystical forward thrust that you experienced after the war.*

G.C.     [*Quietly*] Mm . . . mm. Yup.

*Was that the period you painted that wonderful, full-length portrait of Phyllis with the glove at her feet?*

G.C.     No. That was before. That was before the war.

*Were you painting any of your children at that time?*

G.C.    Yeah. Well, I painted them about that time. I painted them—it was the year before, up in Northeast Harbor. Some of the ones you've seen, for example. The ones of Ben and Poppy were painted along in there some time. Poppy's was painted after that... around in there. But some of them were after that. Ben's was before. Kate's, somewhat after. It was around that period... yeah.

*Were they painted in North Haven?*

G.C.    I don't think any of them were painted in North Haven. Ben was painted in Northeast. Poppy was painted in Boston... uh... the ones I think you're talking about were painted either in Northeast Harbor or Boston. Of course I've got a lot of little sketches I did of them in North Haven. But... uh... not the ones you're talking about.

*And that charming one of Phyllis with the hat. You know the one you keep in the bluebeard's closet.*

G.C.    Oh, that was later on. Yeah, that was done later on. Quite a bit.

*Did you paint Marshall before Lovett?*

G.C.    No, I did him after Lovett.[8] Very quickly after Lovett. I think the same year. I haven't much to say about Lovett. I was thinking about him and I didn't... uh...

*What year did you paint him?*

G.C.    I'd say... Lovett must have been in the summer of '54, I guess. Pretty close. I think that's when it was. He wasn't Secretary of Defense then. He was just through and I painted him for the Department of Defense. He was called back to government some years later. He wasn't in government when I was painting him.

*He must have been in New York then.*

G.C.    Yes. I did him in John Carroll's[9] studio up next to Carnegie Hall. He's a very charming man and I like him very much and was very impressed by him; but I don't have much to talk about for some reason or other.

*Who was John Carroll? Was he a portrait painter?*

G.C.   No. He did ... uh ... he was quite famous in his day along the time of Benton[10] and Marsh[11] and the New York School. He used to do a picture of his wife ... a very consumptive-looking ... very attractive ... very ethereal-looking woman. He was a great big ... uh ... bear of a man and a real swinger ... and ... uh ... quite a lot of fun. He was master of fox hounds up in Chatham, New York, and he used to paint this little frail creature who was, apparently, able to take care of herself in good shape. Her nickname was "Pinkie." He was coming to the end of his career ... I used to use his studio. He didn't live to be terribly old. He died at sixty-three or -four. So Lovett would come in there. I did several there ... Jock Whitney[12] ... several people in there.

*Did you do Jock Whitney about the same time you did Lovett?*

G.C.   Just about. Very much the same time. I did a fellow named Charles Pratt in there. He was head of the Pratt Institute. I never got a photograph of that. The picture was a good one, too. I used the studio quite often. It was a good studio ... very dark, slate-kind of ... dull walls ... gloomy as hell. But it made a good background. People looked very well against it. And I did Lovett there. He used to come in and it was in the summer. He was very attractive and I got some notes on him ... some impressions.

He was a Yale man ... Bones,[13] I think it was. He was a big man about the campus. He'd been very active there, obviously, but the thing about him was he was an intellectual. He was in the Elizabethan Club; wrote a poem and did some translations he was very pleased with, which he told me about. He was a very cultivated, charming man, with many interests and facets to him. The way to characterize him a little bit ... I think of an English statesman. He had the brightest eyes I've ever seen on anybody ... a very bright-eyed man. That's what I remember particularly about him. I painted him rather fast. I wasn't with him a very long time. I didn't use this fly-on-the-wall stuff. I just went at him and took him on. I did drawings, of course, but I wasn't around him as much ... probably one of the reasons I didn't ...

*Did you go to Lovett's house?*

G.C.   I went out to his house one night. That's all. I was wondering why I don't have more to say about him, because he was as interesting a man as any I've seen around for a long time. First-class fellow. He— he'd taken up painting. He'd taken up painting because one night he'd gone over to some place on Long Island for dinner and they ... uh ... had a lot of pictures there. They had Picassos and so forth. He happened to make a remark that's made so many times, "I could do better than that." Or, at least, "I think I could do better than that."

And his wife said, "I'd like to see you."

This irritated him and he thought he'd try. Well, he didn't do better than that, but he did pretty well. He did pretty well. And when I went out there to dinner that night he got them out. He'd taken on things like ... uh ... he liked to garden and he did the tool-covered wall in his tool shed. It was hung there and it was quite a nice picture. It made a decorative picture. Then he tried a very tough one of a cupid in the middle of a fountain and he didn't do so good on that one, but he did the best he could. [*Chuckling*] He took on some tough subjects and he did pretty well in them. It interested me. Here was a very very intelligent man. He put his mind to it ... managed to draw reasonably well, you know. An example of a very intelligent man being able to do what he wanted to ... at least passably well. That's the thing I remember about him as being special.

*Did you know he grew up in Texas with Harriman? His father was general counsel for the Edward Harriman interests. I guess you know he got into Brown Brothers by marrying a Brown ... but it was he who was responsible for getting his old friend Averell Harriman to join the firm, forming Brown Brothers, Harriman. He was about four years younger than Harriman.*

G.C. I'm interested in this. I didn't know this. Where did you find it out?

*I went to the Athenaeum. Through an encyclopedia of famous men.*

G.C. Another thing I could add about him in connection with me painting Marshall. He said of him, "I can tell you one thing about him. If it's his duty, he'll do it. He won't want to particularly, but if it's his duty, you can be sure he'll give you his time." Which he did. That was the introduction to Marshall. He didn't indicate how chatty Marshall turned out to be. Marshall had a reputation for being pretty uncommunicative, but by the time I hit him he was loosening up a little bit.

All the time I was painting Lovett, I was going from New York to North Haven on weekends and midget-racing with my sons. Austin Lamont would take the boys out and get them all set. It was such a considerate thing he did. Austin would get the boat all tuned up and I'd take the morning boat and get over to the island and jump off the boat and go right down to the casino and jump into the sailing dinghy.

*I remember you doing it.*

G.C.    The boys did very well. Yeah. We won a whole lot of blue pennants. They did very well indeed. They were very good. James, particularly, was very concentrated. They won for several years, but I remember that's what was going on that summer. So I didn't do this fly-on-the-wall drawing with Lovett. He just came and sat and got out. It was done quite fast.

*Do you consider his one of your good portraits?*

G.C.    It's a pretty good one. I don't say . . . but pretty good. It all holds together pretty well.

*Was your painting changing at all during this period?*

G.C.:    Oh no. You see these were all portraits. I was doing other things too at that time. After the war, I did a lot of eggs and rocks, you know. And I was doing cobwebs . . . and I was doing crabs sometimes. A lot of other things along with it. More than I have the last few years . . . a good deal. That's when I was in Maine. That's what I did up there a good deal.

*Was the postwar momentum we've been talking about still going strong?*

G.C.    It was when I was doing Lovett. It had been . . . I'd have had periods, you know, when I would be . . . uh . . . well . . . stale or not cooking as well as I might. Be depressed a little bit. Those periods would occur a little bit now and then. And there would be very productive periods, too. But that was a good period, yeah. At least I was going well then. I did a lot of boats, too. I did quite a lot of things. Some of them were sold; some of them were lost . . . robbed and so on. I don't know where they are, but . . . uh . . . I did quite a lot of things besides portraits. Yes. They were pretty good swimmers all around.

*To go back to Lovett: He did more for the air force and the creation of national air defense than anybody else, apparently.*

G.C.    I'd forgotten that. He was a very early flyer . . . yeah. When was he born, Phoebe?

*He was born in 1895.*

G.C.   He's about eighty-three now, then.

*Yes, about eighty-three and four years younger than Marshall. Harriman and Marshall were within four years of each other.*

G.C.   Harriman was about eighty-two when I painted him and that must have been three years ago ... four years ago this time? Three years ago certainly. He'd be about eighty-six now. Apparently, he's OK, too. Well, Lovett was a very attractive man with a light touch. A vivid fellow. Fred Eaton has bright eyes, but Lovett has the brightest.

# 5

# Inside Washington: Acheson and O'Brian

*Our project today is to begin on your Washington portraits. Which would you rather start with, John Lord O'Brian or Dean Acheson?*

G.C.    I think I'll start with Acheson.[1] You see I painted him twice. I did him once when he was Secretary of State about 1950, '51, and then I did him twenty years or more later, just before he died. And ... I did Marshall between these two. Of course, Marshall and Acheson were contemporaneous in the affairs of state. But, I think I'll start now with Acheson.

*The first portrait was done for the State Department?*

G.C.    Yeah. For the State Department. And then I did a replica ... a copy of that ... four years later for the National Portrait Gallery.

*Who was the second portrait painted for?*

G.C.    I did the second for ... Covington and Burling, a Washington law firm of which he was a senior partner. He and John Lord O'Brian[2] were both senior partners. O'Brian should be in here somewhere, certainly. They were both very revered and I painted them in the same couple of years for the board room at Covington and Burling. Acheson died the next year at seventy-seven. O'Brian lasted another year or so and died at ninety-six or -seven. I'll never forget the day I went to Covington and Burling to meet them. I hadn't seen Acheson for twenty years or so, except in the paper and things like that. Oh, I suppose I'd seen him occasionally. There was the time I ran into him at the Metropolitan Club while I was painting Frankfurter and ... uh ... he said, "How are you doing with my little friend?" [*Laughing*] They were like Mutt and Jeff.

Well, that first day he came in the door and God! those mustaches were bristling... and his shoulders and body... like a kind of Steinberg[3] figure. He really bristled right at you. He had a very commanding presence. O'Brian didn't have a commanding physical presence at all when you first saw him. He just kind of came in like the tide at you, but he was very appealing because he had no side whatsoever.

*Where did you paint Acheson the first time?*

G.C.   I painted him... I painted him in the Corcoran Gallery. They had a very good studio there then. It was incorporated in the Corcoran when it was first built, just for the purpose of painting government officials... big shots and so on... statesmen and all that kind of business. It was a very fine studio. You've seen the one I have in Boston. It was about that big... a little bigger. Excellent studio. And I painted him there. I painted quite a lot of people there over the years until they finally used it for something else. So, he used to come there. Of course I went to the State Department to watch him, but most of the painting was done in the Corcoran. I must have gone down to Washington two or three times. I'm not sure, but I did him pretty much on the run. He'd come down to the studio and bring an aide, and the aide would read letters to him... discuss things and... uh... it was very interesting indeed. I remember how impressed the aides were with him. One of them told me how bright he was... told me of a labor board meeting. He said it was a meeting over some labor question... a tough meeting at the end of the day. And... uh... there were fifteen points to be discussed and he... the aide... got kind of worried because he thought Acheson had gone to sleep. He was very tired after a long day and he just wondered if he were sharp enough to handle this. And then, when the time came for him to respond, Acheson suddenly picked up... straightened a little bit... and then he took all fifteen points... one after the other... and dealt with each one right down to the end. This greatly impressed his aides. He was bright. And he knew he was bright. And he was pleased with being bright. I remember that little item right at the beginning, that his aides had a great respect for him.

I did him there; then I went out to his house in Silver Spring, Maryland, to lunch one day. Got to know him a little bit... his wife a little bit... and I had a very interesting time with him. Another thing that has always stayed with me was a conversation we had when he took me to the Metropolitan Club for dinner, one night. His family was away, and we talked, of course, through dinner. One of the things we talked about was the difficulty of his job. And . . . he said that, pretty obviously, the great difficulty always was making the decisions. That was the hard thing. Then he said . . . and this is the thing I remember . . . he said the thing that made it possible for him to make decisions and live with them was that he . . . he felt that nobody else could bring to them any better mind than he had. So that, right or wrong, it would be as good a solution as was available. I've often been asked to talk about these operators . . . these so-called great men in positions of power . . . that seek positions of power . . . what is their common characteristic . . . the universal characteristic they share? I think it is this quality Acheson was talking about. They don't know the answers necessarily, but they all think they'll give as good answers as anybody else would.

He was the first famous man—the first big shot in government—I did. I'd done Conant[4] when he was president of Harvard and Whitehead and others, but in government, Acheson was the first man. Martina Lawrence[5] asked me, before I went to Washington to paint him, if I wasn't going to be nervous around him. I began thinking about it, as you always do. However, no matter what the distinction and glamour of any man . . . he just becomes a problem like any other person. Each presents his problem aesthetically, and . . . characteristically . . . and each becomes just another problem and you take him as such. As a result, you're never nervous around them at all when you go to work . . . at all. Sometimes you wonder how you're going to get on with somebody, but it never constrains me at all.

Acheson was being attacked . . . I'm jumping around here. Obviously [*Chuckling*] I'm jumping around here. Redundant! . . . At that time he was being attacked by McCarthy.[6] He came to pose for me the afternoon after McCarthy in the morning had accused him of being a greater traitor than Benedict Arnold had been. Words to that effect. Acheson never mentioned it. I saw it in the paper later. And of course it didn't bother him particularly. At least, he didn't show it.

At the same time, his most beloved daughter . . . there were two of them. I know it wasn't Jane. Anyway a beloved daughter had had a lung removed at Saranac that day. That's where Mrs. Acheson was. That's why he was alone. It was the day I had dinner with him at the Metropolitan Club. Like all those . . . big fellows, he just compartmentalized himself and talked of other things.

*What you are saying reminds me of your own ability to compartmen-*

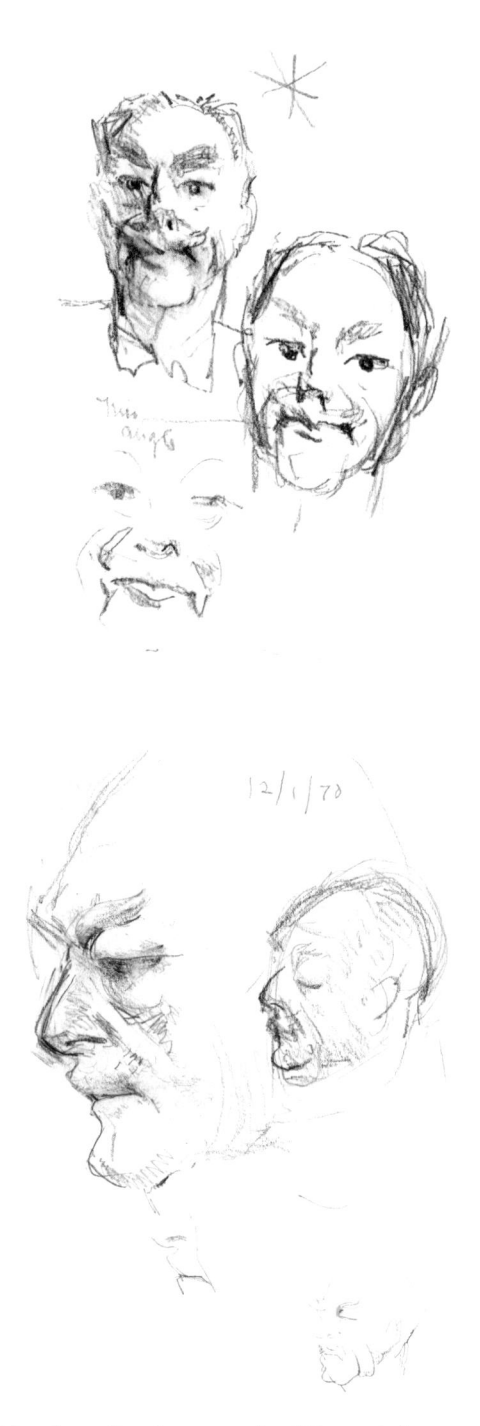

Sketchbook studies for portrait of Dean Acheson, c. 1970

talize. *John and Katherine Parsons told me you came to dinner with them one night in Hartford when you were painting Lefty Lewis. Afterwards, Mr. Lewis told them it was right after Kate's[7] funeral. They said the thing they remembered about that evening was how extraordinarily charming and interesting you were. That is the same sort of thing. You were able to compartmentalize your own tragedy. You said that Acheson was the first big guy in government you painted. Did the Lovett and Marshall portraits come as a result of that?*

G.C.    They came along later. I don't think that . . . they didn't come from just that. As I said, I had painted Conant and Whitehead. Whitehead will probably be known longer than any of them. But Acheson was a very commanding figure and I might have been a little apprehensive before painting him, so I remember him particularly.

*Did you do sketches of him before you started painting?*

G.C.    Not the first time. In those days I didn't do it that way so much. That's something I've done more recently. When I say recently, I mean in the last fifteen years. I must have drawn him while I was doing him. I went and had lunch with him the first meeting at the State Department. It wasn't in Foggy Bottom[8] then. State used to be in the old Army and Navy Building. A whole bunch of them were in there . . . in that old building that is the Executive Office Building now. I had lunch with him . . . saw him . . . I must have seen him around some before I did him, but he came down to the Corcoran Gallery pretty quick to pose. He was always jolly and funny. In fact he'd be funny about the letters his aides read him. It was a different thing when I did Rusk[9] much later. I did three secretaries of state, you see . . . Kissinger being the last . . . the final one.

*Four if you count Marshall, isn't it?*

G.C.    I guess you're right, but Marshall wasn't done for State. He was done for the Pentagon. Anyway, I was around them and knew how they operated. Acheson had a lot more time than they did. Things were pretty hot when he was Secretary of State, but he'd have time to come down to the Corcoran Gallery with an aide and they would work on easy things. Not Rusk. Rusk never got out of the office. He even worked New Year's morning. God! The pressure was building up. You know, Rusk told me they got twelve hundred cables a day in the State Department that needed some kind of attention. Acheson was able to come down comparably leisurely. I've done a lot of cabinet officers since then, but they haven't got that kind of time anymore.

*Do you remember any of his comments on the letters?*

G.C.    I remember one. Some bishop from Texas, as I remember it, wrote him and said, "I can't think of any more appropriate mind to have in the State Department."

And he said, "That's the most ambiguous statement I've ever heard." [*Laughter*]

*What were Acheson's hobbies?*

G.C.    He was a very good cabinetmaker. He'd go to his place in Maryland, in his spare time and on weekends, and do cabinetwork. He didn't like golf. He liked gardening. He didn't see any sense chasing a ball around. He was contemptuous of that sort of thing. He'd much rather garden or make something. Rowing. He thought rowing was great. He was an oarsman at Yale. He wrote a lovely passage in one of his essays about rowing in the New Haven harbor at dusk . . . in the spring . . . and the way he felt about nature and the water and the sky and so on . . . very quiet. I sent it to Geoff Platt, as a matter of fact, because he felt it. These crew fellas have this special thing they get out of it.

Acheson told me an amusing story about his rowing at Yale. Harriman was a little ahead of him, but they both took an active part in it. They got this great coach to come down, he said, to talk to his crew. They waited with bated breath to hear what he had to say. The great coach, you know. Waiting for the word. And the coach said, "The first thing you've gotta be able to do is to sit on your ass for four miles." [*Laughing*] That was about all they got out of him. "Sit on your ass for four miles." This was an example of his good, sometimes ribald sense of humor.

I'm mixing things up with the second time I painted him. The second time I did him I talked to him a lot more . . . saw him a lot more. These are the stories I don't think are generally known, but I'm sure he told them all to me. Lefty Lewis told me at least one or two. I know it was Lefty who told me about his trip to Europe. One summer he went to Europe with a Yale classmate. They traveled around and, after a while . . . they began to get on each other's nerves. Finally . . . I guess . . . one day they just started . . . to slug one another. They went at each other like a couple of wildcats and fought like hell. Then peace was restored and they were all right later on. This was interesting about Acheson because, although he was very elegant . . . a dandy . . . he could be kind of a tough egg. He could be quite combative as well as almost effeminate. You couldn't call him effeminate, really. He was too much of a realist . . . an aesthete, too. A very interesting combination. A very interesting combination considering his Episcopalian background. His father was bishop of Connecticut, but he shouldn't have been, he told me. He was really a sportsman. What his father really liked was hunting and one thing and another. He said he wasn't really a spiritual member of the church, he didn't think. Acheson could also be a little vicious. In spite of the fact he was a loyal man . . . a very warm and sentimental man . . . he couldn't help sticking the needle in, now and then. He had quite a lot of hell in him . . . a little of the devil old Mr. Whitehead used to like so much. It was kind of amusing. He was a great friend of Archibald MacLeish.[10] The year before Acheson died, MacLeish had a play on that laid an egg. I was painting Acheson at the time and I remember he got a little pleasure out of this, as one does [*Chuckling*] . . . as one sometimes does, you know, but won't admit it. But he didn't disguise it particularly.

And then there was the time that he and Jesse Jones[11] drew up their hate list. Jesse Jones had been Secretary of Commerce . . or of the interior. . . in the Roosevelt administration. He was a big shot, anyway, and Acheson liked him. He said that in Jones's office there were pictures of Austin or Dallas . . . whichever big city he came from . . . stickin' up here and stickin' up there, showing what had happened to it because of him. There were pictures of the town when Jones was young; then, in sequence, its development through his efforts. Well, as I say, Acheson was very fond of him and one night, when he and Alice Acheson were driving home after a dinner party, they heard over the radio that there'd been an airplane crash in Texas and that Jones was listed as one of the passengers. Acheson was very worried about this and he made quite an effort to find out as quickly as possible . . . to find out if he was all right. Used some little army quirk to do it. He was greatly relieved to find out that Jones was almost unscathed. He called him up on the telephone to tell him so. And Jones said, "Let's have luncheon together when I get back."

So Acheson said he went down to his office and was so glad . . . so glad to see him again. They had a good lunch in his office . . . drinks and everything. A good old jolly lunch. And about three o'clock, he said to Jones, "Let's talk about people we hate."

And he said they had the best time from about three o'clock to seven o'clock just tearing people apart all over Washington. "Let's talk about people we hate." [*Laughing*] They had *four* hours of it. You know, that's very refreshing, in a funny way, and kind of typical of him. They *rrripped* everybody apart they didn't like. He didn't tell me who they were talking about, but they had plenty of people to work over.

I've told you the story of Ickes[12] haven't I? Yeah. I'll put it in anyhow. This was during the second sitting, and somehow Ickes came into the conversation. Ickes was always referred to as "Old Curmudgeon," but Acheson said he was a very nice fellow and he liked him. Ickes was a very warmhearted man but very outspoken. And he gave me an example of his good and his bad side. He said that Ickes used to pick him up every morning during World War II, when gas was rationed, and take him down to his office. Ickes was doing the driving to save gas. At that time Acheson was Under Secretary of State under Cordell Hull,[13] and one day Ickes lighted into Hull and gave him a going-over ... up and down. Finally Acheson said, "I have my own opinions of Mr. Hull, but I work for him and I can't sit here and countenance that kind of talk."

So Ickes said, "Why the hell don't you get out of the car, then?"

And Acheson said, "That's exactly what I intend to do." And at the first red light, he got out ... hopped out of the car ... really hopped out.

And Ickes said, "Oh, you don't really mean that, do you?"

And he said, "You're damn right I mean it."

And Ickes said, "Oh, come on. Get back in. Come on, get in."

So Acheson got back in and shut the door, and Ickes turned to him and said, "I won't mention the son of a bitch again." [*Laughing*]

I like that very much, and Acheson liked it very much. "I won't mention the son of a bitch again." [Much laughter]

*Where did you do the second portrait?*

G.C.   I did that in Lloyd Embry's[14] studio just at the edge of Chevy Chase way out at Chevy Chase Circle. Embry's a very capable fellow. He's done a lot of portraits ... a lot of portraits in Texas. Comes from around here. He's got this studio outside of Washington and he's got a lot of publicity in his time; but you know, he doesn't take. He's a helluva nice fellow and we're old friends. He's a great supporter of mine. He's very capable and sometimes he does awfully good portraits. He's better, say, than Draper . . . than a lot of those guys. He's done a lot of work, but he just hasn't done a lot around here.

*How old a man is he?*

G.C.   Oh, he must be about ten years younger than I am. He's a wonderful fellow and he's got a very nice studio. I've used it a number of times in the past. That's where I did Acheson. This second time I did drawings of him, too. I did them down in his office.

*Did he have the same sort of charming background that Harriman has?*

G.C.   The Achesons had a very attractive house. A very distinguished house. Just as nice a house as the Harrimans, except for the priceless pictures the Harrimans have around, Cézannes and van Gogh's *White Flowers* and so on. Harriman has quite a collection, but Acheson's house was the house of an educated, cultivated couple. Alice Acheson was an . . . amateur painter. I betcha she didn't want to be called amateur. She was quite good . . . had had an exhibition at the Corcoran. Yes, she was pretty good. I'm sure she was the one who got me to do the picture the first time. I didn't know her, but she'd seen some of my stuff. She was a very nice woman . . . sort of a serious woman. Quite pretty . . . very pretty, but he was much more outrageous than she. She was practically bearing a cross married to this wild man. [*Chuckling*] He spoke out, you know. He told stories. He liked Ickes's attitude very much . . . appreciated that last shot. It suited him fine.

This showed up at a meeting, one day when he was secretary of state. It was a small committee meeting and one of the people there was Senator Jenner.[15]   Senator Jenner was from Indiana. He'd been an undertaker . . . I didn't know he'd been an undertaker . . and all the liberals hated him. They thought he was a bastard. I guess he was a low type of senator. Anyway Acheson hated him, and I guess he hated Acheson. Well, at this meeting they got into a heated discussion and Jenner leaned across the table and kept wagging his finger at him. [*G.C. illustrating with his finger*] And Acheson said it irritated the hell out of him. Then he decided to get mad. He told me, "I decided to let myself go. I could have controlled myself, but I decided to let myself go. I could feel the blood coming up into the back of my neck. It was a wonderful feeling. I leapt up and leaned across the table. And Jenner leaned across the table . . . "

And then one of his aides, an ex-football captain at Princeton, grabbed him from behind and said, "Take it easy, boss! Take it easy!"

He was trying to get to Jenner, and Jenner was trying to get to him, but their aides held onto them. Finally, things quieted down. There were a whole lot of newspapermen outside the door listening to this ruckus and wondering what it was all about. So when they came out of the meeting they swarmed about them asking questions. Acheson kept a stiff upper lip and said, "Jenner will tell you."

And Jenner said the same thing in reverse.

It didn't get any further, but the thing I enjoyed about it was Acheson's description of how excited he got. How he let himself go. He said it was a wonderful feeling. I particularly remember the part of the blood coming up into the back of his neck . . . just tingling all over . . . [*Chuckling*]. . . anticipating taking a crack at Jenner.

Afterwards he said he went into Senator Connally's[16] office to see him about something. Connally was the senator from Texas, you know . . . a real big old-timer and a very well known senator. Connally was on the telephone laughing and laughing. He was saying, "Mr. President, you ought to have seen Acheson and Jenner yesterday. If you could get them on the vaudeville stage, you'd get enough money to pay the national debt."

*Did he talk about Truman at all?*

G.C. He admired him greatly. He admired him very much. His ability to decide things . . . not to pass the buck at all. Marshall said the same thing. They both liked him better than Roosevelt. Anything Truman said, they knew he'd back it up and stick right with it. And, of course, he dedicated his book, *Present at the Creation*, to him:

To Harry S. Truman

THE CAPTAIN WITH THE MIGHTY HEART

He said that Truman was a terribly well read man . . . a fact that is generally known now anyway. That when he was a boy . . . something like twelve years old . . . he had read every book in the Independence library. And he remembered things, too. He really was a student of history and he applied it to current problems. I think a lot of people think he is one of the great ones . . . that he was one of the greatest presidents we've had in our time. I keep hearing this more and more.

But I want to get to Acheson's stories about his children, because I think they say something about him.

He told me his daughter Jane was a big, strong, determined girl when she was a youngster. She liked to conduct school every Saturday morning, with her as teacher and her younger brother and sister as the pupils. They didn't like it so much, and the son didn't like it at all. But, being strong and determined, Jane had her way and they were toeing the line. And this... began to get the little boy down and worry the mother. He was being humbled and taking a psychological beating. Finally, Mrs. Acheson told her husband he oughta... to speak to Jane and set her right on the right course. And he said, "I can't change Jane. There's no use speaking to Jane."

What he did do, however, was to take David, who was about seven ... and he got a friend of David's and he found a professional boxer, a fighter... to instruct them in boxing. They went to this fellow a couple of times a week and David turned out to be very good at it. He had a gift for it. Subsequently he won the boxing championship at Groton and at Yale. So, school continued on Saturday mornings and Jane kept on going. This went on for a couple of years. [*Chuckling*] All this time David was getting really quite good at boxing and he was growing a little bigger. And one day when he was nine, Jane was running school and pushing him around and... suddenly... he ups and flattens her. Lays her out! After that they were the best of friends and got on together like a million dollars. David felt all right and that was the end of that.

There were boxing stories that grew out of this. When David first went to Groton, the older boys liked to set the younger ones at one another. They'd instigate fights, then gather round. I remember the same thing when I was a boy... boys liked to get younger boys at one another. And... uh... David wrote his father and said they were doing this and had set him against this other kid. He knew how to box and it didn't bother him at all, but the other kid didn't know anything about it... and the boys were shouting for blood, you know, and he didn't want to hurt this bird. He kept putting it off... kind of stringing it along, not doing anything. Finally, he gave him a clip. This greatly distressed him and his father was very pleased with this. That was not surprising. Here again was this toughness mixed with tenderness, sentimentality, and great warmth. He was pleased with David's reaction, which he might well have been. This was a nice quality in him. Nice all the way round, how it happened.

Then in World War II, David was on a destroyer somewhere in the Pacific. Sailors from his ship, home on leave, would call on the

Achesons to tell them how he was. They obviously liked him very much. These would be enlisted men, and the Achesons told me some of the girls they brought along were something. These men told them of boxing matches with other ships' crews when they were in harbor. David always boxed for his boat. He'd say to his shipmates, "What round do you want me to knock 'em cold?" And they'd say the fourth or the eighth or something like that, and place their bets. And he'd knock 'em out right on schedule. Again and again he'd do it, and they all won a lot of money.

They also said their captain was a martinet. He'd cancel shore leaves for any noise or drunkenness. The story goes they were in an Australian port ... or some place like that ... and one night a whole lot of them came back from shore leave very drunk. David was the officer on duty, and as they clambered on board he'd tap the noisy ones. They told this with affectionate pride, but Acheson was horrified. Apparently, it's a court-martial offense for an officer to strike an enlisted man. When he said, "What! My son strike an enlisted man?" one sailor replied, "I wouldn't say that, sir. He just kind of soothed them." [*Chuckling*] Just kind of soothed them.

To go back to David when he was a little boy. One day a year Acheson would take him along to some fishing or shooting camp. For this one day a year he didn't say no to anything. David could do anything he wanted ... anything at all. He could stay up all night, if he wanted to. He had one day of nobody telling him anything. He turned out to be a very nice fellow. I don't think he's probably as sharp as his father was, but he's turned out to be a fine man ... a very effective man ... a very attractive man. Certainly not cowed in any way.

We talked about a lot of things while I was painting him. Sometimes there were serious things, too, but you can't talk very seriously while you are painting, you know. Once, I unburdened myself with a theory I had of war and peace. I went on and on about it and thought I was quite good. Elaborated and talked for about ten minutes. Then I said, "What do you think about that?"

And he said, "Not much." [*Laughing*] He said it in such a way it wasn't at all offensive, but also, he didn't think much about it either.

They had an unveiling of the picture of him down at the National Portrait Gallery ... the copy of the one I did of him the first time ....

*Did you paint the copy? Did you copy yourself?*

G.C.   I did what is called a replica.

*Is that hard to do?*

G.C.   Yes it is. Yes. It isn't much fun to do. It's, say, hard to do. You know, you're trying to do something that . . . it's very unpleasant to repeat your own mistakes, because almost everything you'd like to look better. And . . . you can't take off on a copy . . . a replica. You can't suddenly do something a little new, or you don't discover anything. You know what you're copying was done four years before . . . and it's tedious to do it over again. You see a thing that's not very well done and you have to do it. The thing you're trying to do is to make it so you can't tell the copy from the original painting. That's the little problem. So . . . actually . . . I charge just as much for doing one. I've done very few and I charge just as much as I would for a real portrait.

To get back to Acheson: I remember one day he picked me up at the Hay Adams Hotel to drive me out to Lloyd Embry's studio. He used to have gloves on when he drove . . . yellow kid gloves . . . very elegant. He was having a good deal of trouble with his eyes, which I didn't realize at the time, so he couldn't see very well. Once in a while, I'd notice his driving was a little erratic, but I didn't realize until afterwards that he was too proud not to do the driving. He drove every time we went out there, and on the way out we'd talk. This day he told me he'd been to a wedding at St. John's Church right across Lafayette Square from the White House. He'd been to a wedding there recently, when a child of a friend of his had married somebody in the diplomatic service . . . foreign service . . . and they'd had two ministers performing the ceremony: the minister of St. John's and this French bishop. It was a joint service and they conducted it together. Acheson . . . and this is typical . . . noticed something, and at the reception he went up to the St. John's minister and said, "You realize they're not married, don't you?"

The minister was rather flabbergasted and said, "Why not?"

And Acheson said, "That part of the service, 'I pronounce you man and wife,' was taken by the French bishop, who has no legal rights of any kind in this country. He doesn't represent a thing." [*Laughing*]

The minister said, "Oh dear, dear, dear!"

We leave them there.

Then Acheson went into quite a long description of the early custom of marriage. I hadn't realized why all the witnesses were there and so on . . . they wanted to be sure of the legitimacy of the children and the certainty of inheritance. There was a little more than that, but he said, basically, weddings are still performed publicly . . . before all those witnesses . . . so that nobody can come back later on and say they weren't married at all. In this particular case Acheson had picked up that all the children would be illegitimate. That was so typical of him.

Another time he was talking about the Supreme Court and said, "When the Supreme Court convenes, the marshal gets up and says, 'The Court is now sitting. God save the United States of America!'" [*Laughing*]

Like the story of Taft I'll just put in. This is a lawyer story about the Supreme Court. Taft was the Chief Justice. The custom is that when a lawyer is admitted to practice before the Supreme Court, his congressman or, somebody introduces him. The form is . . . he says . . . among other things, that "he is competent and of fair reputation." These two men . . . Texas lawyers . . . were being introduced by their congressman, who went through this business as to competency, but forgot to mention their reputation. So Taft says, "And how about their reputation?"

And the congressman says, "Oh yes. It's fair." [*Laughing*]

Norman Hapgood, the theater critic, was a good friend of Acheson's and he told me how amusing and witty he was. As an example, he quoted one of his reviews. Maude Adams was playing the title role in "Chantecler" and Hapgood wrote of her performance, "Miss Adams is a beautiful woman and a great actress; but she's no rooster."

*Was John Lord O'Brian's portrait commissioned while you were painting Acheson?*

G.C.   Both Acheson and O'Brian's portraits were commissioned at the same time by Covington and Burling. The emissary was Harry Covington. I did Mr. O'Brian first, come to think of it, because he was ninety-four years old and I thought I'd better get to him first. It turned out he lived three or four years after Mr. Acheson.

*Was he still active in Covington and Burling?*

G.C.   O'Brian? Well, he had all his marbles and he was very sharp. He had an office there and so did Acheson, but they weren't very active. They were both in the same boat . . . same situation.

*I suppose they were of counsel.*

G.C.     Whatever you call it. They were active, but they obviously weren't carrying the ball the way they had for years. And as I've said, they were very different. O'Brian had no side at all. He just came in like the tide at you. He was there every day and he'd go over to lunch at the Metropolitan or he'd go over to the Alibi. He was there every day with his devoted secretary, Miss MacParland. Miss MacParland was very nice and she was so devoted to John Lord O'Brian that she wouldn't go down in the same elevator with him.

*Did you paint him in Lloyd Embry's studio?*

G.C.     Yeah. Yup. And he was ninety-four. He was living history. He had gone to Harvard. He then went back to Buffalo, where he was born, to practice. By 1908, he was with Elihu Root.[17] They led the committee to make over the constitution of New York state. Then he went back to Buffalo. He told me he never planned anything. He never schemed or planned at all. Things just happened to him and then he went ahead and did 'em. He wasn't Irish. O' B-r-i-*A*-n. He was an Episcopalian, and he did a great deal for the Harvard Divinity School in his time. He took a great interest in it. Reston[18] referred to him as the greatest lawyer in the United States. And one of my Harvard classmates . . . a brilliant fellow in a big Chicago firm . . . told me at our fiftieth reunion that he had worked with O'Brian and he was the greatest legal scholar that ever lived. He was very good, and he was a very unassuming, charming fellow.

O'Brian told me that one of the highlights of his career was his service on the War Production Board of the United States, during World War II. He and General William Knudsen[19] were co-chairmen of it, which meant they supplied the troops of the whole country. They . . . uh . . . Knudsen was an industrialist and he harnessed industry. O'Brian was in charge of all legal ramifications it required . . . which were two big jobs that went together. And O'Brian at that time got a whole lot of young lawyers to come down and work for him. Laury Lombard[20] was one of them; Fred Eaton was another one. There were quite a lot of them . . . maybe thirty or forty. After the war, they used to have a dinner every year at the Metropolitan Club for him . . . and this has to do with his marbles. He'd go to those dinners and sometimes stay up 'til four in the morning . . . very late . . . later than anybody . . . and they'd talk. And he'd get up and make speeches without notes. Right up to the very end. When I was doing him he went to a couple of them.

He was a most whimsical, gentle, charming fellow, without any pomp and circumstance at all. The first time we went up to Embry's studio, it was a February day . . . a winter day anyway, and it was icy . . . glare ice. We got out of the cab behind the studio where there was a long sloping yard . . . grass . . . sort of country. The glare ice sort of slid down to the studio thirty or forty feet away. He got out of the cab . . . ninety-four years old . . . and I took his elbow. He said . . . very sharp he said, "I'm very sure-footed."

I took my hand off his elbow. I never touched him again. He went slithering down and he got there all right. When he got to the studio, there wasn't any step to get up to the stand where he was to pose. I got a couple of telephone books down, but they were kind of wobbly. I didn't touch him. He put his feet on them . . . wobbled a bit, but he got up all right. [*Laughing*] And I never touched him again. He was proud of that, but he had been very sharp about it . . . the sharpest he ever was with me. We became great friends. He wrote me a very nice letter, after it was all over, which I treasure, and I used to see him every time I went back to Washington.

He greatly admired Knudsen and told me a very nice story about him. During the war some fellow . . . somebody they were connected with down in Washington . . . did a dirty trick . . . a sort of self-serving double-cross which made trouble. It was a crummy thing to do, whatever it was . . . he didn't tell me what . . . and it made O'Brian livid with rage. He was mad as hell about it. And Knudsen was also angry. It affected them both equally. Then finally Knudsen said to him, "You wouldn't have done such a thing . . . you wouldn't have done anything like that. I wouldn't have done such a thing. So let's just forget it." And that was the end of that.

*When you went to see him in Washington, did you go to his house?*

G.C.   No. No. He lived in the Fairfax Hotel. He'd been, apparently, unhappily married . . . as some of my friends who worked with him tell me. They said his wife was kind of a cross, though he never mentioned it, of course. This is just gossip I got from them, but when I asked what was wrong with her . . . did she drink or anything like that? . . . they said no. She'd also come from Buffalo and he sort of came from the other side of the tracks. Apparently she felt a superiority she didn't have in any way. Anyway, he didn't have a particularly happy time, that way, though it never prevented him from achieving a helluva lot.

Studies of John Lord O'Brian's head and hands for portrait, c. 1973. G.C.'s sketches are in crayon on dark gray paper.

*Did he have children?*

G.C.   Yeah. He apparently had several children who were very fond of him and who he was very fond of. Miss MacParland told me about the time he got pneumonia while he was staying at the Fairfax and he'd gone to the hospital without telling anyone. He never told his children or anyone and specifically told her not to let them know. He didn't want to bother them to come down and see him or any of that kind of business. He was...a very happy-looking guy. Did you ever know him?

*I had dinner a couple of times with him at the Lombards'.*

G.C.   So you knew him, then. Small, round, bald. Everybody had the greatest respect for him. And I did. One of the things of interest he told me about was the resignation of Oliver Wendell Holmes. O'Brian wasn't there personally, when the resignation occurred, but somebody very close to him ... one of his law clerks or somebody who knew him very well indeed ... was there. He was right next to being there, so this is an accurate account.

It was a Saturday afternoon. Justice Holmes's doorbell rang and it was Chief Justice Hughes at the door. Hughes said to Justice Holmes, "You remember you asked me when I came to the bench ... when I became Chief Justice ... that if I ever felt you weren't able to carry your weight I was to let you know; because, you said, people generally hang on too long." And Hughes said, "I've come to tell you."

And ... uh ... Holmes turned to O'Brian's friend, who was a very young lawyer, and ... uh ... he said, "Go over to that file and get out the resignation."

He took it, made it out, and signed it. Then he said, "I'd like to go back Monday morning. I'll give it to you at one o'clock."

And there were tears in his eyes and tears in Hughes's eyes; but Holmes took it OK and that was all there was to that. That was about all that was said. Of course, O'Brian knew Holmes well. He knew them all well, and he got this from the horse's mouth, so it is an authentic account of a minor historic moment. A dramatic moment, too. The ending to a man's career. It doesn't seem so surprising to me at that age, though. At the age he was getting to be. It wouldn't be such a blow. Well, he did go down Monday morning and sat through the morning session. When it was over he got up and went out to the robing room, and he said to the black man who was on duty ... who disrobed him, "I won't be needing this tomorrow." That was his good-bye. Pretty laconic; but these are all big men.

Speaking of the Supreme Court reminds me of a John Harlan[21] story. I did a number of justices in my time. I think I did seven of 'em for different reasons. Harlan was a very nice fellow and this is just an in-court, amusing joke.

There was a very fresh, sassy guard who'd been there a long time. I'd been down there so much I'd gotten to know most of the guards. And this one said to me, "This Harlan's a funny fellow."

"What do you mean?"

He said, "The other day I was going down the corridor and I ran into Harlan and Harlan saluted me. Chief Justice Warren told us we weren't supposed to salute justices, so, when he saluted me, I said to him, "We aren't supposed to salute justices."

And Harlan said, "Who the hell said you were a justice?"

You know he was a funny fellow and this got the guard puzzled. He wasn't sure Harlan was being funny or not. [*Laughing*] I get that story balled up usually, but I got it right this time.

*How did you happen to do seven justices? Were they all done at the same time?*

G.C.   No . . . no. I did Frankfurter first.

*When was that?*

G.C.   About '59 or '60. It was commissioned by an old student of his named Arthur Colin. He was a great operator who died subsequently, but he raised the money and then paid for it as a gift to the Harvard Law School. Then there was . . . uh . . . Arthur Goldberg[22] when he was Secretary of Labor; and Harlan for . . . uh . . . himself and then for the court when he died, subscribed to by his law clerks. They none of them had anything to do with the commissioning. Byron White[23] was done for the Yale Law School. All the law schools paid for them. Soon as any law school gets a fellow on the Supreme Court, they do something about it. I may have left one out.

*Which was the most colorful?*

G.C.   They were all very attractive in one way or another. Oh, the other one was Chief Justice Warren, which was done for the National Gallery. The National Portrait Gallery wasn't in existence at that time. Speaking about the National Portrait Gallery, did I tell you I got a medal? Well, I went down and got a medal . . . .

*When was that?*

G.C.   Oh, about two weeks ago. I got a very nice little gold medal, honoring their tenth anniversary. It has a copy of Copley's[24] self-portrait in bas-relief on it. A very good bunch got it. Harriman got one. Paul Mellon[25] got one and . . . uh . . . Barry Bingham.[26] He's on the board there. John Nicholas Brown[27] got one. I was the only painter who got one . . . no, I guess one other. I think it was because I gave them some things. I gave them the Bobby Kennedy portrait . . . and so on.

*Are you giving them the Kissinger portrait, too?*

G.C.   No. I think they're going to buy it. That's what Sadik[28] said. I told him I was going to change the background and the clothes somewhat. I won't change the head at all. Not an item. Barry Bingham saw it. Yeah, I think they'll take it. I think they'll buy it.

*Where did they have the banquet, when they gave out their tenth-anniversary gold medals?*

G.C.   It was in the long, narrow gallery on the floor above the portraits where Lincoln gave his second inaugural address. He had his inaugural ball in another part of the building, but his second . . . his second inaugural address was in that room where we held the banquet.

# 6

# Marshall and Harriman

*Gardner, can we get on to your memories of painting General George Marshall?*[1]

G.C.   The portrait of General George C. Marshall was done for the Pentagon... for the Department of Defense. And it was done in the late fall of 1954 and extended into 1955. It was done... uh... at Pinehurst, North Carolina, where he'd gone to retire... gone into retirement in a little house where he lived with his wife and a grandson... stepgrandson. The big hotel... I can't remember the name of it now, but it was a big caravansary which is quite well known... I did the picture there because the house he lived in was a very small, suburban type of house. There was no place whatsoever in it where we could do anything... paint... so he came over every day. He wasn't very well. He was in bed somewhat every day, but he'd come over for two hours and sit there... pose in this room in the hotel. He'd never take a rest. He was like a soldier and sat there and didn't want any quarter. When I asked him, "Do you want to get up and move around?" he'd say, "No, I don't need any rest." I worked on him in this room with a north light and a rather big window. I remember it was high enough so I could cut off the bottom part of it and make a sort of field-expedient studio light.

*Wasn't this room your own bedroom?*

G.C.   Yes, my bedroom. The room was... uh... eleven by fifteen. A small room. I had the bed up at one end. He sat facing the window. It was done pretty much in profile... a three-quarter face view. I don't like people looking at my work while it is progressing, because it bothers me to have them checking every day when you're doing things you know are wrong, waiting to change them and make them right.

You don't want to have people peering over your shoulder at that time. Also, it disturbs them. They get somewhat more self-conscious. So, all in all, I generally don't let them see it at all . . . never let them see it as it progresses. In his case, I could put the easel up right at his feet and he sat up against the wall looking out the window. I'd go over and look at him and then go back and paint, and he couldn't see it because the light glanced from the window over the canvas. As happens in oil paintings, it glared in the light, so he couldn't see the painting at all. Never did . . . never did until the very end.

His biggest gripe was an eleven-year-old stepgrandson who was feisty enough to stand up to him. He'd often start the morning off with little bits about him . . . getting it out of his system, so to speak. He'd been commander-in-chief of all the Allied armies, his word law to millions, and this cocky little boy stood up to him. To this grandson he was nothing but an old gaffer and it irritated him. [*Chuckling*] One particular morning he came in and said, "Do you know what he did today?"

And I said, "No."

And he said, "He wants his socks washed every day. When I told him I had my socks washed only twice a week, he said, 'You don't run around as much as I do.'"

This irritated the general. It irritated him a great deal. It also annoyed him that this boy ate with his elbows on the table. This amused me because it was not what I expected of him.

He had a reputation of being very reserved . . . very dignified . . . very impressive. A man of few words who went right to the point, but he proved to be very talkative and I had an extremely interesting time with him. He could be very blunt and direct . . . forthright, of course. I'd heard about this. When he was . . . say . . .Secretary of State, people would come into his office. They'd come in and he'd be writing at his desk. The person who came in would sit down and start talking, and the general would stop writing for the moment and listen to him. As soon as the fellow had covered the subject he wanted to talk about . . . made his point . . . the way he knew the interview was over, was that Marshall was writing again. Didn't even say good-bye. So I knew he could be direct. A story he told me very early in the game illustrated this point.

He said this Balkan diplomat from behind the Iron Curtain came to see him one day and . . . uh . . . he said to Marshall, "General, why can't we get together? Why can't we be friends—trust one another—get on better?"

And Marshall said, "I said to him, 'Because you're a goddamn liar!'"

That was all there was to that. The diplomat left. This was, apparently, his style.

Another example he told me about was during the war when he went out to the Walter Reed Hospital to see a friend who'd had a nervous breakdown. This was another general, a close friend of his . . . a West Pointer . . . who had been historian of the army. He was an intelligent fellow and Marshall was fond of him. Marshall told me, "He sat there worried about everything: how awfully the war was going, how awful the world was. Goddamn it! Here I was running the war and I wasn't worried. He was sitting there doing nothing but worrying. I was disgusted and got up and left."

I imagine that put the fellow back a year, at least. With all Marshall's sensitivity, he didn't get that one and he let him have it. Outrage! Outrage!

I am apt to put questions down on a piece of paper and tack it on the canvas so that, if I want to stimulate my sitter a little bit or if things flag, there's a topic I can start him off with without having to think of something. Because, after all, if you're trying to paint somebody you're using a side of your brain . . . a great weight . . . and you can't carry on a highly intelligent conversation with a highly intelligent man while you're doing something as difficult as it is to paint anything well. This is a great help. Sometimes I ask something out of the blue such as, "General, what do you consider was the most hazardous . . . the most crucial moment in World War II?"

Without hesitation Marshall said, "Two years before we entered the war when the draft was almost abolished. It survived by only one vote in Congress."

He went on to say that this gave us a chance to prepare. People saw the war coming. He could see it coming. If we had abandoned the draft at that time, we would have had to scramble so hard, and the Germans could have gone so fast, that we couldn't have mounted anything to oppose them. He said he was very very much aware of this at the time and, for him, it was the worst worry of the whole war. He had felt that the mothers were a big influence in bolstering up the draft, so he would go out to mothers' clubs and talk to them about the importance of sacrifice and so on. He even went out to Seattle to talk to them. He was sensitive enough to realize the importance of this area. He implied that if the draft had not been extended . . . if one vote had gone the other way

... it would have been like the Newton Country Day School, or Park School's second team, playing the Boston Patriots. Against the German army we wouldn't have had a chance.

He was not only sensitive, he was a very cunning fellow. I don't mean cute. I mean cunning. He gave examples and he was rather pleased with them, too. He was a great friend of Queen Frederika, the Greek queen. After the war, when they were having a lot of trouble with the Communists coming in from the north, there was a great struggle to keep them out. He told me when she was over here she asked him, "What can I do to help the resistance in this?"

He said, "When you get back to Athens and you hear there's been a fight ... active fighting in some little village ... you get into a jeep and get there just as fast as you can. In a place like that," he said, "in a small town there'll always be somebody who has distinguished himself ... a local hero or a couple of them. You find out who he is, or who they are, and have them brought to you. And then you hug them in the public square. That's the thing that will fire them up," he said. "That's the thing you can do to help."

This again showed a sense of symbol. A sensitive sense of symbol. It interested me. Another example: Anthony Eden[2] gave a luncheon for him in London when he was between official offices. Between ... say ... Secretary of State and Secretary of Defense. What happened at that luncheon was a par-excellence example of his style. Eden himself had just been married to some relation of Churchill's ... a niece or something like that, and, at the luncheon, Marshall was placed next to Lady Eden. She was pretty cold and snooty. She had been over here for a while when Eden was sick, and I met her at Arthur Schlesinger's. I thought at the time that she was worried about Eden, but it was more than that. She was pretty arrogant. Marshall sat next to her at that luncheon in London and he felt this right away ... her arrogance. I guess right off the bat he didn't like her, but he tried to make conversation and he mentioned Lady ... I always have trouble with that name ... Lady Bentinck who was a great friend of his. He asked Lady Eden if she knew her and she said, "I never heard of her."

And he was pretty damn sure ... pretty damn sure she had heard of her because this woman was a very well known member of the British nobility. It made him sore. He really began to dislike her then. He hadn't been drawn to her before, but now he began to dislike her. Dinner went on a little bit longer and then, suddenly ... at one point, he heard her talking about Eddie Devonshire. Well! Eddie Devonshire was the Duke of Devonshire and Lady Bentinck was his sister, so then he knew she had been putting him down, and he decided to get her. This time she was really proven guilty. So he told me, at the end of luncheon and in the face of the fact, as a guest, it was not de rigueur to give a toast ... it was bad form for him to do this ... he suddenly stood up and said, "I want the men to stand up."

The men stood up.

"I want to propose a toast." And he looked down at Lady Eden, suggesting by this action that he was about to propose a toast to her. And he said, "She looked at me with absolute withering scorn. At this vulgar American who was going to propose a toast to the new bride."

And then he turned away from her and said, "To Mrs. Marshall, because it is her birthday."

He told me this *crrripppled* ... *crrrrumpppled* ... Lady Eden. She shrank down and was humiliated. He had embarrassed her ... made an ass of her ... and he was delighted. [*Chuckling*] He said he'd done three things: he'd humiliated Lady Eden; he'd pleased Mrs. Marshall; and, because he'd put in that business of the birthday, he knew Winston Churchill would hear about it. They were having dinner with him that night, and he was sure that Churchill would give her a present. Which he did. He claimed he had thought about all these possibilities and he'd got 'em all. He was very pleased with this.

He told me something else which obviously pleased him. He told me that once Eden had been asked who was the greatest man he'd ever known, and Eden had said, "Marshall." He was very pleased about that. It was rather immodest, it seemed to me, to tell it; but it was all right ... he was an old man then ... and there it was. It was quite complimentary considering the people Eden had seen. He'd picked Marshall over Churchill, over Stalin, over Roosevelt ... over the lot.

He was a very unusual man ... a very impressive fellow. In that connection ... vaguely in that connection ... it amused me when he talked about his early years ... when he was young ... a boy in school. He didn't do very well. He rated more or less low in his class for a while, and he said it worried him because it was such a catch-up in the end. It was such a tough thing getting back in good standing that he found it much easier to work every day and keep at the top of the class than it was to struggle along and come back from behind. He got to the top of the class and stayed there because it was so much easier. So much easier!

General George Catlett Marshall, sketch for portrait, c. 1954

I've told that story to many people since then. Boys like that story. It was very characteristic of him. It was logical . . . better to be at the top . . . more restful.

He'd begun to lose his memory a little bit . . . not much . . . but just a little. The average way a person does at that age. I'd kind of shoot questions out at him, as I told you I do from the piece of paper pinned to the canvas, and one time I asked him, "General, what do you consider the five most important battles in history?"

Starting with Thermopylae, he reeled off four, couldn't remember the fifth and, without worrying the issue, passed on to something else. He just said, "I can't remember," and that was that. This happened again and again and every time he couldn't remember something he didn't bemoan the fact, but went right on. Again, it was like a soldier . . . going up hill, you know, taking his losses and keeping right on going without a moment's hesitation.

There's another story which illustrates something about him. You can draw your own conclusions. I said to him, "General, were you able to leave the problem and the agonizing decisions of war behind you when you left headquarters at night and returned to wherever you were staying?"

And he said, "Absolutely. One had to be able to do it to do any kind of a job."

Then I said, "After issuing commands that would send thousands and thousands of soldiers to certain death, do you mean to say you could slough it off . . . forget it?"

And he said, "Oh, yes. I had no trouble doing that at all. Nobody could stand it if they couldn't do that. They'd go crazy."

Then he said what enabled him to do it was a trick he'd learned in the First World War, when he was in the trenches. He was just a young officer . . . maybe a captain. A low rank anyway. He was fighting in the trenches . . . in the carnage . . . very rough stuff. He said he always made it a point at the end of the day . . . or when he had a chance . . . to get down in a dugout somehow, get a candle, and read Frances Hodgson Burnett's *Little Lord Fauntleroy*, or that other one of hers, *The Secret Garden*.

I said, "Jesus, General! You mean to say Little Lord Fauntleroy put you to sleep after all that blood and gore?"

"It did," he said, "and I always went to sleep with nice thoughts in my head and slept perfectly soundly until morning. I also did that in World War II."

I said, "General, a lot of people wouldn't be able to take their minds off war that way."

He said, "Well, it did for me."

"Of course I went to bed with nice thoughts on my mind" is an example of how he could concentrate, you might say.

*Were you ever influenced by a wife's opinion?*

G.C.   Yes, in fact it was General Marshall's. At his second sitting. As I've told you, the first time I went down to Pinehurst to paint him early in December of 1954 . . . he sat for a week . . . maybe a little more . . . ten days.

*Did he ever see that first portrait?*

G.C.   No. At the end of that week, I told him, "General, it isn't good enough. I can do a better one if you'll give me more time. Let me do another."

And he said, "How much time do you want?"

And I said, "Six sittings," just to give him something to answer to.

He said, "Come down again and I'll sit for you."

This was just before Christmas, so I went home and came back a month later. Same situation . . . same room in the hotel. I'd gone pretty rapidly and about the third day . . . on Wednesday . . . I asked Mrs. Marshall to come in and take a look. It was coming along pretty well, I thought; but I wanted to be sure nothing had escaped my notice . . . proportions . . . something like that. I wanted to see how it struck somebody else. This was a wife again. She thought it was pretty good, but he took one quick look and said, "Looks like somebody with influenza." [*Chuckling*]

He went back to his chair, sat down, and didn't look at it again.

Actually, he wasn't very well. He'd often be in bed before he came over to pose. Be in bed most of the morning and come to my room in the early afternoon. He'd been ill and was taking good care of himself. He lived several years more, but he'd slowed down. This turned out to be a great advantage to me because he was a lot more talkative, apparently, than he'd been before he retired. I got the impression he'd been pretty laconic. Bob Lovett warned me that he didn't talk much, but this turned out not to be so. He talked a lot about a lot of things.

One of the things I remember him saying was that he had learned never to appoint a fellow to a job if he hadn't seen him for some time. He told me of an appointment he'd made of a man he hadn't seen for ten years. This fellow had shown great promise... had had a lot on the ball when he knew him. But he went to pieces on the job he gave him ... didn't have it anymore. This taught him never... never get anyone to do a job if you hadn't seen him recently. To check up on him, no matter how good he'd been once.

He also talked about not having gone to West Point. This also had to do with choosing people. He'd gone to the Virginia Military Institute, and it had been a great advantage to him, he said, because when he was chief of staff he had no leftover obligations at all.

General Somervell,[3] for example, was a very good man, and Marshall made him quartermaster general of the armed forces. Somervell was the only one he'd known as a young man and he considered himself lucky not to be tied down by old associations.

He talked about MacArthur,[4] too. A couple of years before the war ... "and we all knew it was coming," he said... he, Marshall, was due for promotion to brigadier general. Apparently if he wasn't appointed by a certain date he wouldn't make it. Just before the promotion was due he was appointed by MacArthur, who was then Chief of Staff, to the command of the Illinois state guard. This appointment called for the rank of colonel. If he got in there he was a frozen man. So he wrote MacArthur a letter.

"In all my years in the army," he wrote, "I've never questioned or asked for a change in orders. I've gone where I was asked to go... told to go... without complaining." Now, because of this situation, he requested a change of orders. He wanted an assignment that wouldn't stand in the way of the promotion that was due him. Either MacArthur refused or he didn't answer. Marshall was good and burned up. He was bitter, but he went out to Illinois... took the job and did his best. Here was this able man sidetracked with a war coming on; but Roosevelt knew of him and put him in command of Fort Lewis, Washington. This was the huge place where men were processed for duty in the Pacific. Its command called for the rank of brigadier general, and in short order, Roosevelt walked him up to chief of staff where he was telling MacArthur what to do. He was not unknown at the time, you know. He'd been Pershing's aide at one time, and Roosevelt wasn't going to allow this able man to be sidetracked.

*Was Marshall bitter about MacArthur?*

G.C.    He wouldn't say much about it. Oh sure he was. The feeling

I got... and it's really just my feeling... is that MacArthur wanted to keep him down. When one ear of corn sticks up too high, lop it off—that kind of stuff. MacArthur didn't want another dog barking around. But it's all pretty well documented. This wasn't an intimate thing he was telling me. It's all in the books.

*Did you see Marshall outside the sittings?*

G.C.   Yeah, I did. I went to church with them and I went to their house for dinner a few times. With just him and his wife and his stepgrandson. Their house was too small to entertain in... a little bit of a suburban house... so there was no wining and dining, and I left pretty much after dinner. I remember Marshall would get terribly annoyed with this grandson because he kept putting his elbows on the table. I did go to one cocktail party with them, however, where he became very courtly. Now was the time to be light and witty, and he was light and witty.

There's a story he didn't tell me... I read it somewhere... about the night he first met Mrs. Marshall. He was a widower and she was a widow and they were at a dinner party in Richmond, I think it was. He asked if he could drive her home and, although her house was only a block away, she was glad of the offer. So they drove around for a while. Suddenly she realized he was driving her all over town. They'd been driving around for a half an hour or more. It was his way of getting to know her... a typically corny move, as far as women were concerned. Something like that evening at the Edens' dinner in London that we've already recorded.

*How did Marshall like the second portrait?*

G.C.   He didn't say... didn't see it while I was around. I worked on it the six days he'd promised me, and then I said, "I'd like another day."

He said, "No. You said six days and the six days are up."

I didn't have to have another day. The portrait was essentially done, but I can always take a little bit more time. As Bob Lovett had warned me, he'd do his duty like a soldier... keep his word... and that would be that. So he went to the door and I said, "General, would you like to see the picture?"

It was only ten feet away, but he said, "No thanks."

He'd had this little glimpse of it the day Mrs. Marshall came in, and he may not have wanted to see it again because he was afraid he might not like it, but I never knew anyone else who wouldn't take a look.

When Marshall had died, Dean Acheson wrote a . . . an appreciation of him. At least, a memorial appreciation. It was printed out. It came out. It was the main one, I guess. And in it, as an example of what he was like, he cited the time that Marshall didn't look at his finished portrait. He didn't mention me. Just said Marshall was having his portrait painted and he used that as an example of what he was like. When a thing was done, it was done. Absolutely finished. Marshall hadn't even bothered to turn around, but had just walked out of the room. So this was an example of how a person can use an anecdote like that. Acheson knew Marshall very well, but he'd never seen an example of this kind . . . quite like that. That's about as far as you can go that way, in the sense that people usually want to take a look at a portrait just out of vanity or maybe curiosity. Maybe vanity would keep them from looking at it; but mostly they'd be curious enough to walk ten— eight feet to look at it. Even to be polite they might look at it. [*Chuckling*]

*It was done for the Pentagon, wasn't it? Not the State Department?*

G.C.   Yes. It's in the Pentagon.

*What were his relations with Harriman?[5]*

G.C.   I didn't know Harriman when I painted Marshall and I don't remember him ever mentioning him. You see, I painted Marshall in '54-'55 and Harriman in '72-'73, almost twenty years later. Why?

*Well, as Harriman is next on our agenda, and as they were close associates during World War II, I wondered what they had to say about each other. Who commissioned the Harriman portrait?*

G.C.   First let's go back to the first time I met him. It was at a reception in Washington. It was our host, Bill Walton[6] . . . who introduced us. He said to Harriman, "You ought to get him (meaning me) to paint your portrait."

All Harriman said was, "He costs too much."

I thought that was pretty funny coming from him. Actually it was his third wife, Pamela, who commissioned the picture and it hangs in their house in Georgetown. It's in very good company, I'll say that for it. Harriman's second wife had a famous gallery in New York, the Marie

Harriman Gallery... French Impressionists, mostly. That is the main thing... the foundation... of his collection. But he has bettered this. The house is full of things. In the hall is a very good bust of him by Jo Davidson.[7] Across from it... facing it... is another Davidson bust, a head of Roosevelt who, as you know, he admired very much. He presented one of these Roosevelt heads to Stalin in 1944.

*Did he talk about Stalin?*

G.C.   Not that I remember particularly, although he did boast he was known as "The Crocodile" by the Russians. He seemed pleased with this wily and tough image. Unlike Marshall, who talked about a lot of things... personal things, anecdotes and so on... Harriman's overriding interest was politics and he really didn't want to talk about anything else. Since it's a subject I don't know much about, we didn't talk very much. While you're painting, it's almost impossible to carry on a serious conversation, especially with such a highly intelligent man. You're concentrating too hard on what you're trying to do. So, although everything was natural and easy and we had meals together and saw a lot of each other, I can't remember any particular conversation with him. He was an old man when I painted him three years ago ... eighty-two; but he was still very charming... very bright... very in touch with things. While I was there, a lot of people were always coming to the house: foreign diplomats and government officials coming for advice. He was very vigorous and a part of things. I saw him just the other day and he seemed just the same.

*Can you think of anyone particular you saw there?*

G.C.   Paul Nitze,[8] whose hawkish views he distrusts, was there quite a lot; and Dobrynin,[9] who is still the Russian ambassador to Washington, came a couple of times. When he stayed for a meal I didn't eat with them. Then there was the birthday party for Ethel Kennedy which was lively and fun. I met Bob McNamara, who I am now painting, for the first time that night. And I sat next to Roger Mudd's wife... you know one of Walter Cronkite's substitutes on the CBS's evening news? All kinds of people were in and out.

But to go back to his art collection: Harriman is a man who has concern for the fine arts... appreciates them... you know has respect for them. At the far end of his living room is an enormous picture of white flowers by van Gogh. And there are Picassos and so on. It is a very elegant house in this way, but also cozy and very pleasant. My bedroom overlooked the garden and heated swimming pool; and the food was terrific. Terrific! I lived high off the hog there for over a year... dragged the picture out, you might say.

*Did you go home on weekends?*

G.C.   Yes, and I was doing other things... painting other portraits, of course. But I was in and out of that house and kept my room there for over a year. When I first came they said, "Take all the time you want. It doesn't make any difference to us. We love to have you here."

Finally it was, "You know, sometimes we could use that room...." [*Chuckling*] The picture was done by that time anyway.

They had a butler named Michael who I enjoyed very much. He always served me breakfast downstairs and everything would be just right. He told me that before he went to work for the Harrimans full time he'd been a police sergeant down at Washington headquarters. He said he'd moonlighted around a lot... worked up at Dumbarton Oaks for Jack Thatcher. Often, his little beeper would go off in the middle of a dinner party and he'd have to leave immediately... just take off. He was a rough character... not the old house-butler type in any way; but, although the Harrimans' standards are very high, butlers are hard to come by and he is still there.

*Where did you do the portrait?*

G.C.   In a house next door, where Harriman has an office. They own two houses: one where they live and entertain, the other where he works. There is no inside connection. You have to walk outside to go from one to another. I worked in a sort of studio next to his office, and it was very convenient for him. He had a secretary named Lilian, a ladylike old career employee who'd been around for a long time. He'd be sitting for me and he'd call out, "*Lil-y-aan! Lil-y-aan!*"

She'd come tearing in. He'd give her some instructions and out she'd go. Pretty soon... he loved to yell at her.. was always yelling like this. It was always, "*Lil-y-aan!*" with little smile on his face as he let it out. Sometimes it irritated her. One day I remember particularly. She came running in as usual and he said, "What's the name of the capital of ..." some obscure country I can't remember the name of now. We all tried for this one.

She'd say, "Is it Oomfar?" Or something sounding like that.

Sketchbook studies of Averill and Pamela Harriman
prior to G.C.'s portrait of Averill Harriman, 1970s

"*No!*" he'd shout.

"Is it Mangora?"

"No. *No !*" Of course, he couldn't think of it himself. Every time she'd think of something he'd yell, "*No!*"

Finally she got mad. "Damn it! Go find it yourself!"

But of course she did find it for him by calling up the State Department. It was comical, and he thought so too.

*So he had a sense of humor?*

G.C.   Not a ready one, but certain things made him laugh. I remember one time saying to him, "Are you getting tired?"

And he said, "I can stand it. After all, I've got to get this damn thing over with."

I said, "Couldn't you express that a little more felicitously?" He laughed.

I enjoyed him very much and we became friends. I still see him once in a while when I am in Washington, and I still have an open invitation to their house.

*How about Mrs. Harriman? Did you see much of her?*

G.C.   Yes. We had dinner together a couple of times when he was out. She is a lively, gallant, amusing woman ... warm, and a very entertaining hostess. Everybody likes her. Her first husband was Winston Churchill's son, Randolph, and later she was married to Leland Hayward, the Broadway producer. She told me she ran an interior-decorating business when she was married to Hayward, but gave all that up when he became sick. I've heard she nursed him like a slave through a long illness. She takes very good care of Harriman, too, I guess she likes cash and glamour, but she's a very good wife.

*Did she talk about the Churchills?*

G.C.   She never said anything about Randolph, but she was very interesting about Churchill. Apparently they were very fond of one another. She said he liked pretty women ... wasn't a womanizer, but enjoyed their company. She also said he loved gambling and often took off on male vacations or long weekends without Lady Churchill. Pamela thought this was very hard on her, but she told me these all-male excursions were an acceptable British custom to that generation.

Geoff Platt knew her when she was first married to Hayward. He did over his Mount Kisco house, "Haywire," for them.

*Is that the "Haywire" of Hayward's daughter's book? The place where he and Maggie Sullivan lived with their children?*

G.C. Yes. And Geoff told me that when Hayward first introduced Pamela to Mount Kisco, people went, "tsk, tsk, tsk." She was too lively and glamorous not to be suspect and they didn't know what to make of her. It turned out that her old man was Sir Kenelm Digby, of one of England's most ancient baronages. As soon as that became known she was accepted, and this amused Geoff.

After Hayward died, she married Harriman. Everybody knows she had been his mistress in London during the war, and by now he was a widower. So they got together and "Haywire" became their summer home.

*Did you ever go there?*

G.C. Yes, one July. I drove down over the Fourth to deliver a picture. My car broke down, so I had to stay on a day or two while it was being fixed. Here was the same comfortable elegance as in Washington ... a swimming pool ... and lots of people around. There were a couple of big shots staying there, and then people who weren't big shots at all. A very pleasant mixture. One young man, named Holbrooke, was Assistant Secretary of State for Foreign Affairs. He had with him an attractive girl in some kind of government job, who he wasn't married to, but as is the way of life now they were given one of the little houses by the pool.

We did various things over the weekend. One day the Harrimans took us over to New Canaan to see Philip Johnson's glass house.

*Philip Johnson,[10] the architect?*

G.C. Yeah. He's a great friend of the Harrimans'. A charming, likable fellow about my age. I saw quite a bit of him when we were both active trustees of the American Academy in Rome. He's very original ... very positive and autocratic, and because he has money of his own he's done a lot of experimenting. Some good things, some bad. This irritates a lot of architects who haven't the financial security to take his chances. But whatever else they say about him, he is one of the bellwethers of modern architecture. He and Pei. His Connecticut place is full of creative buildings. Just inside his driveway is an old farmhouse where he lives most of the time, I think, but most of the stuff is way-out, is way-out.

The glass house is down a slope about seventy-five yards from the drive. It looks like a small, oblong box. There is a shaft inside for bathrooms and such but otherwise it is entirely of glass, very simple—very chaste. But in spite of curtains that can be drawn you wouldn't want to live in it. It's too exposed. This overlooks a pond where he has built a sort of a gazebo . . . a little pier over the water. Then further on down the road . . . a country road . . . there's an underground bunker where he has pictures. And there's a small, glass, steel-beamed museum for sculpture. Near this is a huge, outdoor piece by Judd,[11] I think. This looks like a half-submerged cistern. You wouldn't know it was a piece of sculpture without being told. He's pretty far-out, you know . . . original.

But to go back to the "Haywire" weekend: On Sunday, we went across the Hudson to see the old Harriman estate, "Arden." Harriman had spent his summers there as a boy. The big house now belongs to Columbia University, where they hold meetings and seminars, and the grounds have been made into a public park. There were a lot of people there swimming and having cookouts and having a wonderful time. He took us to a secluded pond with an old broken-down boathouse. He told us he used to swim and play there. As I said, it was very hot and we swam and picnicked. Very pleasant, as all Harriman hospitality. I was sorry to leave it.

# 7

# Wives' Eye View—and F.F.

*When I was in Washington last week, I visited the National Portrait Gallery and couldn't find your portrait of Acheson.*

G.C.   It isn't up there because he hasn't been dead long enough. It isn't there yet. There are two in the State Department. As soon as he's been dead for ten years one of them will go to the National Portrait Gallery. The original one was done for the State Department.

*Speaking of originals, another original I'm thinking of is Eero Saarinen,[1] Lily's ex-husband. I love his TWA terminal at Kennedy Airport.*

G.C.   Actually, he took the idea of that from her. From one of her eagles. She's done quite a few of them. There was a small, metal one in that exhibition she had with Maude Cabot and me at the St. Botolph Club. Eero is awfully clever at taking other people's ideas and transposing them. There's nothing wrong with that. It's quite correct.

*Why isn't Lily better known as a sculptress?*

G.C.   Mostly because she isn't very good at promoting herself. She's taken life a little bit easy ... enjoyed herself ... and she's had rather bad luck. She did some very good things with him but didn't get any credit. She certainly should have been in the Institute of American Arts. She's far better than some who are in there.

*I think the head she did of you ... the one that was exhibited at your joint exhibition with her and Maude Cabot last month at the St. Botolph Club ... ought to belong to the National Portrait Gallery.*

G.C.   It's rather immodest of me to try and bring it forward, but if you think so, I'll mention it. I'll mention it to Sadik. It's a good piece. That's the point. I wouldn't mention it except it's a good piece. I'll just say, "Do you want it?" And he might for the hell of it. He just might. You've seen it before, haven't you?

*I saw it once before in that other exhibition you had with Lily ten years ago in Cambridge. Each time I see it, it's you. A much younger you, of course...*

G.C.   It's not much younger. Well, yes, I suppose it's somewhat younger.

*It's exactly the way you carry your head. Does Lily own it?*

G.C.   No. I own it. The Fogg[2] owns one. There were three made.

*Three from the same cast?*

G.C.   Yes. The Fogg owns one and I have one. And I think mine is in the cellar of her house. Nobody knows where to put it. [*Chuckling*]
   She's got two down there, I think. I could give mine to the National Portrait Gallery. She's funny, you know. [*Chuckling*] She has this thing she did for St. John Smith... a fox... God! [*Laughing*] She's had that fox back for years... may have sold it. You know, to her they're hers. She's done my children. I said to her, "You better not sell anything of mine."
   She's got these things of mine around and I've told her if anything happens to me, I've told 'em to go over and get them. The children like that head all right. Did I show you the little pig of hers I've got? A little bit of a thing?

*No not yet. Gardner, how much influence do wives exert in the acceptance or rejection of a public portrait? I am thinking especially of Judge Bailey Aldrich you've just finished for the United States District Court of Appeals.*

G.C.   Well, actually, in that case, she liked it very much indeed. Sometimes they don't, but she did. She was really very rhapsodic about it, although if she hadn't liked it there's nothing much she could have done about it. It was commissioned and paid for by his clerks and they thought it was good, so it would have been hung in the court house no matter what she thought of it. It's been quite successful, you know. It's one of the better ones I've done. I had an awfully good time with Bailey. He had an unexpected ribald sense of humor and he knew the words to all the old songs. I know a lot of them, too. He'd start humming, "Five

Foot Two, Eyes of Blue," or even "Darling, I Am Growing Old," and I'd join in and we'd sing together. We had a great time, but I'm sure it took longer to paint the picture than it would have otherwise because of it. But to answer your question: I've never known a public portrait that the wife had the influence to refuse.

*How about Nancy Kissinger?*

G.C.   You have a point there. She said to me she liked his portrait very much when it was first finished; but certainly one of the reasons the State Department gave, when they refused it, was that she didn't like it. You never can tell with wives. I've been leery about them. I've said to many men who couldn't wait for their wives to see their portraits, "Don't get too excited. You never know how they'll react."

They see their husbands in situations nobody else sees them in, and they like something in him nobody sees very much ... if ever. So, you can't tell. I learned that in the very beginning. It happened with Roger Merriman[3] when I was just out of college. He was a colorful history professor at Harvard ... a character. He looked rather like an elephant, with folded eyes kind of peeking out. He was the first master of Eliot House, I think, and his wife wanted his portrait painted to hang there. She was a nice lively little woman and was arranging to have him painted by Iacovleff,[4] who was teaching at the Museum School. Billy James[5] had been influential in getting him in there to teach as head of the drawing department, and he was an extremely good draftsman ... extremely good, but he was nothing particular on portraits. Mrs. Merriman was much taken with him. She thought he was very charming. A Russian ... a foreigner ... that kind of mystique. It irritated me and I thought I could do better. I knew Merriman quite well because we were in the same club at Harvard. He was sort of an honorary member of the Spee and was around a lot when I was in college. So I went to him and said ... I'd never done this before ... but I went to him and said, "I'm sure I can do you. I'd like to take a crack at it."

He said, "All right, I'll give you an hour." Something like that ... maybe "two."

So he came up to the studio ... the one in the Cambridge house ... and we started off. I worked very fast. Not because of what he said. It just went fast. In those days, I let them see the portrait as I went along. He got very interested in it and liked it very much right off. It was a very good likeness. Everyone felt this and he was tickled pink. He couldn't wait to have his wife see it. So he brought her up to the studio and he was jumping around like... well, if he'd been a dog his tail would have been wagging like lightning. He thought it was terrific, you know, and he was so pleased he was rubbing his hands. She looked at it and went, "Tsk, tsk, tsk. Just as I thought. *Just* what I was afraid of."

He stopped jumping around. He stopped wagging his tail and said, "What do you mean?"

"He's got that worldly look about you." She said, "You have a dreamy side. This doesn't have your dreamy quality. He's got your worldly look."

He said, "You never see that look on my face except in the bedroom. *God damn it!*"

And he left the place, slamming the door as he went out. She kind of chuckled, but that was that. You see, he'd been maladjusted when he was young . . . awkward and maladjusted . . . one of those late-developers who get to be very popular when they're older. So he liked the fact he was one of the boys and a good fellow . . . all that kind of stuff. This was the side I saw of him. I'd never seen the dreamy side. That's the reason he liked the picture. Iacovleff did a bad one, [*Chuckling*] which they got for Eliot House. For example, Merriman had an eye shot out in a hunting accident when he was a boy, so he had a glass eye. I did a three-quarter face and put the glass eye at the far side . . . didn't make much of it. Just an eye in there. Iacovleff did a three-quarter face, too, but the glass eye was the one you could see. The glass eye was the prominent one. He just reversed what I did. It was a crummy picture, but they got it.

*Where's the one you did?*

G.C. It's around somewhere. I've shown it several times. Then sometimes, wives like something you don't expect them to. I did a guy once who was a real stinker: General Harold Talbott, Secretary of the Air Force under Eisenhower. He was a tough, aggressive man and had a great many enemies because of his rudeness and toughness. I did a picture of him and it worked. It felt like him and it looked like him. A little bit nasty. He had a very charming wife and I thought she wouldn't like this, but she thought it was great. She liked this quality in him. You just can't tell.

Then there's a very common reaction. An old wife may be keeping before her the silver-threads-among-the-gold stuff. No matter how old he gets, he's still young and fair to her. And then they see him on canvas and they get some kind of a shock. I can think of one good example: Dr. John Enders,[6] who isolated the measles and polio viruses. He had a very nice wife. She was his second wife and had been his secretary before she married him, so she had been around a long time. Dr. Enders looked the way he always had to her. When she saw the portrait she was quite shocked. She thought he looked old. It was a very good portrait, if I do say so ... made him look younger if anything. His younger colleagues who worked with him and had commissioned it disagreed with her. They liked it very much and it was accepted and hung in the Jimmy Fund Clinic of the Children's Hospital in Boston. I was sorry for her— not angry or irritated; but she wouldn't let me show it for a long time in outside exhibitions. Wouldn't give the hospital permission to show it publicly.

*How does your work go with McNamara?*[7]

G.C.   I get on pretty well with him. I'll go down to Washington again to work on him some more. A funny thing happened to me there. I thought I was locked in for the night at the top of the World Bank[8] Building. It's terrible to get out of there after they've closed up.

*Do they have any dogs wandering around?*

G.C.   No. Maybe they do. I never thought of that. [*Chuckling*] I don't think they do. McNamara has a big suite on the twelfth floor. You come into it off an elevator bank, through the glass end of the corridor. You open the doors there and go into this large foyer. Very nice, indeed ... very tasteful and so on. Rooms go off it and I have a little room there. Well, one night I came out to go home about a quarter to seven, and, oh my God! the glass door ... the whole glass thing was tight as a drum. I shook it and banged it and nothing happened. And I began yelling and nothing happened. I went yelling around the offices. [*Laughing*] Finally I found a fire exit. There was a little passageway out to it. I suddenly realized if I went out into this and the door closed behind me I wouldn't be able to get back again. It was one of those funny situations that I finally got out of.

*You couldn't telephone?*

G.C.   I didn't know who to telephone in the building. I didn't know who to call and let me out, and I didn't want to wait around until nine o'clock for some guy to get me out. I wanted to go home and get a drink and dinner. It was very irritating. [*Laughing*]

*Where were you staying?*

G.C.   With Jimmy and June Byrne, Phyllis's brother and sister-in-law.

*Did you finally get out through the fire exit?*

G.C.   Yeah. I got out all right through the fire exit. I just had sense enough to take off my raincoat and put it down in the door going into the passage, so the door wouldn't close until I was sure I could get out. If I hadn't been able to get out and the door closed behind me, I would have gotten stuck in the passage, and that would have been a *lousy* place to be. [*Laughing*] No books... no bathroom... nothing there. At least I could have lived in the other place for years if somebody'd given me food. There were couches, obviously, and books and all.

At any rate, the work on him is going very well.

Oh, various things have happened since I've seen you. Nothing in particular... just going about doing things, you know. But I feel fine. I feel good... am working well. I'm working now on Ed Mason.[9]

*How's it going?*

G.C.   I've just started on him. Do you know him? He's a professor at Harvard, an economist. I see him at the Saturday Club. He's a very nice man. I guess I told you that Galbraith and a fellow named Carl Kaynes are promoting the picture... among his ex-pupils. He's obviously got many.

*Where will it go?*

G.C.   It'll go in the Littauer Center.[10] He's a big... quiet... kindly ... deep-feeling man. Kind of shy. I find him very appealing. Sort of the same appeal as... uh... Paul Freund.[11] You're kind of drawn to Paul Freund... I always was, anyway. Something nice about him. This fellow has this kind of feeling. I'm doing pretty well with him.

And the Aldrich picture has been accepted and they all think it is very good. His wife hasn't seen it. She's the only one. But they've accepted it, so they can't back down now.

*Where is it going to hang?*

G.C.  It'll be in the court house in the United States Federal Building in Post Office Square. In the courtroom of the First Circuit Court of Appeals. He's a senior judge there. And I told you, I saw the Kissinger picture for the State Department. Oh boy! It's a dog. It's a real dog!

*Could they refuse this one, too?*

G.C.  Oh, I don't think so.

*Where do you suppose Kissinger found the artist?*

G.C.  He must have seen him someplace around in Texas. He particularly wanted him to do it. It's lowered him some in my eyes. I thought he had more cultural taste.

*You asked me if we'd done Frankfurter, and I said yes, we had done a little; but I don't think we did him up the way we should have. We were talking about Lippmann and we fell into Frankfurter. Now, what you did tell me about him was that you sketched him in his living room in your underwear, because he had a cold and kept the room so hot.*

G.C.  *Without* my underwear. I just put on my shirt and trousers. I didn't have any underwear on under them.

*And you also mentioned how he couldn't stand Douglas and had an antipathy for Warren. And then the other thing you gave me was that lovely quote from Carlyle that meant so much to him. But that's all we've got on Frankfurter.*

G.C.  Oh, we can do better than that. I hope I can piece this together in some way, because there's quite a lot more about him. If I start coming at it now, I can think of things right away that are just items about him; but I'm sure when I leave today there will be quite a lot of things I haven't thought of. So, I don't want to feel I have to get it all in today. All right? All right.

Oh, there are quite a lot of little items about him. To put them in helter-skelter . . . you mentioned the quote about Carlyle. He made another quote . . . it wasn't a quote. It was just a remark he made. Just right off . . . it doesn't need any context . . . he said, "The most difficult art in the world is to persuade men to live in peace together."

It's a very good remark. I've suggested it to many others since . . . this is relevant to that remark . . . that statesmen or people who work in affairs of state . . . are faced with that kind of problem. It's like a piano player. I don't know how many keys there are in a piano. Let's say one hundred and eighty-seven or something like that. It would be like a pianist sitting down and having one hundred and eighty-seven keys on Monday, and then something happens in Iran or Phnom Penh or some place like that, and the next day they have only fifty-six notes. And the next day they have two hundred and seventy and the next day they have five. They constantly have to keep playing this terrible shifting keyboard. This is rather a good analogy. In that connection, I remember George Kennan saying . . .

*Did he say this to you?*

G.C. No. I heard him say this. He said it at Walter Lippmann's. That's something we might talk about sometime, Walter Lippmann and Washington. I used to go there and work when he was alive and lived on Woodley Road. I used to go and stay there once in a while— work from there and go to dinner, because they sort of had to have me. There were always interesting people there . . . almost always interesting. The level of candlepower of some of the luminaries was considerable. [*Laughing*] You'd look around and there'd be three *Time-Life* cover fellows. You'd sort of recognize the faces vaguely around the room. [*Chuckling*] They wanted to come and impress him . . . get ideas across he might do something about. And he wanted to pick their brains and so on. George Kennan[12] was one of these and one time he said . . . it was pretty obvious . . . but he said that people were always expecting answers and there never were going to be any answers. You'd go up one rung and then there'd be another problem. And the problem changes. In foreign affairs . . . world affairs . . politics . . . there never never never would be any answers. People will expect them and think everything is solved, but . . . but to get back to Frankfurter.

*He split with Lippmann, didn't he?*

G.C. He split with Lippmann. Yes he did. Indeed he did. One of the first things Frankfurter did with me in that room where I had my underwear off . . . where he had the fire going because he had a cold— was to start in on Walter. I think he knew he was my brother-in-law. They fell out over Walter saying he didn't think Hitler was totally bad. I think that's what it was. He didn't condemn him utterly in the early stages. I don't want to get this wrong, but . . . uh . . . he didn't defend . . . Walter did not condemn Hitler enough, in Frankfurter's opinion. Did not stand up for the Jews enough. Frankfurter was a Jew and he was proud of it, conscious of it. Walter wasn't sort of anything along that line. Most of Walter's friends were not Jewish.

*Was Walter Jewish?*

G.C.    Oh gosh yes! Totally. One hundred percent. Oh yeah, oh yeah. Obviously he was a very distinguished man. He came from intelligent people. But he never emphasized this at all. He was very cool in all his judgments, you know. Frankfurter got disgusted with him and angry with him and really didn't like him after that. They never got together again. Walter tried to be... uh... pacify him a little bit, but he was out. Frankfurter really had a file on Walter... how Walter was cowardly about facing up to situations with people. How he'd kind of duck out when the crunch came. I'm telling you things now that Frankfurter told me. As I said, Walter didn't like to face up to scenes. Everybody knew this about him. He didn't like fighting and that kind of thing at all. He was brave enough about other things... but... Frankfurter had a list of things he had against him.

*Can you give me an example?*

G.C.    Yeah. Walter married a girl named Faye Albertson. Mr. Albertson started a kind of experimental community like Brook Farm when Walter was in college... or about that time... and he was out there with a number of other people... I've forgotten who exactly. A little intellectual community went out and started a kind of Bronson Alcott[13] kind of thing. And Faye was a pretty, attractive young woman ... not an intellectual at all. She was charming and she was Mr. Albertson's daughter. And Walter married her. Apparently it was an unsuitable match from the beginning. Judge Hand told me it was very unsuitable. Walter was cerebral and she wasn't cerebral at all. She was sensitive and a very warm woman. And eventually they broke up. Walter never faced up to her. He'd gone off and was going to marry Helen, my sister-in-law, Phyllis's sister. He went to Mr. Albertson—and said, "I think you'd better break this to her. You can do it better than I can."

So he left her, and he got his father-in-law to do his dirty work. This burned Frankfurter up. Now, as a matter of fact, Walter may have been right. It could have been easier for her, you know. But he wouldn't have any false sense of honor about this... of going to her himself... but actually, doing it this way might have been better. I don't know.

Frankfurter took it very bad. [*Chuckling*] He made jokes about it, you know. How Albertson had given and now Albertson taketh away. "The Lord giveth and the Lord taketh away." [*Chuckling*] Walter ducked that one, all right. And then Frankfurter dwelt on the time he let Croly[14] down when he was on the *New Republic*. He was on the *New Republic* with Croly, and he left him to go somewhere else without telling him. He didn't give any warning. He just left. Again, he didn't want to make any scene.

All these things Frankfurter held against him. And he didn't like Helen. Helen, of course, *adored* Walter. Anyone who was Walter's enemy was her enemy. And she began to give Frankfurter a hard time.

*In other words she had the Byrne fire.*

G.C.   Yes she did. She certainly did. [*Chuckling*] I remember Frankfurter saying, "She's not my favorite woman." He didn't like either of them at that point. And . . . uh . . . he used to quote his wife on Walter. She would say, "He was too clear to be good," or something of that sort. In other words, it was there-was-less-than-meets-the-eye kind of criticism. It was criticism of his lucid solution of things. And I can remember her saying, "We'll have to wait to see what we think until we've read Walter." Frankfurter's wife was a . . . have I talked about her?

*Not at all.*

G.C.   Well, his wife was a . . . a gentile. Her name was . . . I can't remember now. Putnam . . . Loring . . . something like that. It was a New England name.[15] And she was a very beautiful woman. She was a very pretty woman.

*Was she tall, because he was so short?*

G.C.   She wasn't very tall. She was taller than he was. You didn't have to be very tall to be taller than he was. I never saw her standing up. I just saw her in bed . . . lying down . . . so I don't know whether she was tall or not. Lots of people know what I'm going to say here now, but it's rather interesting. He married her . . . oh . . . uh . . . probably early in the century. He might have been thirty or so. But when she married him, she'd been to Vassar, I think it was, or Bryn Mawr . . . one of those colleges. She was sort of an avant-garde girl, I guess. And she married Frankfurter, who was a Jew. In those days it was like a person marrying a black today, a little bit. This was a proof of her progressiveness. This is me speaking now, but I think it must have happened somewhat that way. She was very attractive and he was a long-established professor at the Harvard Law School. I guess that's about when she married him. I'm not sure when, but someplace in there. And they lived in Cambridge quite a long time. He was very proud of her.

Then he got on the Supreme Court, and when they went down to Washington she became an invalid. She withdrew and ... uh ... stayed in bed all the time. She would go out in the afternoons and have little automobile rides, but she withdrew from social life entirely. There's all kinds of theories you can bring up about this. There didn't seem to be anything the matter with her. But very few people saw her. I was greatly honored by him because he wanted me to go and see her. And he adored her. He'd talk about her and say things she'd said. She was always sniping at him and it amused him. But the cuts were quite nasty. I don't remember any particularly now, but there were little criticisms—little criticisms of him that he'd quote with glee. As I say, he adored her and he gave me the honor of saying he'd like me to meet her. So I went in and saw her in her Washington house. She was in bed and ... uh ... I'd expected to see somebody probably, you know, in ill health, emaciated, but she was as pink and rosy and pretty as she could be ... for her age. She was obviously very rested and her face was pink and there was no sign of illness* whatsoever, except that she was staying in her room all the time. Everything was very nice there. It was a shrine. He'd come in every day; and he'd come in when he went to parties and tell her about it. But finally these stories of her sniping at him made me feel a little funny. In the end ... that would be 1961 ... and he didn't die for a number of years afterwards ... eight or nine years afterwards ... I used to go see him when he was dying. He was a very warm man. He made me feel ... he made one feel as if he was very interested in you. That he appreciated you. He did this with many many people. And ... he liked me sufficiently so he wanted me to come and see him. And this was an honor coming from him. But of course he had many much closer friends, but he was a very warm man and I used to go and see him. I remember once ... these are derogatory some of these things ... but I'll put them in ...

*They give a rounded picture.*

G.C.   One time ... and I was surprised at this ... and then not

---

* Arthritic left hip kept her bedridden for her last two decades.

surprised . . . he was lying in this . . . uh . . . they had left that house in Georgetown and were in an apartment on Massachusetts Avenue . . .

*Was she alive?*

G.C.   . . . she was alive . . . which Dean Acheson got for them. Dean Acheson was a very good friend of Frankfurter's. He took care of him and helped him all he could in every way. By this time, Frankfurter had had his stroke, and Acheson went out and got the new apartment for them. Frankfurter was in one room . . . it was quite a big apartment . . . and his wife was in another. I went to see him and he was in this bed . . . this hospital bed that had been put in . . . and I remember he took my wrist in his hand and said, "You had more fun while painting me than you had with anybody else, didn't you?"

Here's this very famous man . . . able man and so on . . who really wanted me to say yes.

And I said it. "Yes."

But I've had just as much fun with some other people. Just as much. Acheson . . . Hand . . . quite a number of people. He certainly was one of the ones I had a nice time with and I liked him, but he wanted me to say I'd never had as good a one. This was kind of amusing, you know, to take it for what it's worth. Another time . . . and again this was not long before he died . . I went to see him and he was up, sitting in the little sitting room. And . . . he got talking and he said . . . I was doing a picture of Mr. Rusk at that time . . .

*What's the date here?*

G.C.   This would be about '63 . . . someplace in there. I think I did Rusk in about '63 . . . '64, in there.

*After Kennedy died?*

G.C.   No, Kennedy was still alive. No, wait a minute. No. No. It was after Kennedy died, because I remember Rusk saying to me, "You know, this Johnson is a more powerful man than Kennedy ever was. Maybe this won't be so bad."

Rusk liked Kennedy, but he thought Johnson knew his way around and was a very good leader. He did know his way around. As Reston once wrote, "Kennedy was rather in awe of the senators before he became President, so he approached them with a certain amount of awe. But," he said, "Johnson runs the place."

No awe whatsoever. [*Laughing*] Just shoves 'em around . . . you know, twisting their arms and so on. Frankfurter shared this view a little bit.

Anyway, I was talking to Frankfurter that day, and this came up about Rusk . . . so it was after Kennedy died. It must have been '62 or '63 . . . and Frankfurter said, "Who did that picture of Acheson down at the State Department? Who did that terrible picture? Do you know who did it?"

And I said, "Yes, I know who did it."

"God!" he said, "it's a terrible picture." [*Laughing*]

He went on a bit how bad it was. How it made Acheson look arrogant and pompous and one thing and another. He didn't like it in any way and he really went after it hard. And then he said, "Do you know who did it?"

I thought a minute. Am I going to humor this fellow and just let it go? And then I thought, he's too good a man. Obviously his mind was going a little bit because he had known before that I'd done it. He'd kind of known it, but he'd forgotten it. I didn't want to dishonor him by hoodwinking him . . . or trying to hoodwink him . . . and later on have him suddenly remember. He was too strong a man to humiliate that way. So when he said, "Who did it?" I said, "I did it." I said, "I did it." Not belligerently, just, "I did it." There was nothing else to say. [*Laughing*] He said, "Oh."

There was no way to say anything else. He'd gone *way out too* far. There was no way of him going back and saying, "Well, you know — I . . . ." [*Laughing*] Then we went on with other things and it was forgotten. It was funny. I couldn't stop him. Like the Walter Lippmann thing. He used to rip into him and I couldn't stop him, as I told you. I guess he didn't know I was his brother-in-law. Very quickly I'd told him. But I didn't worry about Lippmann. He could take care of himself. He didn't need my defense. Obviously a lot of people used to knock Walter. Some revered him, others didn't. But this had nothing to do with me. I didn't go to his defense particularly, unless it was something 'way off on him. He was fair game. To get back to Frankfurter's wife. About this time . . . I didn't know this . . . Lefty Lewis told me . . .

But to get back to Frankfurter . . . where I got this from was from Lefty. I'd indicated to Lefty that Frankfurter's wife was critical of him in a kind of sarcastic, humorous way. I don't remember the cracks now, but they would be there. They were rather witty . . . a little subtle and a little derogatory, most of them. He was so bouncy he could take this stuff. Like he had a cook that he liked very much ... a black cook. She did the same kind of thing to him and he enjoyed it.

For example: He was reading the paper, one morning, and he said to the cook, "I always leave the newspaper the way I got it." He said, "Very few men do this and no women."

And the cook said to him, "It's wonderful working for a perfect man." [*Laughing*]

He thought this was great. The cook was always giving him stuff like that, and she was fond of him, too. He would quote her again and again. And Mrs. Frankfurter made the same kind of remarks, only they had more bite to them. They weren't quite comfortable sometimes. Most of them were pretty snappy, snide little remarks.

Now, remembering she'd gone to bed like that ... after having been quite a belle in Cambridge ... in Cambridge she'd figured pretty much, but when she hit the big spot she began to wither ... withdraw. Then comes Lefty Lewis at the last. He told me this particular time he saw Frankfurter when he was dying. He would be wheeled into his wife's room in his chair or whatever it was. He went in one time and she began to be nasty. And then she said, "You little Jew." She said in utter contempt, "You little Jew."

And he went out. Lefty saw him later and he told him. When Lefty said, "How's Marion?" ... I think that was her name ... "Can I see her?" Frankfurter said, "I don't know." And then he told him. Frankfurter told him this story. It was a very brutal thing to have done and I assume it's true.

My own interpretation in the crudest kind of way is that she married him ... she married him as a kind of gesture. That is, probably loving him and so on, but influenced greatly ... like the debutante who marries the captain of the crew and maybe doesn't love him very much, but the whole thing is exciting. I'm holier ... I'm more sensitive ... I'm-more-aware-of-the-great-values-than-you stuff. And then in Cambridge, everything was fine. She held her own. She was a bright, college intellectual ... or at least an intelligent, educated woman. Then he got to the Supreme Court ... went down there and he was the big shot and she was nothing at all. She was just the wife of ... this is just what I'm saying. She took to her bed, and there wasn't apparently anything the matter with her. Nobody else ever said this, but this kind of fits together in a general way. And then this final turning in the end. The nastiness really getting nasty. They had no children, which was too bad, and he was a very exuberant man. He was very high-powered. Probably a very hard guy to live with, in some ways, he was so full of piss and vinegar. And he loved to go out. He went out a lot. And he loved people. She was just not the same kind of nature. She couldn't sleep with him, that's what it really amounted to.

*Where did you paint him?*

G.C.   I painted him in the Corcoran Gallery. I painted there for years, when I went down to Washington. For quite a long time, you could take a government official or anybody important there; and if you were professionally acceptable you could go and get a very good studio for nothing. I painted Acheson the first time in the Corcoran. That was the one for the State Department. I forget what year it was they finally used the studio for another purpose, but it was a very good one and had been built when old man Corcoran built the gallery. That was one of the great museums of the country. It's still a very good one. It's just been overshadowed by the National Gallery and all the other museums that have sprung up in Washington. But when I was a boy ... uh ... it and Chicago and New York and Boston were the big museums.

*Where did you stay while you were painting him?*

G.C.   I stayed at the Hay Adams Hotel, which I did for years. When I painted Frankfurter he'd had a heart attack. He had a bad heart and wasn't supposed to go upstairs, so he'd come into the Corcoran by a back door where there weren't any steps. He'd come up a ramp where they brought in the heavy pictures and crates. So he'd come down, and I painted him down there and it went fairly well ... pretty quick.

*And that's in the Harvard Law School?*

G.C.   That's in the Harvard Law School. Then there's a replica of it in the Supreme Court, which is a pretty good replica. If you don't see them together, they look pretty much the same. That picture did me a great deal of good. It got all over the place in a quiet way ... in a lot of law books. Max Freedman wrote a biography and published Roosevelt and Frankfurter letters.[16] It's the frontispiece of that book. It's been the frontispiece of quite a number of books and I've ... done quite a number of lawyers because of it. I'm doing one right now for this fellow Toepfer[17] ... Lou Toepfer, who's been president of Case Western

In May 1953, Gardner Cox was in the audience when the Welsh poet Dylan Thomas gave a reading at the Fogg Art Museum, Harvard. Afterwards, G.C. was host to a very distinguished gathering at 88 Garden Street, where Thomas proceeded to get drunk, answering questions with long silences punctuated by obscene non-sequitur remarks. This portrait is the result of sketches done on the spot; there was no formal sitting.

G.C. used hotel stationery for this impression of Felix Frankfurter on the bench, 1960s

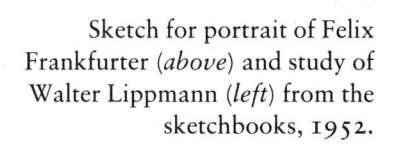

Sketch for portrait of Felix Frankfurter (*above*) and study of Walter Lippmann (*left*) from the sketchbooks, 1952.

Reserve University now for eight years. He was vice-dean of the Harvard Law School for quite a long time before he went out to Case Western Reserve Law School as dean. That portrait is on account of Frankfurter. He remembered the picture, so when it came time for him to have his portrait . . . oh, that Frankfurter led to quite a lot of things.

*Do you think it led to most of the justices of the Supreme Court?*

G.C. No, I don't think it did. It helped with the Harvard ones undoubtedly. I don't think it had much to do with the Yale ones. Yes, it would have helped some. It helped with Levi, the president of the University of Chicago. It helped there. . . . One of their best men in the law school . . . a very eminent fellow . . . he had it on the frontispiece of his book about Frankfurter. A lot of lawyers knew about it. But now to revert to other little things about him.

That remark he made about Carlyle has always stayed with me. There were other ambiances about him that gave me a feeling about him, too. But of course they were just little items. He used to sit on the Supreme Court and he was so small that you'd see just the top of his head. I drew a picture of him of just the top of his head lookin' over . . . you'd see the other justices sitting there and then you'd see just this little dome. I used to get these very good seats in the Supreme Court for big cases. They put me in there so I could look at him. When I was there he made a point of getting up and asking questions . . . leaning forward so I could get a good look at him [*Chuckling*]; because you'd come in and all you'd see was this little . . . this little pink thing over the top of the front of the bench. [*Laughing*] But when I came in, he'd put on a little something for me. He could be very comical in court, too. Wish I could remember some of the funny remarks he made . . . I almost can . . . .

*Can you remember any of the cases they were arguing?*

G.C. Not under him. I remember a few of the others. I remember the great case of the Taft-Hartley Law, when the railroads were striking. The place was packed then so you couldn't get in.

*Who were you painting then?*

G.C. At that time I was painting Arthur Goldberg. He wasn't even a justice. He was a lawyer for the unions. I did that one of him for the Labor Department. Or was it one of the other justices? I did eight in all. Frankfurter was the first. Potter Stewart[18] was fairly early on. I better get a little order in the thing. We better leave the justices for another time.

*By the way, Gardner, I was at a New England Poetry Club meeting recently where your friend Dave McCord read some of his recent poems. They were just wonderful. As an octogenarian he seems as fit as ever. The only way he showed his age was he talked too much.*

G.C.   He can talk quite a while. He's a hard man to get away from if you're in a hurry, but I'm very fond of him and I agree with you he's just as good as ever. I don't see any signs of falling off. He's got a whole lot of things coming his way too, which he richly deserves. He was taken into the Saturday Club last year, and he's just been made an honorary member of the Tavern.

*Wasn't he always a member of the Tavern?*

G.C.   Oh, yes. But he doesn't have to pay dues now. The point is that it was a nice thing ... it was a testimonial to the fact that a lot of people are fond of him. It doesn't happen very often. It's very rare it happens there. These are little things in his community, but, as you say, he's getting recognition in other things, too.

*What is the purpose of the Saturday Club and how old is it?*

G.C.   I just saw something yesterday or the day before that came out of a book about it. Emerson started it and Longfellow and Holmes Senior. I think it's a little bit over one hundred years old. Founded in 1864 ... about in there someplace. There are now forty members altogether. You get in and you don't pay any dues. Somebody ... some members who have more cash than others subsidize it sufficiently so nobody pays any dues. And nobody pays any initiation fees. It doesn't cost anything at all; so, if you're a member, you just stay for life. They don't all come to every meeting by any means.

*Is it a group of scholars?*

G.C.   No. No. I think it's varied a great deal over its history. They have three big volumes of ... uh ... of biographies. Small, short, five- or six-page biographies, written by members about other members from the beginning. And ... uh ... all the fellows in it are on the local scene.

*Is it just Cambridge?*

G.C.   No, no. It's Boston. It's always been Boston. A lot of Cambridge men have been in it, but we meet in Boston at the Union Club in the room where President Lowell was born. [*Laughing*]

*I didn't realize the Union Club was a Lowell house.*

G.C.   It was a Lowell house before the Civil War. I think the club was started right after that and its name is connected with it.

In the beginning it was very literary. There've never been many painters in it. Sargent was in it. William Morris Hunt[19] was in it. Charles Hopkinson was in it. William James Jr. was in it and I'm in it. That's it. But they've had a helluva distinguished bunch of people in the past. Whittier . . . all the great poets over the time. Whittier was quite shy. He didn't come much. James Russell Lowell went a lot and Agassiz[20] went a lot. Agassiz was one of the early ones. The volumes of people who've been in it are very impressive. It looks to me as though they were giants in those days and now have come down a little bit.

*Who's in it now?*

G.C   Archie Cox[21] is president. John Finley[22] was president before him. He was president for several years . . . was in there when I came in about five years ago. He was very graceful and Cox is good at it. They're both teachers. They know how to bring people out. It's done very easily and very gracefully. Enough people pitch in.

*Is Galbraith in it?*

G.C.   Yeah. And Moynihan's[23] in it. Elliot Richardson[24] is in it and so on. As I said, forty in all. There're a lot of lawyers and economists. Bob Bowie[25] is a member. He's a lawyer. And Charlie Wyzanski, a lawyer and a judge. Then there are the technology men. This fellow, Jay Stratton[26] is a helluva nice fellow. Wiesner . . . all the M.I.T. ones . . . good ones are members of it.

*Howard Johnson?[28]*

G.C.   Howard Johnson. Yeah.

*Is he one of the bright ones?*

G.C.   Yes. Very. He's the most undistinguished-looking fellow. He doesn't look like anything. He looks like a real Babbitt, but he's not.

Not one little bit. So when that group talks, I just sit and listen. I don't open my kisser.

*Do they give papers?*

G.C. No. No papers. Nothing's prepared. There's general conversation during lunch . . . sherry and wine . . . then after dessert the president picks some specific subject and asks somebody around the room . . . someone who knows about it . . . what he has to say. This leads to discussions. Last Saturday . . . I had a cold and didn't go . . . Archie Cox asked Joe Meyers to talk about Vietnam. He'd just been there. They talk a lot about world affairs. John Enders told me he doesn't go much because he's more interested in something else. And Bok[29] doesn't go much. His family are still young and he wants to be with them as much as he can. When he gets older he'll come more. I've heard some very interesting conversations there. Sometimes I can't follow them all, sometimes I can, but I like to listen and it's a damn good meal.

*Do they ever ask you to speak?*

G.C. Oh, sure. They asked me about the Kissinger thing . . . you know the time when the portrait was turned down by the State Department. Occasionally I have something to talk about. Frannie Moore's[30] a member. He pitches in in good shape. Then there's a new member, Krister Stendahl, the retiring dean of the Harvard Divinity School. He's got that stiff neck. And, representing downtown, lawyer Charlie Coolidge and Bill Claflin,[31] although they're getting on now. But it's changed. At one time it was all literary. But it's an interesting place to go. It's just talk and it usually goes on until about four o'clock.

# 8

# Kissinger

*Weren't we going to talk about the Kissinger portrait today?*

G.C.    All right, but let's start off with Warren. It's Earl Warren.[1] He was Chief Justice of the United States and he was painted . . . I'll get the date . . . it's a waste of time wondering about when it was now. It was done because, as Chief Justice, he was automatically chairman of the board of the Smithsonian. Chief justices are always head of the Smithsonian, by courtesy, you can call it or ex officio. And they always get their portrait painted and put in the National Gallery. The National Portrait Gallery of the National Gallery. They don't have it on the main floors. They have it down in the executive part. It's a very nice place to have it, as a matter of fact. So, it was commissioned by the Smithsonian for that purpose. And . . . er . . . I went down and had the usual negotiations, so to speak. I went down and saw him in Washington and had lunch with him and saw his suite. I'd done this before. I'd done Frankfurter and, I think, I did Potter Stewart. I think the chief came along during the course of doing the seven. I did seven justices altogether. I'm not sure what the sequence is, but I don't think he was the seventh. Am I talking loud enough?

*Just. Don't go any softer.*

G.C.    The reason I mentioned this is because he had a different setup than the rest of 'em. He had two clerks. The others had one. In those days, justices would have one clerk. He had two and he had a bigger office and a bigger anteroom connected with it. On the right was his office, anteroom in the middle and then the room . . . the big room where the justices meet every Friday and discuss the cases; and where all the arguments between the justices, in any formal shape, take place. That goes on all Friday, every Friday. And nobody is allowed in that room except them. There's not . . . there's no secretaries, there are no tape recorders, nothing. Nobody there that can repeat outside what's been said.

*Were you allowed in?*

G.C.   Yes, but not when it was in session. Nobody! They can knock on the door when there are messages or something important, and come in when nobody's there; but you get little tidbits, little impressions of the formal format, you know. The first thing they do is to all shake hands together, apparently. They might not shake hands when they get through [*Laughing*]. I don't know whether they do or not, but they certainly do when they start off. Apparently they get very angry. Things get very hot at times. I think the sequence, as I remember it, is that . . . er . . . the Chief Justice calls on the youngest, the newest member of the court to speak first and so on; and then goes on up the line to the senior members. Obviously, the reason being to get the fresh ideas of these young men, rather than have them cowed by the older members if they went first. You can imagine it would make quite a difference, as a matter of fact, if all the big ones sounded off and then the little ones . . . .

[*Interrupted by the telephone*]

*You were talking about the Friday sessions.*

G.C.   Well, it was just interesting to see the room. And . . . er . . . Warren and I had lunch in his office and discussed things. And I said I'd do it. We decided to do it at the National Portrait Gallery. It was Gallery 14, as I remember it, because I've used it many, many times over the years. It was an empty gallery, not yet filled with acquisitions. Warren came down usually about nine o'clock and he sat for about an hour and a half. He was very, very business-like. And . . . er . . . I don't remember anything about that first lunch particularly beyond we had a pleasant time getting familiar, describing how I worked. Then setting it up. When he came to sit, he was all business. There was very little talk. I talked . . . I talked some, as I always do, and he rather discouraged it by not talking, not taking things up very fast. I realized after a while that he . . . that he posed for an hour and a half and he was going to get *one hour and a half's work* out of me. Work. No playing around. And

...er... that was the feeling I got out of him. I didn't expect much out of him and I didn't get much out of him, except... well, there are a few things. I may recollect some as I go along.

You mentioned about the light in that gallery. Of course, we had the light from above, as all those galleries do. It casts light down across the pictures and they look well just because of the light. But it is overhead, like the light in the subway, so it casts shadows down very strongly—under the eyes and the eye sockets, and under the nose and under the chin; and it makes a very strong illumination. You see the planes exaggerated, to a degree. That's an extremely good thing. It's a good thing for somebody like Abraham Lincoln or .. er ... Just using an example where it would not be good, it would not be good for Charles Laughton, or for a fat face. It's good for some people, but not for all. I remember it was all right for Warren. I put him in a corner. I usually put them in corners, far away from the light so it isn't coming down on their heads, in which case they would be almost all in shadow. For his particular kind of face it was good . . .the face structure, the head structure. The things I remember that stand out were his business-like attitude and then a couple of questions I asked him. The ones I told you I ask sometimes:

What would he endow a child with if he could endow it with just one quality?

And he thought for so long that I thought he hadn't heard what I said. I was about to—to wake him up, so to speak, try it on him again, when he finally answered. He must have taken two or three minutes. He took a helluva long time. And then he said, "The ability to tolerate opinions that don't agree with his own." The ability to tolerate opinions at variance to his own. Now the answer to this question... is generally a very good clue to their character.

And...er...when it came to the other question of what he thought was the motivating force behind men... people... mankind, he said, "the desire to learn." [*A lot of mumbling through here.*] I think the best definition was Judge Hand's, later on. He said, "The desire to impose the self on the non-self."

Well, these two things about him come out distinctly. Oh, yes. I remember another thing in the course of conversation. It turned out that he had been in the habit of having two cocktails every night. He was then about seventy, seventy-one, no more. And he found out that

... er ... that if he laid off those two cocktails, he was a little sharper the next day. So he had done so. And he said, "Don't tell my wife." [*Chuckling*] I never saw his wife. I guess I must have met her just once, but I never had anything to do with her whatever. I suppose ... I assume that she'd been after him herself to lay off 'em, and he didn't want to let her realize she'd been right all the time. It was pretty funny to have the Chief Justice of the United States tell me please not to tell his wife. [*Laughing*] An advice I took myself eventually, about twelve years later.

*I think I should take that advice.*

G.C.   [*Laughing*] You're so lively I don't think you'd get drunk on a quart of whiskey and you'd be all right the next day. God knows, I take a cocktail plenty of times, but I just work better if I haven't the night before. Each person has his own reactions. And Warren began to find out at seventy years old he was better off without it. He wasn't really conscious of it, but he found out he was just a little bit smarter the next day.

*The other thing you brought out in that lost tape was the lighting of Lincoln's statue in the Lincoln Memorial.*

G.C.   Oh, yeah. They first lighted that statue with footlights. Stage lighting. It was very good stage lighting, but it was very, very bad for the statue. It made the whole thing kind ghastly looking, because you could see ... er ... he has rather hollow eyes, deep-set eyes. That was all lost. And the shadows cast look the opposite of what the sculptor had done himself. Sculptors' studios have, for their kind of work, light down from the top. Painters' studios always have light from the north side of the house ... the north side of the room. The sculptor has it right overhead from a skylight. That is the tradition. That was how Saint-Gaudens had it and French ... Daniel Chester French, the man who did the Lincoln statue. So the stage lighting from below reversed his effect. A travesty. Impossible. And they turned it around and lighted it from above. Now it is a very fine thing. It's the way it should be. All the modeling of the face, the eyes, comes through.

*Gardner, weren't we going to talk about Kissinger today?*

G.C.   If we're going to talk about Kissinger[2] today, we'd better start at the beginning. I've been thinking about the Supreme Court justices a lot, lately, and I'd rather talk about them than about Kissinger, because I enjoy them more. But we can talk about Kissinger if that's what you planned.

I saw him three or four times, over the years, before I painted him, and each time he was quite different. The first time was long ago, when he was getting his divorce and living at Marian Louthy's in Cambridge. This was before he *was* anybody and he was teaching at Harvard.

*Had you known them around Cambridge as a couple?*

G.C.    I never saw her. They lived in Belmont. I understand she's very nice, very attractive. Lily Saarinen was with me the evening we dropped in on Marian. He came in around ten o'clock and, instead of going up to his room at the top of the house, he came in and talked to us for a couple of hours. He was very generous in answering questions. He would elaborate and explain as best he could the things we didn't know much about; but he was very humorless. His eyes were like Mussolini's, wide open with the whites all around them. I guess he was under a strain and he didn't have any of the vanity he had when I saw him the next time. Later, we heard how funny he was, but that evening there was no sign of it at all. He was a very tense-feeling man and, as I said, his eyes were the main thing.

*Do they bulge?*

G.C.    A little bit, kind of part of his Jewish configuration, but not particularly. The main thing was they were like little huckleberries or little blackberries with whites all around them.

The next time I saw him was at the Century Club in New York. This was just after he'd gone down to Washington as Nixon's head of the National Security Council. I was in the club looking at an exhibition that was there when Ken Galbraith came in and Lippmann came in. Walter came over to say hello to me, of course, and he knew Ken. We chatted a bit and then went into the big room there. Suddenly, this little guy came tearing in and it was Kissinger. He had changed from the first time I saw him. He was more relaxed, stood quite straight, a plump little fellow, sparky, spruce, feisty like a little terrier. Not aggressive, but on the ball. They greeted him and talked. I didn't say anything because I was just on the tail of this thing, but Walter and Ken congratulated him, and I remember him saying that he hoped they'd be speaking to him at the end of the year.

Then I remember seeing him a third time outside Nelson Rockefeller's

New York apartment. Rockefeller had put together a committee of prominent citizens to review the fundamental problems confronting the country.* Sort of a think tank, I think it was. Your son-in-law, Jay Iselin, was on it, wasn't he? I know Geoff Platt's son-in-law was secretary. And Kissinger was one of them. It was about seven in the evening, and I was walking up Fifth Avenue, eating peanuts out of a paper bag. There was a meeting of this group, apparently, inside the apartment, and a red carpet was laid from the curb to the entrance. I stood with the crowd and watched the cars drive up and the people get out and go inside. Pretty soon this long, black limousine drove up and Nancy swept through. Then Kissinger and Hugh Scott[3] got out. Neither had a hat on, and Scott had his arm around Kissinger in a familiar manner. Poor Kissinger was glued to him like a real buddy. He was engulfed by this great bear of a man and he had a sick smile on his face. His eyes were heavy-lidded and he looked quite sinister. Quite reptilian, in fact.

*And all this time you were eating peanuts?*

G.C.   I was eating peanuts and dropping the shells on the sidewalk. A newspaperman came up to me and said,
  "Don't you know whose apartment you're standing outside of?"
  And I said, "Yeah, Mr. Rockefeller's."
  And he said, "You barbarian! Don't you know enough not to drop shells all over the place?"
  I was very humiliated. [*Laughing*] I always thought newspapermen were very free and easy, but this one was shocked by my mark of disrespect.
  I saw Kissinger one more time before I painted him. This was at the presentation of the replica of Dean Acheson's portrait that was commissioned for the National Portrait Gallery. The original was painted for Covington and Burling, his law firm. I think they picked up the tab for this one, too. I had flown down from Boston the day before, and all the way down I had sweated out my speech. I spent the night at the Harrimans' so, naturally, I drove down to the presentation with Averell.
  I said to him, "God! I've worked over my speech."
  And he said, "I don't, you know. I just get up and do these things." Speaking didn't worry him at all, but then he did it all the time.
  When we got to the gallery, Kissinger was already there and the

* The Commission on Critical Choices for Americans–PBD

others. All of a sudden, it became apparent who was going to speak: Mrs. Acheson, Kissinger, Harriman, Sadik (the head of the gallery), and myself. I was to speak after Kissinger and Harriman — terrible acts to follow — and I remember thinking to myself that this was fast company for a fellow to be in. Kissinger spoke well, in that rather deep voice of his. He talked about how much he'd admired Acheson and what a trenchant way he had of expressing himself. He said he'd never forget Acheson's description of a certain foreign diplomat as a man practicing the boomerang in a crowded ballroom. A terribly dangerous fellow to have around! Thank God, I'd prepared something! Harriman, it turned out, wandered about quite a bit. He said some appropriate things, and then told how Acheson had bullied him at Groton. Acheson had been a class ahead of him, I think, and apparently had made his life miserable.

So I saw Kissinger there. We didn't speak and we didn't shake hands. We just nodded. Then I didn't see him again until a year later, when I went down to Washington to talk over painting his portrait. It was in November, 1976, just after Ford had lost to Jimmy Carter, and I don't think it had entered either his or Ford's head that they'd be out of a job. This first interview was the most interesting, and the longest talk I had with him while he was Secretary of State. It lasted about half an hour. I told him how I worked and he was respectful. He's very respectful of the arts and there was no arrogance at all. He did ask if I would consult his wife when I'd come to the concept I was choosing. Discuss it with her a little bit. It was an unusual request, but there was no reason why it shouldn't have been made, so I said I'd be delighted to do it. Actually, I thought it would be fun to see her; and, remembering the moods I'd glimpsed him in over the years, especially that expression on his face outside the Rockefeller apartment, I figured there were all kinds of things I could do with him. He asked me if I would paint him while he was still in office. I said no way, but I would make a start. I was in the middle of painting Coleman,[4] Ford's Secretary of Transportation, so I was in Washington a lot anyway. I told him I could sandwich him in between the Coleman sittings. Sketch him. Do fly-on-the-wall stuff. This suited him fine, so we went on to talk of other things.

He said he was very pleased because he didn't think anything could happen before he went out of office. After that, he couldn't be sure, but it wouldn't be his problem. This suggestion of the temporary nature of things came out very strong. Indeed, he said at other times that they never knew what was going to happen. They *don't* know. They just do their best and hope. The other thing he said was that, before coming to Washington, he'd always had eight hours' sleep (thought he couldn't do without it), but for eight years now he couldn't remember a night when he'd had more than four, but he'd gotten along just fine. In fact, he'd gotten a little plump and this was worrying him. When I was painting him, he kept asking me to make him thinner. I couldn't do that and I'd say,

"I wouldn't insult you by prettying you up."

You can give them a little break, but you don't say, "Yes, sir!"

So I went down and sketched him in his office at the State Department. When things were too secretive (for instance when the Chinese, in their little jackets, were in there) it was *Out!* I spent a lot of time sitting in the outer office waiting to go in. It was a large, rather handsome office, with his desk facing you as you walked in. On the right of this was a bank of windows, and between them was a couch flanked by two armchairs. He'd get up from his desk and sit down in one of these chairs. He always lounged on the end of his spine, very relaxed. He wasn't comatose in any way, but his hammer hands hung loose as he squirmed around. It was an impossible pose. It would have been a waste of time for everyone, but I made a lot of drawings of him like that. Got his profile, took notes on his head, got the feeling of him, and so forth. One day, there was a group of Africans, I think it was, in there and I asked him to get up and sit in one of the straight-back chairs. It was an elegant chair with arms which made it impossible for him to lounge. In other words, I moved him from one place to another in the middle of a conference, and his aides were astounded. Afterwards, one of the said,

"That's the first time I've ever seen anyone tell him what to do." Apparently, they were scared stiff of him.

All this time I was following him around to receptions and luncheon meetings. I always got the best seat, usually just below the podium, so I could get a good look at him. He's pretty chesty standing up, you know.

*You keep saying "chest." Do you mean chest or tummy?*

G.C.    Both.

*Did you get the pose from the way he stood at those luncheons?*

G.C.   No, but he had some very symbolic gestures. It's characteristic of him to hold out one hand, and, often, he has one hand behind his back, sometimes two. I thought to combine these gestures, one hand offering, the other withholding, was characteristic and symbolic at the same time. And it made a good composition. But it didn't come to that. I didn't get the pose until almost his last day in office. Finally, just before the inauguration at a farewell luncheon with the press corps, I think it was, I got it. He was telling them what he thought was happening as far as he could make out and I've never seen him more forceful. I remember him saying that the Russians weren't as much of a threat as you might think, because the men in power, the Politburo, were plodders. They weren't brilliant people, and they didn't have the imagination for brilliant strikes. It wasn't their style. He couldn't tell about future generations, however. They might be different. He said he could imagine in twenty-five years or so, not an atomic attack, but a bunch of Russian paratroopers dropping down on New York. He believed China was the one to worry about, not now, but later; and his advice was to cultivate the Chinese now to keep the Russians in control. He was very forceful about all this and it was there, then, that I got the pose.

So I went over to see Nancy as I'd promised; and, also, to see if there was a suitable place to work in their house. There were Secret Service men all over the place. One of them came out from under the stoop as I stood at the front door and said,

"What do you want?"

I'm not sure he touched me, and he wasn't rude, but I'm not used to being asked what I want when I go someplace. It reminded me of a friend who said he must look like a thug, because he never got by a doorman without being asked his business. I know how he felt. It feels very insulting. The guard kept me waiting out there on the cold steps for about five minutes while he got another fellow to call inside to see if I were expected. At last, Nancy opened the door herself, in bare feet and bluejeans! Kissinger wasn't at home, so she and I and Tyler, their golden retriever, wandered all over the house looking for a room with a good light. In a townhouse like that, you know, there isn't much light. There are too many trees and buildings around it, so it was hard to find a room with the right exposure. One possibility was a bathroom.

*Was it big enough?*

G.C.   It would have been a very tight place to work. Very tight stuff, but it did have a fairly good light and a north exposure.

*Why didn't you paint him there?*

G.C.   Well, as you remember, there was some question of my doing him at all. When he first called, I was feeling kind of crummy and I wasn't sure I wanted to do him. Then I thought it would be kind of fun, so I sandwiched him in among other things. I told him I'd do him after the inauguration, but then I postponed it, and he agreed. Anyway, after he left office, he and Nancy were going here and there. They discussed going to Laurence Rockefeller's Caneel Bay resort in the Virgin Islands. It's very remote, and he started to worry about it. He's a guy who likes to see the newspaper, and this place didn't even have a phone. At first it had sounded like heaven, and then it began not to sound so good. They talked it over with friends who'd been there and he decided he'd go crazy. So they went to Acapulco, with all their staff. We corresponded a little, and it was decided we'd work in New York when he got back. But it turned out I didn't paint him until early spring; and, by that time, he was living on the Rockefellers' estate, Pocantico Hills, on the Hudson.

He was living in a simple, white clapboard house which Nelson had lent him. Very nice, with trees between it and the river. The house was connected by an areaway to another building where his guards lived. This was a little, clapboard guesthouse with a living room and kitchen, and bedrooms upstairs. The living room served as a security command post.

The problem for me was where would I work? There wasn't a room in the Kissingers' house with the right light, so I had to look around outside. About a hundred feet away was an old, abandoned garage and stable. The garage had a concrete floor and the door wouldn't come down; and the stable was crammed with odds and ends. Nearby was a third building: a hen house with old nests, roosting rails and crates. This was the most likely place to work because it had the best light.

*Didn't it smell of hens? When I was a little girl, we used to keep hens. Years after we gave them up, we still knew they'd been there.*

G.C.   Hens are quite sweet-smelling. It didn't smell bad at all; but it was hot, dusty and hot, and it wouldn't have been a good place to work. Finally, it boiled down to the garage, and I went outside the gate to the huge maintenance building to look for the things I needed for a makeshift studio. I needed a table, obviously, and two strips of tarpaulin: one to put the paints and brushes on, and the other to hang across the lower part of the garage door to create a make-shift studio light. Maintenance kept a crew of carpenters, painters, and people to do repairs on the place and I must say they made things awfully easy for me. They'd tell me where to go to get anything I wanted, and then they'd call ahead so I'd be expected. They even went so far as to send the things I'd collected over to the garage in a truck. But it was an awful catch-as-catch-can studio and only possible when Kissinger was sitting down. In the old days, I used to be able to get down on my hands and knees and look up, but I can't do that any more. So it wasn't one of the easiest places to work, and that was one of the reasons I didn't go back when Kissinger rejected the portrait, but asked me to go back and "fix it up." If circumstances had been better, it might have been different. Anyway, I don't do that sort of thing. I don't fix up a painting if I feel right about it.

*You mentioned the guesthouse where the guards lived. Were you conscious of tight security while you were there?*

G.C.  Except for Kissinger's guards, the only place I noticed it was getting in the main gate. You weren't allowed in till word came down you were OK. Kidnapping is the thing they worry most about, and they have to withdraw behind the encircling wall to protect themselves. It makes one conscious of their great wealth and gives a feeling of reclusiveness rather than exclusiveness. There's a very forbidding atmosphere outside, but once you get in they're very friendly.

I remember my first approach. I had come from New Haven, where I'd stopped on my way down to see the Kingman Brewsters at Yale. Phyllis called me there to say security had been trying to reach me to tell me not to come down that day. Ex-President Ford had just arrived and the combination of him and Kissinger there at the same time had complicated their problems. So I spent the night with the Brewsters and went down the next day. I took the wrong turn getting on one of those interstate highways; and, as you know, if you get going in the wrong direction, you've had it! You have to go for miles and miles before you can get off and try to reverse yourself; and, in so doing, you can get completely lost. I'm very nervous about this sort of thing until I know my way; and this time I knew very quickly I'd made the wrong turn.

Henry Kissinger, sketch for portrait, 1976, and (*right*) the chair he posed in.

Consequently, instead of taking the shortest route to the main gate, I found myself approaching Pocantico downriver from Tarrytown, and I had to drive around the whole thing. It's a helluva a big place and it must have taken me twenty, thirty minutes to get around it. Imagine how long it took old John D. in a horse and carriage; but in his day all the gates in the surrounding wall were open and he could get in from any direction. I got a glimpse of these gates through the trees. As big as the one at Massachusetts Hall. I got the impression of a big enclosure, a little county, that I wouldn't have had if I hadn't lost my way.

*Did it seem as enormous inside?*

G.C.   Once you get through the main gate, it's less formal. After driving a couple of miles, there are these little, white, Victorian houses, one of which, as I've described, the Kissingers lived in. Nelson lived in the big, formal, family house on the top of a hill. The grounds around this are full of pieces of sculpture, kind of like pre-historic animals lurking in the trees. There's a Calder, a Lipchitz, a Moore, I think, very much like Maeght Museum you visited in the south of France, with the same big pieces, many of them by the same artists.

Then there's the so-called "playhouse," where maintenance sent me for the table. This would do for an average-size country club. It has a nine-hole golf course, two swimming pools, and I don't know how many tennis courts. The playhouse itself is big enough for dances and big dinners and is equipped to put them on. And, upstairs, there are guest rooms. It sounds ostentatious, but it's not. It's what it is called: their playhouse.

*Did you stay with the Kissingers?*

G.C.   No. I stayed about an hour's drive away. I commuted either from the Geoff Platts' in Bedford or from the Willy Chandlers' in Golden Ridge, Connecticut. It worked out very well for me that way.

*To go back to security, how many guards did Kissinger have?*

G.C.   There were three in Pocantico. They didn't follow him around all the time, but if he went somewhere (walked over to Nelson's house) they were aware someone could climb over the walls and take a potshot at him, so two would go along. The three Pocantico guards went everywhere with him. Then there were three more in New York. Their job was to case the places he intended to go and to give added protection

SKETCHES FROM LIFE                                     161

in the crowds. Kissinger would sit for me in the mornings and usually go into the city in the afternoon to write his memoirs, I think it was, leaving me to work on the portrait without him. One of the guards told me that the New York duty was very tiring. You just watched and watched until your eyes almost came out of your head. When I asked him if anything ever happened, he said,
  "Yes, once in a while some nut tries to jump out of the crowd."
  The guards used to come in and chat with me after the sittings and I got to know them quite well. The third was attractive, in an Errol Flynn sort of way, but he was lean and mean. The other two were actually baby-faced, charming young men who had worked with an organization with a name something like S.M.A.S.H., a rescue sort of thing. They didn't seem to have any nerves or imagination. While a poet can get excited by a flower or a blade of grass, it seemed to take a shotgun blast to get these guys going.
  But they all hoped nothing would happen to Kissinger.
  "I like the chap," one of them said. However, it was clear that, if they lost him, the first consideration would be that they'd muffed it.

*Was the government still paying for them?*

G.C.   No. Carter had taken his guards away, after the first month or two. It was costing Kissinger $100,000 a year out of his own pocket to keep them on; but, apparently, it was necessary. He knew he was on the American Nazi Party hit list and, as he told me, "There are a lot of people out there who want me dead. Veterans, people like that."
  Then he said that everywhere he went, he was instantly recognized, which was a danger in itself. I asked him if this worried him and he said no, he'd gotten used to it and also he felt secure with the guards around. Usually they kept daily threats and details of that sort away from him. This fact was brought home to me one afternoon when they were all in town and I walked over to the guards' house to use one of the telephones there. There was only the cook around and, as I wandered over to the table where the telephones were, I saw a yellow pad with lots of notes on it. Just lying around. So I read them.
  There were reports from the chiefs of police of New York and New Orleans; and other reports that added up to the fact that the American Nazi Party planned to assassinate Kissinger on the 7th of July. It was the middle of June and I was kind of jolted. I asked my friend the guard about this, and this was the kind of thing they kept from him. They

wouldn't burden him with specifics such as this. What they would do, as the date came closer, would be to change his pattern or do something nobody expected him to do. I couldn't get my mind off July 7th; but, as you know, it came and went and nothing happened.

*What was Kissinger like when you were painting him? Was he full of interesting information?*

G.C. Not while I was painting him. I was working pretty hard, concentrating, and there wasn't much conversation. There were interruptions though. One of the most irritating was Tyler, who would wander into the garage waving his enormous tail around, but I'd yell, "Out! Out!"

One day Tyler disappeared and Kissinger was frantic.

"My God!" he said. "We'll never see him again. He's so friendly he'd go off with anyone."

Everyone was sent looking for him. The guards. Everyone. Then I remembered seeing something that morning that looked like Tyler streaking out the gate while I was coming in. Immediately everyone was sent outside the gate to look for him. Finally, he was found at a neighbor's pool, enjoying the fun.

*Did you have any meals with the Kissingers? Luncheons? Dinners?*

G.C. Occasionally. The first Sunday I was there, Kissinger's sixteen-year-old daughter was at lunch. She was very beautiful and obviously devoted to her father. Then there was a dinner in July, a Tuesday, I think it was, with Nelson and Happy and Jerry Ford. It was a reunion of sorts. It didn't seem like a reunion of old friends, but rather a meeting of top guys who'd run things together. It reminded me a little of the fellows in my class at Harvard, the big ones who always ran things. They become friends because of this, but there isn't much warmth to their conversation when they get together. The meeting of Ford and Kissinger and Rockefeller reminded me of that.

*What did they talk about?*

G.C. Before dinner, supper really, the conversation was a little stilted, of no significance. We walked down to the pond where there were some geese and we talked of geese, that sort of thing. At dinner, there was nothing of significance that I heard, but I was sitting next to Nancy and talked mostly with her. Rockefeller quite obviously preferred Kissinger to Ford and talked to him. You asked me what Rockefeller was like. That evening he was very hearty, reminding me of something I read which described him as an enthusiastic basketball coach. He was a back-slapper, a politician, but what I remember most is that he was fish-belly white. Here it was the middle of July and, in contrast to Ford, who had just played eighteen holes of golf and was russet red, he had no color at all. Apparently he was perfectly healthy, but for some physical reason had to keep out of the sun.

After dinner, there was more general conversation. Ford thought Carter could make a good president, but he wasn't sure that he would. Someone asked why.

"Because he's too much like Nixon."

"How?"

"He's egocentric. Doesn't think things through and he thinks he can save the world."

*Did the subject of painting Rockefeller ever come up?*

G.C. No, but Happy indicated she'd like me to do her. I let that one drop. I wasn't interested in painting her, but I'd've liked to have a go at him.

Another dinner I remember particularly was when Rockefeller's osteopath, Dr. Kenneth Riland, and his wife were the guests. Dr. Riland used to stay at Pocantico when Nelson was there, and Nelson often lent him to Kissinger. He was very much a personality in his own right. He'd rubbed all the best bottoms and took no guff whatsoever in his own field. That evening, he told a story about a trip he'd taken with Kissinger when they shared the same bedroom in Rome. Kissinger had gone to bed early because he had a morning audience with the Pope. Riland went out on the town. He returned to their room around four A.M. and had just fallen asleep when he was awakened by Kissinger who wanted a rub. He told him to forget it and went back to sleep. About a half an hour later, Kissinger shook him awake again. Riland got out of bed went into the bathroom and came out with a roll of toilet paper. This he rolled down the middle of the room between the two beds and said,

"If you put so much as one toe across that line, I'll break your jaw. No further disturbance," he said.

Later in the meal, Kissinger said to Nancy,

"Why don't you go upstairs after dinner and have a good rub? It will do you good."

Riland told him it was between him and Nancy and really none of his business, and Kissinger let the matter drop. After dinner Riland said to Nancy,

"How about it? Would you like a rub?" She said she would, so they went upstairs.

*During all this time, did either of the Kissingers ever indicate they didn't like the portrait?*

G.C.   No, quite the contrary. What was so confusing later was at the time they seemed enthusiastic. Just before I took the picture back to Boston, Nancy said she liked it; but maybe she was just being polite, because she was the main reason for its refusal. He didn't like it either particularly, but wanted to give me a chance to change it.

*Because of Carter's cutting off Federal funds for portraits, didn't you have a deadline?*

G.C.   Yeah. That was December 30th, but I had to get it off earlier to give the Federal Art Commission time to pass on it. I sent it off on the tenth, which was a little tight on time because I had had to have it revarnished, and also because of holiday schedules. It was finally crated in two days by Huntington Frames and sent down air freight.

*As I remember it, State called you on the 26th, the day after Christmas, and told you it was unacceptable to the Kissingers. Awful timing. Didn't it upset you?*

G.C.   That didn't bother me so much. Anyway, I wasn't all that surprised. Most people would be ashamed to say their portrait wasn't good enough of them. Kissinger, by saying just that, was either more vain or less vain; or, perhaps, just more honest. Dean Rusk wasn't crazy about his, you know, but he never said anything about it. He just accepted it. And Dean Acheson never said anything about his, but that one was pretty good. In fact, it was because he liked it so much that Kissinger wanted me to do him. Anyway, Kissinger's refusal was a trait common to him, so it didn't take me completely by surprise. I'd had a feeling it would happen.

*But, still, wasn't it upsetting?*

G.C.   Not particularly. That's not the kind of thing that bothers me.

*Where is it now?*

G.C.   Right now it's sitting in my studio. At the time of all the publicity over its refusal (the articles in *Time* and *Newsweek* and in the papers), I could have sold it to a couple of people for twelve, fifteen thousand dollars. That is, done it right away. A real smart-money fellow would have cashed in on it, but I didn't. Now, I'm going to wait and see. I may fool around with the clothes and the background, but I'm not sure. Bobby Kennedy's portrait was refused by his family and it wound up in the National Portrait Gallery, so I wouldn't be surprised if this one ended up there too.

*Will you give it or will they buy it?*

G.C.   Eventually, I guess they'll raise the money to buy it. Up to now, his friends wouldn't contribute anything because he didn't like it. But I think somebody will crash through because they haven't any other portrait of him, except that awful one he finally had done for the State Department. That one's a real dog, you know. What's so discouraging about it is that people with supposedly cultivated taste like the Kissingers will settle for something like this. I think the technical advances in photography have something to do with this. In fact, I think photography is one of the main reasons behind the decline in portrait-painting.

*I have two questions I'd like to ask you. While you were doing the preliminary sketches of Kissinger, he was still Secretary of State, wasn't he?*

G.C.   That's right. It was after the election and before Carter's inauguration. He was on his way out.

*And during this same time, I understand you were painting Coleman, Ford's Secretary of Transportation. He is black, isn't he?*

G.C.   Right.

*Now my question is: What difference is there in painting a black man and painting a white?*

G.C.   Well, it's a different thing. You can almost make a joke about it by saying you do a light-skinned person by putting the head against a dark background. With a black person, you do just the other way around, like a negative. It's a different thing, but not a difficult thing to solve, in that sense. The difficulty for me is that I'm never sure I have the likeness of feeling. The way I work is I try to get the likeness of feeling. To do something that, when I see it, it feels like the person I'm painting. With blacks you're not so sure a judge, although I've been quite successful at times.

Judge Hastie[5] was black, actually very light, café au lait; but his eyes were dark and he was a negro with strong negro blood. Coleman, on the other hand, was chocolate. Maybe a little lighter than that. In both cases it came out quite well, but I wasn't sure of the feeling of these men. I didn't quite know. This would apply to the Chinese, too, or anybody who was not of your own race. It's probably why we think the Chinese are so inscrutable. We just don't know them well enough to recognize them as individuals and pick up the feeling behind them. It's like a cowboy who can look at fifty horses and tell them apart in no time at all, whereas a greenhorn might pick out two or three, but certainly not a lot. So, you see, I'm not accustomed enough to blacks to get the very subtlest points.

*That's well put. Now for my second question. I remember the Kissinger picture was done in the alla prima technique. Very straight forward.*

G.C.    Right.

*How about the Coleman portrait? From the photograph I couldn't tell. Did you use any of the Venetian technique in his portrait?*

G.C.    [*After a pause*] I'm trying to think what I did. Noooo. I don't think I did.

*What guides you in this?*

G.C.    It's some whim, I guess. No, it's not exactly a whim. I did a lot of it, at one point, and then, for some reason or other, I didn't quite like it and stopped doing it. I've started doing it again now and then. I definitely used it in Bailey Aldrich's background.

*Again: What is the Venetian technique?*

G.C.    The Venetian technique is powdered paint mixed with egg emulsion and put on the prime canvas, which is a lead-white or a zinc-white base. Egg emulsion is a combination of varnish, oil, egg yolk and water; and the technique comes in when you put it on with a tone. Where it usually shows is in the background, but sometimes I've used it in the clothes. Kissinger's portrait might have been better if his clothes weren't so somber. The feeling and the face I wouldn't change, but I'm not satisfied with his suit.

In many cases the egg emulsion is all covered up. You paint over it, but some of it is left. I'll give you an example you're familiar with: Seybolt's[6] portrait. His background has a buff tone all over. That's the egg emulsion. There's some, but very little, in the rest of it.

*How about Dillon?[7] That's one of my favorites.*

G.C.    Dillon is egg emulsion all over. I scumbled paint over it, but it comes out very strong in that portrait.

*And Enders? I remember that first all-white background you painted in later.*

G.C.    Maybe a little. Mostly, no. There's a lot of egg emulsion in Whipple's[8] portrait and Ed Mason's.

*I always liked the Whipple portrait. You lived with it in your studio for a long time, didn't you?*

G.C.    I didn't change it much, though. It's about the way you saw it. Did I tell you about that opening? It was a week ago last Friday at the Smithsonian Observatory at Harvard. You know where it is? It's just above Radcliffe on Garden Street near my house. I never saw such a response to a picture in my life. People *really* went overboard over that one. The opening was from five to seven. I figured I'd get there about half-past five, a quarter to six, so I wouldn't have to stand around while people looked at it and tried to say something nice. Unfortunately, I didn't realize Whipple was going to speak, and he spoke before I got there. He said some nice things about me, apparently, and I'm sorry I didn't hear them. When I got there, his eyes were sparkling and he said, "People really like it. They really mean it."

I was surprised. I've never gotten more enthusiasm from any picture.

*What is Mr. Whipple's full name and what is his position at the Observatory?*

G.C.    I think his name is Fred and he was director of the Smithsonian astro-physical laboratory at Harvard. He's emeritus now, of course.

Professor Menzel,[9] who I also painted, was head of the Harvard Observatory when the Smithsonian was looking around for someplace to put their laboratory, and he was responsible for getting it for Harvard. The one stipulation was that the head of it should be a Harvard professor. At that time, Whipple was Harvard Professor of Astronomy, an astro-physicist, and he was made director. He got the Presidential Medal, you know, and knows more about comets than anyone else in the world. He's seventy now, and he's got some new theories he's working on. Exciting boys, these astronomers!

*One more question related to the Kissinger portrait which I hesitate to ask. The winter you finished it, you were in one of your cycles of depression. Do you want to talk about it?*

G.C. Well, I'm not going into details, psychoanalyze myself. It would be a great bore, and I wouldn't do it right; but I will say that the men in my family are a little neurotic, although they have been pretty effective people. My grandfather was a wonderful fellow as a person. A much-beloved family doctor. But there was some deficiency of endorphin, or whatever they know so much about now. Some little imbalance that makes us less effectual at times. Certain things will trigger it in me, such as too much trouble or too much worry about certain things. I recognize it coming pretty well, by now, and I try to do something about it in time. Psychiatric advice will help if it hasn't gone too far, hasn't taken on a life of its own. That one you mentioned during the last months of the Kissinger portrait was a bad one. It got a little out of hand, but finally it went away after five or six months.

*So you think it is chemical?*

G.C. Definitely, it's physical. They say that depression is the common cold of psychiatry, you know, and that's a very good definition. It's not character. It has nothing to do with character at all. I'm prone to it occasionally. Certain things will throw me for a while and then it passes. It always passes. People get so depressed they actually kill themselves, but if they would only live through it, it goes away. Something about it wears out.

*Does it affect your work?*

G.C. Oh, yes. It affects my wanting to work. I've done a lot of good things when I was feeling bad, but I enjoy it more when I'm OK. I started Bailey Aldrich, fly-on-the-wall stuff, but I didn't paint him until I got over it. And when Kissinger asked me to go back, I didn't explain all that, but I wouldn't have done any different if I'd been feeling all right. I let several things go by at that time.* Oh, well, it's a fact of life I have to live with. Perhaps I'll never have another. Perhaps there'll be one in two or twenty-five years. I never know.

---

\* On September 9, 1977, Gerald Ford's office in Palm Springs left a message with G.C.'s answering service to call his secretary. G.C.: "I hope it wasn't Betty. I wouldn't be particularly interested in doing her; but I'd like to do him, not as an artistic challenge . . . he's a nice guy, but uncomplicated . . . historically, it would be an experience." G.C. returned the call on Thursday, September 15. Ford's secretary was unavailable, so he left a message. She called later in the day to confirm that Ford wanted his portrait painted for the Smithsonian.

The first appointment was to be on December 4 in Palm Springs. G.C. postponed it to January 8th and then again to March. Ford himself initiated the last postponement and had his portrait painted by someone else.

# 9

# From Olympus to the Backyard

*What have you been doing since I saw you last?*

G.C.   I had dinner with the boys[1] last night.

*Where did you take them?*

G.C.   We went to Ferdinand's.

*Is that in Cambridge?*

G.C.   Yeah, that's in Cambridge. On Mt. Auburn Street. It's pretty good. It's one of those . . . you know . . . quite expensive . . . ten, eleven-dollar-a-plate things. Whatever you order, except chicken. Chicken is cheaper, as you know. Not very cheap, but say chicken was about seven ninety-five, making you think it must be terrible . . . leftovers, three or four days old. We had dinner there, and I've not been drinking very much. I've been drinking vermouth instead of gin. But last night I had a couple of martinis. You know, a fellow never gets a hangover who drinks a lot. I never have a hangover, but when I'm working I think vermouth is better.

*I'm sure it's better when you're working because you wake up feeling like a fighting lion. You must feel better and keener, don't you?*

G.C.   I won't say like a lion . . . [*Laughing*]   I wouldn't say like a fighting lion.

*When we were in South Carolina, I must have been drinking a lot. We always had martinis at our picnic lunches, and a dressing drink—which I never have. And I never felt better.*

G.C.   You do look very well.

*I'm sure it was the exercise, because we played eighteen holes of golf a day.*

G.C.   So you got pretty good at it, didn't you? Did you break a hundred? That's the great criterion. I did it once.

*Well, if I say I played well it's comparative. Compared to who? Compared to me. [Laughing]*

G.C.   I think the proof was when I said, "Did you break a hundred?" You had to think a bit. Normally you would have said no immediately.

*What's been happening professionally?*

G.C.   The Mason portrait is a great success. I'll bring the photograph out to you next week. This is one of the good ones. This is a great one.

*You really are hot right now, aren't you? That's two hot ones in a row.*

G.C.   Well, I'm doing pretty well on stuff I'm doing in the studio. I've got plenty of time on them. But McNamara ... going back and forth to Washington ... I'm working under a little difficulty. It's going slow as a result. I know a lot more now than I did. In some ways I'm better, but I take longer. The portraits are better ... richer ... and even though I'm slow most of 'em stick around.

*We've talked about the Warren portrait. Would you like to talk about Judge Hand now?*

G.C.   In regard to Hand,[2] it was 1947 ... in the fall of 1947 ... I did him in New York. I was doing old Mr. Lamont at the same time ... finishing him up ... the second portrait. I went back and forth between the two places a little bit ... at that time, over a period of a couple of months. Hand was commissioned by his son-in-law, Norris Darrell. He's a lawyer with Sullivan and Cromwell. He's still alive, but I guess he's retired now. Maybe not. He's a great big attractive fellow. He married Mary, Hand's daughter. Darrell wanted it done, just for the family. Have a picture done of him. And I'd known Mary, Darrell's wife, at architectural school when I was there. I'd met the judge a couple of times at picnics at Northeast Harbor the year before. And I would be delighted to have a crack at him. And ... he didn't want to do it. He ... Darrell persuaded him ... Darrell persuaded him because ... they took a walk up on the mountains on ... Mount Desert Island and discussed it. Hand refused on the basis of modesty. Darrell pointed out

Judge Learned Hand, study for portrait from G.C.'s sketchbook, 1947

to him that he was being much vainer by refusing to do it than he would be to do it. And the judge saw the point of this and then he said he would. Holding off was really much vainer than going and doing it. Which is true. But he recognized it and when it was pointed out to him he gave up his objections. So I went down to New York and painted him in his house.

*Did you stay with him in his house?*

G.C.   No. I stayed at the Harvard Club. I stayed at the Harvard Club and I ... we arranged the times over the phone ... and we decided to do it ... let's see ... He had court in the morning around ten o'clock. We decided to do it at eight-thirty in the morning. Two hours. Eight ... nine ... ten. He didn't have to leave right on the dot. But the thing was to do it at eight-thirty so's he'd be free for the day. So I went down ... and we did it on the fourth floor, in a little room he had on the top floor. It had a north light because all the houses in New York in the ... let's see ... yes, on the south side of the street, of course had north lights.

*What street was this on?*

G.C.   It was about Forty-third Street. And there was an unobstructed light at the top of the house. We made a studio out of that. And ... uh ... I got up every morning around half-past six at the Harvard Club. I would get my breakfast and get down to him every morning at half-past eight and work right through. In those days I worked differently. I worked right straight through and did it. It took about eight days, I guess. I think I did it right straight along, every day. And ... uh ... when I got through, it turned out he didn't want to do it at eight-thirty at all. [*Laughing*] And I didn't want to do it at eight-thirty, God knows. The two of us were getting up every morning ... didn't need to at all. [*Laughing*] He thought I wanted to do it at eight-thirty. The last thing I wanted to do ... He thought I wanted it at that time because of the light. I had told him any time between eight-thirty and four o'clock this time of year is all right. And he got the idea it was eight-thirty I wanted. So we were both torturing ourselves. But I had a lot of fun with him. He was extremely responsive. He was a very comical man. Comical! There was a famous act he had of getting up from the dinner table and going over to the sideboard and being a Catholic priest. He'd go over and turn his coat around, look more like a priest, you know, and he'd get up and he'd conduct a mass, ringing a little bell and putting things around and it was [*Laughing*] terribly funny. He was very serious about it and it was just a farce on a mass. He would dance little jigs. He was very lively. Very ebullient man ... and ... uh .. had all kinds of stories. He was lots of fun. And, apparently, in a very good mood. He had black depressions ... subject to them, but he happened to be in a very ... a very mellow state when I was painting him. And ... uh ... he was a great friend of Judge Swan's.[3] These depressions didn't incapacitate him or anything like that, but he ... had a very dark side.

*Did he tell you about it?*

G.C. No, he didn't tell me about them, but I know about them. 'Cause a lot of people like Wyzanski and all these people said "you got him at a good time," but he had periods of gloom. But this happened to be a period when he was feeling good. And he was like a boy. He was exuberant. And of course he looked sort of like Daniel Webster. Very ... he could get very grim, too, beetle-browed and Websterian. [*Chuckling*] He was comical and complicated.

*What was the portrait like?*

G.C. Oh, I got a good picture of him. That picture did me a lot of good. The Century Club had it around, and a lot of people saw it, and I got a very nice letter from Charlie Hopkinson about it. It was ... it was one of the good ones. You've seen it, I think. I'm sure you've seen it in Washington, too. You probably don't remember it but it was in the Corcoran exhibition. You've seen photographs of it.

*Was he amusing while he was posing?*

G.C. Yes he was. Again, I could tell you all kinds of anecdotes about him. I'm trying to think what they were about now. I used to work on him and then I used to stay and work afterwards myself, sometimes all day. Be around with it. And in the afternoon one time he came back and he had Judge Swan with him ... Tom Swan ... and ... uh ... the door slammed way down stairs ... you could hear it up all the way up the house, and he shouted up, "I have a friend. I have a friend. [*Laughing*] I have a friend. I have a friend." And he brought him upstairs.

And his wife was nice. She wasn't as brilliant as he was, but she was a charming woman. And they had a sort of ... they had a situation *à trois*. ... It couldn't have happened except in a Victorian group. And ... this other man was devoted to his wife, Mrs. Hand, and they did things together. Unquestionably nothing happened. Hand and he ... this fellow ... they used to go down to a burlesque house.

*Can you remember his name?*

G.C.   I can't remember. He was a very respectable fellow. He'd go up and visit them in Maine and he was around ... not all the time, but quite a bit. As Helen Platt[4] said, it couldn't happen except in that period with people like that. And it was accepted, and there was no scandal of any kind. But I remember being told about this, and then I remember him speaking of this fellow affectionately and nicely and they, the two of them, would go off and go to these burlesques like a couple of dirty old men. [*Laughing*] Old Howard[5] stuff. And ... he was high-minded as we all know. I remember him saying when he was young he worked in a lawyer's office ... apparently it was a very good law firm, I guess. But he referred to it as a "bucket shop."[6] ... He said he just worked in a bucket shop until he was forty years old. He was depressed and felt terrible ... he didn't think there was any point whatever in doing what he was doing. [*Laughing*] Then they gave him this judgeship.

*What court was it?*

G.C.   Well, he was a Federal judge. He was a very famous Federal judge. He should have been on the Supreme Court.

*Why wasn't he?*

G.C.   I don't know. He and Augustus Hand[7] ... Augustus was his cousin and ... Augustus and Learned were both judges on the U.S. District Court of Circuit Two in New York. They were federal judges on the final court of appeals before the Supreme Court.... The next court was the Supreme Court. I think it was a district court they called it. He ... they were district U.S. judges. That came up from time to time. When it did come up, I remember him saying, "The way you get to be a Supreme Court justice is you know somebody. You play golf with somebody. It's just luck." Of course it isn't just luck. You've got to be a good lawyer. A good judge ... a pretty good judge. No, I guess you don't ... but whether you get it or not is just like ... like Paul Freund is a Jew. He'd 've made it, but they already had a Jew on the Supreme Court, for example. He told me a very good story about that. Many people thought Learned Hand should be on, and Augustus should be on.

Funnily enough, many business people apparently thought Augustus was the better . . . the quote was, "Read Learned and do what Augustus says." Learned had flair and he made quotable statements and epigrams and had a great literary quality about him. Brilliant. Augustus was apparently very solid. They had a dinner for them at one time and I saw them both together. And about Augustus . . . he stood up like an old beaver with his hands at his side. No élan whatever . . . just a lump of integrity, speaking out what he thought. Of course, Learned had plenty of integrity too, but he was much more volatile. I don't imagine Augustus ever had any black moods, particularly. But when he was standing he was just pear-shaped . . . reminding me of a penguin or a beaver. A beaver. No legs . . . no nothing . . . with his hands hanging by his side like this. [*Demonstrating*] Just hanging.

Well, Learned Hand said, anent being a Supreme Court justice, he worked very hard for Woodrow Wilson when he was running against Hughes. He worked with Herbert Croly, Walter Lippmann, in this group of New Yorkers who worked very very hard to get Wilson back in and defeat Hughes. And do you remember that was when they thought Hughes had won?

*Very well. I was in the sixth grade.*

G.C. You know the situation and there it was; on the night of the election apparently Hughes had won about midnight. They all were talking down at headquarters, and Walter Lippmann came over and saw Hand and said, "You know, if we had won you were going to be on the Supreme Court." Hand said, "That's the last I ever heard of it." Well, you remember Wilson won, but something happened . . . to this chance theory. But . . . this was just one man's story.

He had a good ribald sense of humor . . . for those days, certainly. He had one little thing . . . he must have been in college in the class of around . . . and he was married to Reggie Fink's sister.

*Could it have been his sister? Reggie Fink was our age.*

G.C. Maybe Reggie's aunt, that family at any rate, and I think his brother-in-law was in the Porcellian.[8]

*I know our friend Reggie Fink was.*

G.C. And Hand wasn't in the Porcellian.

*Did he go to Harvard?*

G.C. Oh, God yes! Yeah . . . yeah, one of the great alumni. And—

he came from Albany and so did Augustus. And Mr. Brandegee came from Albany. He knew all the boys in Albany. He wasn't a nobody thing, but I guess he was in the Pudding[9] but he wasn't in the Porcellian. He used to be sarcastic about the Porcellian. He referred to it as "the brotherhood of the sons of Christ." [*Laughing*] You know that's a blast at them. My Porcellian friends didn't think that was so funny. No, they didn't think it was funny. I know Prissy Hallowell took quite an exception to it when I said this is what he calls it. Pen didn't mind it; but Prissy got quite feisty about it.

*Was his house attractive?*

G.C.   Yes it was a very nice . . . a very nice brownstone . . . modest brownstone, the regular. Attractive living room in the back . . . and a little garden in the back and . . . it was a regular . . . typical New York brownstone.

*Would you have your luncheon there?*

G.C.   No. No, I'd go out, because he would go downtown at ten o'clock, see . . . with all this early starting in the morning. [*Laughing*] Flying early start . . . He was gone long before lunch. And I went around the corner to a coffee shop, which is what I wanted to do anyway . . . wanted to be alone after a morning like that. So I ate out and I'd come back and . . . .

Then I remember I did Maudie Kernan . . . Frannie Kernan's[10] wife. I did her in that same room. She lived right across the street . . . I did her the same time I did Mr. Lamont. I did him up at his place, and along around the same time . . . that fall and winter.

*Did Frannie commission the portrait?*

G.C.   Yes, Frannie commissioned it. It's in their house.

*Was Maudie a good subject?*

G.C.   I don't remember the picture very much. I saw her not long ago. Just happened to run into her. She lived right across the street and I painted her in the same room in Hand's house. I was around there—in and out of there—quite a while.

*Do you know where the Kernan picture is now?*

G.C.   I think it's in the New York house, if they've still got it.

*Can you remember any of Hand's stories?*

G.C.   Yeah. I think so. It was a very pleasant relationship and I used to see him afterwards. And as I say, I got on with his wife, and I knew Mary very well before, just as a friend. So that we kept up that way. I'd see him at the Century Club . . . and so on. But it was a very lively warm relationship and he was exuberant. He was boyish and we didn't have any very serious conversations, as I remember it . . . he had his little anecdotes. It was a serious thing about the Walter Lippmann thing, and it was a serious thing when he was trying to tell about things . . and so on. But it wasn't long protracted . . . that kind of thing. He told me about one literary anecdote.

I'm pretty sure I've told it to you . . . We were talking about Henry James. He was talking about writing opinions. He had difficulty sometimes, and he said that it recalled to him what Henry James said to him about writing. And he said. . . I'm not quite sure of whether he said it to him or he said it to a friend of Hand's. Anyway, Hand quoted James as saying this as to how he wrote. "I walk up and down and I walk up and down and I walk up and down, and finally I shit it out!"

He would be in a position to hear this kind of thing, and he'd use four-letter words, but he wouldn't say "fuck," that kind of word, but he said "bitch" and he said "shit." Then he was describing how he arrived at very difficult opinions. How all judges have to write such opinions. (This was at the same time he was telling the story about James.) He said, he goes over the case and over it and over it . . . and if he just can't make his mind up, which way to go, "I say 'shit' and declare for the defendant." *[Both laughing]*

Oh yes. He was a wonderful mimic. He was a very funny man. He was an actor. He described Oliver Wendell Holmes,[11] who he was a great admirer of, and he always called him Holmesy. Holmesy did this and Holmesy said that. Affectionate . . . not disrespectful . . . just the way that would sound.

There was a very pompous . . . sort of foghorning lawyer that used to appear before the Supreme Court. He always wore a cutaway He was very pompous and he was arguing about a case . . . something to do with prohibition. The Volstead Act or whatever it was, and . . . Hand said . . . this pompous lawyer gets up before the Supreme Court and roars out, "I have the blood of Cromwell's soldiers in my veins. And every drop of it boils with indignation when I think of this infamous enactment."

And Holmesy, you know, said, very measured, "Who is this goddamn fool?" [*Laughing*] "Every drop of it boils with indignation when...."

Then he told about going ... to a judge in Connecticut who had ... gotten very old. This was when Hand was a young man. They decided this old judge was getting too old. He was losing his marbles a little. They wanted him to step down, but there was no way they could unless he resigned. So this delegation waited upon him. And when they went in they said, "Now, Judge So-and-So, we admire you so and you've given such great service to the state and the bar, we think you should now be entitled to rest as a reward."

And the old fellow said, "No, I don't feel like that at all. I feel fine. I don't feel tired at all. I don't want to rest." Hand said the fellow said he never felt better in his life.

But this same old man, when he was young, had been in a group who went to another old judge to do exactly what they were trying to do to him. He'd gone with a delegation to Judge So-and-So and they'd ... persuaded this old gentleman to get out. Hand's group said ... "Judge ... do you remember the case of old Judge So-and-So?"

And the old gent said, "I certainly do, and a dirtier day's work was never done!" [*Laughing*]

They all bowed their way out. And that was the end of that. He was a wonderful mimic; telling those stories his way.

*Gardner, I have been waiting for you to mention painting women before asking you why you seem to enjoy painting men so much more, and why you have painted so many more men than women?*

G.C.   Is this the first time you've asked this?

*We've talked about it but not while we were recording.*

G.C.   My reasons are ... well, I guess there are several reasons. I suppose I'm more comfortable when I'm painting men because I'm not worried ... about hurting their feelings. Nor am I worried about getting involved with them at all. These two things are the things, I guess. Funnily enough, when you paint women, they can get very fond of you. Whatever the reason, there's a tendency for the person to be quite attracted to you, even though there's no fooling around or flirting. Ministers have this ... and painters. After all they are making quite a lot of a person ... seeing them in quite a natural way. You just go in and work in a friendly way, so you can get mixed up quite naturally.

I guess I'm kind of scared of that . . . a little bit uneasy about that . . . and then I'd be more and more aware of them, not quite dispassionate. The last thing I ever want to do is any kind of society woman stuff, with bare arms and bosoms . . . that kind of thing. That kind of painting I don't like. I didn't want to get mixed up in that at all. And also, again there would be a tendency *not* to hurt their feelings or . . . lean over backwards *not* to flatter them a little bit. Too often they'd expect you to do something you just couldn't bring yourself to do. This applies to some women but obviously not to all. My most successful portraits of women have been of types who did not have this particular brand of self-consciousness. My friendships with them have been very rewarding. Martina Lawrence was completely natural . . . didn't need to be flattered. And others like Mrs. Schlesinger[12] and Miss Marian Valliant, the headmistress of Buckingham School. Miss Valliant was the most delightful of unmarried ladies, and we had a wonderful friendship. I remember she said, "The loveliest experience is to be painted by Gardner Cox in the spring."

I'm not sure these are all the answers. There may be some more; but I can make a stronger statement with men than I can with women. I don't worry about hurting their feelings at all. As I say, my relationships with the women I painted have been very rewarding.

Except for one. There was only one where we didn't get on at all. And she quit. Come to think of it, there was just that one. Again, she wanted the kind of work I wasn't able to do. She was quite pretentious, avant-garde, and wanted something advanced, mannered.

*Vogue*, or some magazine like that, in their "hints for women," advised, "When you walk into a room think, 'I am loved, I am beautiful,' and you'll take 'em by storm." [*Laughing*] And this is the quality in them you are sensitive enough not to want to hurt.

*I remember you did several portraits of Sarita Kellogg.*[13]

G.C.   Yes I did. I did two or three. She came in, off and on, and I did one until I got one that was right.

*She was a beauty, wasn't she?*

G.C.   No. I had trouble painting her. I had trouble with her because I don't do women very well. I've done a few well. That one of Miss Valliant was a good one. Martina Lawrence's is a good one. I did Martina for quite a while before I succeeded. I just loved Martina. I loved Martina. It was what you call very pure love. There wasn't any ... I never just thought of her that way at all. And I think she was very fond of me. She got fond of me. They see you struggling, you know. You're working away ... and you're paying attention to them ... in a very wholesome way, so to speak. But ... I had an awful lot of trouble with Sarita. Finally got something that was good enough. It isn't very melting ... very feminine looking ... although it's kind of handsome.

*I love the two I've seen of Phyllis.*

G.C.   Yes. I did some of her. I did her. I didn't mind doing her. She was very hard to do. She was very hard to do ... she was beautiful. She had good bone structure.... big eyes ... and everything. Yes. She was a ... she was a very good-looking woman. They were pretty good of her. I did some good ones of her. But she had a pitfall and that is, you could make her look too soft. And she wasn't either one to that extent at all. That was the ... the ones I got, they looked pretty well. But that was the place you could go wrong with her. You could get it too tough or you could get too sweet. But the ones I did get, I did pretty well with. About right, I think.

*How about the one you did of Daggy?*[14] *I like that one.*

G.C.   I like it, but I don't think she likes it. They don't pay much attention to it. I don't know. She never said anything about it at all. But I like it. I told you a fellow tried to buy it out of that Athenaeum show. It's very rare when somebody else who is no relation tries to buy somebody's portrait. So it did something to somebody.

*About painting women, one of the reasons Phyllis is so good, and Daggy, too ...*

G.C.   Mrs. Schlesinger was quite good....

*Is that because they are your family, so there was none of this ....*

G.C.   Self-consciousness. I've done Poppy, too....

*Oh, Poppy's is enchanting....*

G.C.   And I did Kate. Kate was easy. Kate and Poppy were easy. The only one in the family that I had trouble with was James. When James was a kid he was awful cute, and I never got him quite right. When he was a kid he was the cutest little bugger you ever saw ... a manly little

Studies of his family from G.C.'s sketchbooks: James seated, 1952 (*at left*) and Phyllis holding Ben — "Mop and Ben at piano," 1946 (*below*)

Study of James Cox (*right*)
and Poppy (*below*) from
G.C.'s sketchbooks, 1952

fellow and I never got him quite good enough. He had a very peaceful smile like Eisenhower. [*Laughing*] He looked like Eisenhower. And I never got him quite right. I got pretty close, but not quite right. But the other three children were easy.

*That one of Ben sitting in a chair is charming. Wasn't the reason that Phyllis and your daughters were easy was because you weren't conscious of them as women?*

G.C.   You're right. I probably wasn't conscious with them. More self-conscious with women, that's what it amounts to. I'm not really self-conscious with women, you know. I'm just talking in a general way. I'm not particularly afraid of women, you know.

*As I understand it, women have meant more to you . . . have influenced your life more than men have.*

G.C.   That's right. What are you getting at? [*Laughing*] Ooooooo, you just stepped on a twig. [*Both laughing hard*] Stepped on a twig.

*I thought it was a good time to sneak it in.*

G.C.   [*Still laughing*] It was. It was a good try. We'll go into it some other time.

*It's one of your charms, actually, that women are terribly fond of you and you respond to them so marvelously.*

G.C.   You can tell 'em that. I can't.

*I'm telling them right now.*

G.C.   I can't exactly say myself, "Now let me tell you of my charms."

# 10

# Changes in the Arts (I)

*For whatever reason I am often tense—when I paint
I have to be—to feel like a tiger before I put the highlight
in the tiger's eye. True—otherwise the work lacks
something—what I feel—and it does.*

—from G.C.'s notebooks.

G.C.   Today I'd like to address myself to changes in painting. Go back and enlarge on it a little bit. Changes in painting as related to changes in architecture. These things don't go along absolutely parallel, of course. Some changes start a little earlier... or the effects are felt... or begin to be shown and so on—not obviously, at the same time exactly, but they go along more or less the same way.

The best way to start with changes in painting, I think, is through my personal knowledge with a man named Jaegel. John Jaegel. His father was quite a celebrated singer. I went to teach at the Museum School in 1954. I went there and took over from Karl Zerbe, who had been head of the painting department for a number of years. He had started kind of a Boston school. Well, he had a sabbatical and he asked me would I take his place and I thought I'd try it. I took it for two years altogether, and the first year I ran into Jaegel. He was a fifth-year student who had been there for four years under Zerbe. He was very bright. That is, he was charming—still is—a charming man. At that time, he was in his mid-twenties. He had won a prize the previous spring at the Boston Arts Festival for an abstract, non-objective painting. I make a difference between abstract and non-objective. I might just as well make the point here as any other place. As I see it. As I think it should be seen.

All painting is abstract by its very nature. It isn't the thing itself. It's an abstraction of whatever you are painting, whether realistic or non-realistic. Some paintings have their source in simple design—or in inner feelings of color, like Abstract Expressionism. That's what I call non-objective painting. Its source is non-objective. Now, all sources that have anything to do with visual reality, or objective reality, are objective. In other words, source is objective or non-objective. It's a distinction that should be made more often, because they're always talking about abstract painting and it's really a very loose term. It's not an accurate, not a good use of the word. It doesn't describe it.

Jaegel's pictures were non-objective painting. But, just to split a little hair here, funnily enough, they were objective in the sense they were derived from non-objective paintings. Now, you can get objective about non-objective painting if you want to. In fact, that's a very common thing to do. [*Chuckling*] There's an enormous amount of that. And, in this picture that won the prize (and there was pretty good competition at the Museum School in those days), Jaegel had combined three or four artists without knowing it. Oh, there was Tamayo,[1] some of Matta,[2] a little work of Gorky.[3] You see, he'd combined these people the way Picasso combined. Picasso combined rather classical stuff like the African masks and the Greek; and then Cézanne who, of course, was an unclassical fellow. Anyway, Jaegel had done that kind of thing and the date's important. It was 1954. The date the art historians seem to give as the peak of Abstract Expressionism. The fifties are given as its high-water mark. In the sixties, it began to break up a little and pop art began to come in. The date's important, too, because this young man was aware that he was using other people's symbols and combining them. And at that time, too, art books and the media had disseminated the work of people like Miró[4] ... Gorky ... you can name them. There's no use belaboring this, but you can jump through the Abstract Expressionist list: Pollock[5] ... de Kooning[6] ... any of them.

*Kandinsky?*

G.C.    Yes, Kandinsky[7] comes in there. All kinds of that very free, non-objective work. The minds of Jaegel's generation were filled with other people's images; so when they went into that closet and shut their eyes to pray and to think and to work, what their minds were filled with was other people's images. They couldn't get rid of them. They tried to self-consciously, which is not a very good way to work. Jaegel didn't know what was bothering him. We talked about it, and he realized he was using other people's images. Actually, he was very upset about it.

In the early stages of Abstract Expressionism, you see, a man like Miró made up those little bones and those little forms and they were quite original. They originally came out of him. But as soon as he did it, of course, other people got those things in their heads and it's damn hard to get it out of your head except by just leaning over backwards, and instead of making a soft shape like a bone with round ends, you might make a horizontal, sharpened thing. You get away that way, but it's running away. It's self-conscious. It's trying to be original another way. Miro wasn't being self-conscious, and this happened to all the early ones. They came up with their thing and, pretty soon, there was a glut of this stuff.

From Jaegel I figured out (well, I'd been thinking about this for a long time) that one of the things that would change this movement would be that the bright boys would want to have their own thing, and they'd know they wanted it. They would finally renounce Abstract Expressionism because it was robbing them. At least they couldn't get out. Jaegel couldn't get out. He's never gotten out. There's nothing bad about this. He's a good man and all, but he's still adapting from other people's work. He probably has a particular propensity for it.

*Is that why we don't hear more of him?*

G.C.   Yes, because he's quite talented. Of course, Picasso did this too. He was the first, and it was a very original vein with him because *he* did it.

*But Picasso's a genius, so there was always something of himself in it, even when he was adapting from others' images.*

G.C.   Yeah, he was a genius. He was an extraordinarily gifted man. But, although he could paint without doing it, he did take from other people. Jaegel's pretty good without it, too; but I think your way of putting it is all right: Picasso had more to put into it.

And here's where I, as a critic, should be good; because I know what it is to be in the pits. I know what it's like to feel these things and how quickly you can get something in your mind, and how an artist's mind works. But I wouldn't want to use another man's symbols. A person like myself, born in tradition, thinks of Rembrandt. I think of Velásquez.

I think of Giotto, Goya, El Greco. I think of hundreds of people in the past, but that isn't using their symbols. It's an approach. Eakins[8] is another one. All of them were objective painters, but they painted totally originally. Everything they did had their own mark and their interpretations.

Think of poetry about love, for example. The poets are writing about something they've all experienced, but they lend it something totally original. The early abstractionists, however, have been scraped down to actual mannerisms in a sense, intellectual mannerisms, so the movement was bound to change, and indeed it has. It was the desire to get away from the symbols and images that started it off. It got more and more minimal and then just conceptual which, of course, was no good for the very talented fellow.

In that quote I once gave you from a talk by Robert Morris,[9] he proposed an art that anybody could do and didn't even need to be seen, just described, to be appreciated. Rembrandt, right *out!* There are too many people born with ability to buy that kind of thing, so that's what made the change come; and, of course, it's operating now and increasing.

*Do you think it's back to more rather than less? Has conceptual art run its course?*

G.C.  Well, I should say it has. People will do it now and then, but it certainly has. Even at the time it appeared, exponents of it said it couldn't last more than two years. Obviously, they didn't expect it to last.

*Wasn't conceptual art phony, Gardner? I thought it was phony as hell.*

G.C.  It's hard to say. A very large part of that movement was gimmicks and invention and being original. There was a critic around 1956, 1957, who wrote, "Let's face it: unless a painting is original, unless it's new, it's not modern art."

That's a terrible thing for a student to read. That meant you had to think of something nobody'd ever thought of before. You couldn't go around looking at things and getting your own reaction. You had to come up with something really original like a blank canvas. That would be an answer to that. A blank canvas. There were things of that sort that were being done. Some people were being inventive, but some were pretty stupid.

*How about Christo? You know the guy who hung a sheet across a canyon and had a wall of canvas that stretched for miles and miles?*

G.C. Christo? He sounds like an awful ass to me, but I don't know that he's phony. He got his ideas the way Mondrian[10] got his. Christo's came from doing camouflage during the war. He was commissioned to camouflage haystacks and from this he got the idea of making something look like something it wasn't. And, of course, he used gunnysack and cloth. But I don't think he's a great artist. There's nothing new about packaging buildings. You see them covered by a tarpaulin all the time in winter to protect the workers from the weather, but he was the first one to think of bundled buildings as a work of art. Who cares? Who wants to cover them? I certainly don't, but they were able to raise an awful lot of money for doing this.

His exhibition of drawings of the buildings he proposed to cover had charm and were quite stylish. I saw it at the Institute of Contemporary Art some time ago, and they were very dramatic. They were big and decorative and had a ghostly quality about them. There was the shape of the buildings under wraps with the wings coming out like a museum; and buildings way off done darkly in charcoal.

"Phony?" That's a word used all the time. I think it's more that the artists delude themselves they're great when most of them are not great. Only about five great ones come along in a hundred years. Christo's not one of them, believe me. His ideas are too simple to be great and he doesn't even do the work himself. He's kind of a half-assed architect with a crew of people doing things for him. He gets a building and then he gets a crew of people to cover it. What's so great about that? Where does it lead to except to have someone say, "Jesus! I'm going to cover a tree or the Washington Monument if they'll let me." [*Chuckling*] Can you imagine that starting a big movement? No, there's nothing to learn from him except to go out and do something original.

But originality, per se, is never any good. It's only good in the service of an idea. It's a by-product of something that's worth while.

*Originality is only good in the service of an idea. That's good! How about Oldenburg?*[11]

G.C. Oh, he's much more original and varied than Christo. He was a first-class student at Yale. One of the brightest students they had there, and he's done a lot of things. He's a satirist and a joker, but he's not pulling your leg. Did you ever see his *Lovers*? He had a show at

Tech, and I saw it there. It was done with clothespins, great big ones, the kind you pinch open. He had two of them about as high as those trees out there, with little things on top and wires for arms. When you saw it you thought, "God, it *is* the lovers!" Damned amusing and very graceful. Then, at the same show, outside, there was a big ash tray with crumpled shapes in it made of lead, I think, which were burnt-out cigarettes. [*Laughing*] It was ridiculous, but it had a kind of jumbled action. Oh, he's fun!

But this kind of art, especially pre-conceptual art, is very temporary. It's the kind of thing that will be talked about for a year, and next year they'll be talking about something else.

If you want an example of phoniness, there was a guy, less than a year ago, who had an exhibition at the Institute of Contemporary Art here in Boston. I can't remember his name now, but it doesn't make any difference because nobody's going to remember him anyway. Well, a little bit of chic got him in, and there was a film on him that went with the exhibition. He'd take a canvas about as big as that picture up there [*Gesturing*] and he'd paint white on it, maybe a little gray-with-white, and that's all. In the film he was a dull, unattractive, pathetic little guy. Frightfully humorless and he'd say, "Man, you do this because you want to do it. You want to get the feeling of . . ." He went on and on and it was very boring. His pictures were nothing, and he added nothing.

*But he was recognized enough for the I.C.A. to put him on and make a film of him.*

G.C.   Now, that's an interesting point. A good example. You say the I.C.A. thinks he's good enough, but the I.C.A. would be Gabriella Jeppson.[12] She picked him. You see, it's who picks them. This goes for the Museum of Modern Art in New York, too. Incidentally, it never should have been called the Museum of Modern Art. That term is premature of the timelessness of the work that was selected, or even the work selected that didn't turn out so well. Alfred Barr,[13] who started the museum, is a bright critic and art historian and a very good chooser, but he isn't time itself. So it was Gabriella Jeppson who picked that guy, not the I.C.A. And when you put a picture up in a museum, it gives people who don't know much about it (the public, in other words), the impression that this must be hot stuff. So of course some artists are phony. Picasso certainly had his tongue in his cheek, at times. They say he'd watch people rush up and get it as soon as he left the table. He was witty and he was fun, but he was one phony, now and then.

I had a personal experience, back in 1931, that had a lot to do with this. It was when I was at the architectural school at Tech and there was this fellow there named Webber. He was in the periphery of the group I used to go around with, and he was quite an intellectual. He was a theorizing fellow and considered himself very avant-garde. He was always looking for the chic, looking for the new, theorizing. One time at lunch he said, "Beauty is entirely what you choose to call it." Eye-of-the-beholder stuff. I remember he took a piece of paper and made just a squiggle on it and said, "Now, if I say that's beautiful, it's beautiful."

I said, "You're full of you know what, Webber." And he said, "No, that's the way it is."

One vote. Just one vote. That became common practice after a while and it's been going on for a long time. You know, a lot of people at the top of Abstract Expressionism didn't know any better than Webber. In fact, an awful lot of people weren't any better. Jackson Pollock did a lot of those.

*But I like him. Don't you?*

G.C.   He's OK. I might buy one of his pictures if I had enough money, but his things aren't very deep.

*How about de Kooning?*

G.C.   I like some of de Kooning better. He's more talented than Pollock in certain ways. Much more capable. There was an amusing incident of a kid, who had never even heard of him, who painted the way he does. He even had the same technique. It got into the papers and either *Newsweek* or *Time*.

*How about Motherwell?*[14]

G.C.   He was original, some, but the only original thing he ever did were those black balls and that black sweep which had a sort of machismo feeling. He does the same thing over and over. [*Laughing*] He happens to be one I don't like, you know. I don't like him chemically.

But the very best of Abstract Expressionism was spontaneous and very pure. I remember particularly this fellow, let's call him Forsyth. Actually, I can't remember his name. He was a very nice man, and I met him when I was painting someone in the Corcoran Gallery and he was teaching there. We'd have lunch together, from time to time, and he told me that before he went to the Korean War, he'd been a commercial artist. He was an honest, attractive, vigorous young man and very capable; and when I asked him, "Were you good at it?" he said, "Yes," and I believed him. Well, he was drafted and got married before he went overseas; and, while he was over there, he began to think less and less of what he'd been doing. When he got back he didn't like commercial work anymore, and he was kind of at sea. He was beginning to have a family and he told me it was a very bad year.

Then he went to an exhibition of Abstract Expressionists and he said he knew right off that's what he wanted. That said it for him. He had two kids by that time, but he gave up his job, and this was quite a thing to do. It was a real piece of conscience. Here he was with a wife and kids living out in Virginia, teaching at the Corcoran School, and he didn't have much time to paint during the week. He wasn't an oddball; he wasn't any crazy saint-type; he was like you and me: warm-blooded, liked a little fun, liked a drink, a good fellow by nature; but every Friday, he went to bed early to get into condition to paint the next day. When I ran into him at the Corcoran, he'd been doing this for years.

He had a little studio in the garage, and every Saturday morning he'd get up early, nice and healthy, and go out there and paint. He'd take a bare canvas. Then he'd take a brush, he'd put it in a can of paint, say a can of blue paint, and here's where he was in that closet we were talking about, all preconceptions peeled off, and he'd draw the blue paint right across the canvas like this [*With a wave of his hand*]. Or he'd draw it across like that. So, here's this blue line on canvas. What's that make him feel like doing? He grabs a brush of black paint and goes *Whoops!* like this [*Again illustrating*]. Then what does he feel like doing? He takes some white paint and splatters it across here. He goes and does these things, responding to each situation as it changes. Just as he feels. Just as if he were being analyzed on a couch. And he told me when he thought that was it, when he didn't feel it anymore, he'd quit. So that everything he did was very pure, just out of feeling.

And out of the fact that he had had long training at art school and had been a commercial artist too, he did things that had great weight behind them. And his pictures were good. Frankfurter and I went to an exhibition he had, and Frankfurter nearly bought one. They were kind of deep and quite beautiful. There was nothing phony about this guy at all. As soon as he wasn't feeling it, *Stop!* And there on this canvas would be how a man felt from nine to twelve on April fifteenth. It had a lot of virtue; but for a person who didn't have his background of study and experience, maybe not. You can see how it would appeal to people who didn't have much on the ball. And the sad thing is I'd never heard of him and can't remember his name. This is an awfully tough-field.

*Do you remember you tried to make me do just that? Put paint on paper the way you feel?*

G.C.   That's right. That's right. The best painting I do is done that way. I don't do it Forsyth's way; but the best I do is when I'm not thinking of anything except trying to get the feeling at the moment of operation through position, composition, and various other things. That little portrait of Poppy is a good example.

There's another way of putting it which I've thought about for a long time and written down. It's firmly in my mind and it's absolutely true. That is: a great deal of painting is Abstract Expressionism. Rembrandt's full of it. When he does something like this [*Illustrating a squiggle*] it's in a different context, but it's the same thing. He does an earlobe. I used to show pictures of it when I lectured to the whole Museum School at lunchtime, every damn week. They ate while I talked. Well, in this slide of an earlobe you could see he just took a lot of paint and went *whoop!* Then he'd give another *whoop!* and it was action painting if you ever saw it. It was beautifully-controlled painting in his case; but it was the same impulse, the same response as the expressionists. I blew it up and threw it on the screen, and the students saw this wonderful, juicy piece of work.

Another thing the Abstract Expressionists did was to take one or two factors of, say, a Titian and make a whole thing of it. The Renaissance fellows, painters like Rembrandt and Titian, the good ones, used all the factors I've talked about: color, texture, line, value, and so on. Now the Abstract Expressionists would use one or maybe two. Pollock used just texture and a little bit of color. Mondrian was just line. His principle was good and evil as opposing forces. This occurred to him while looking at an apple tree, funnily enough. And here's a lesson for Mr. Jaegel. Mondrian saw those branches going this way and that and he got this through his thick head (or whatever head he's got, [*Laughing*] because I've heard he got awful boring and obsessed with what he was doing) that this was it: good and evil in opposition. He thought he'd solved the world. The basis for everything good and evil in proportion. But it was original. He got it from just drawing an apple tree as well as he could . . . good old objective piece of work . . . and it suddenly occurred to him, why don't I really get simple about this? Why don't I reduce it down to its essence? And there he was. [*Laughing*] He never did anything else in his life. I'm glad this came up, because it's a good example of how you can get something out of something else that turns out to be original. Now Mondrian's influence is all over the place. On linoleum and many other things. If he hadn't gone out to that apple tree, the idea would never have struck him. And after it struck him, it struck a lot of people and they began to imitate him.

So I told Jaegel, "Why don't you go out to nature and see what she suggests? Study a blade of grass, a leaf any old thing. You might come up, like Mondrian did, with a symbol of your own; not just a predigested idea of Picasso's or Miró's."

Of course, going back to nature and objective objects for inspiration is the basis of a great deal that's been done in the past. The impressionists tried the system for light. Light was what they were after. Turner saw beauty in those slums, you know, and in those dirty streets and the lemon peel in the harbor. There was some pretty dirty stuff in there, but the river and docks were beautiful. Cézanne, in his attempt to get the feeling of nature, evolved those cubes which Picasso took and made cubism of. It was rich enough for that.

But Abstract Expressionism isn't very strong anymore. Back in 1978, at the American Academy in Rome, only one picture was submitted, and it was a very bad one. This from three or four hundred submissions from all over the country; whereas, ten, twelve years ago, there would have been a great many Abstract Expressionist pictures submitted.

*You know, I have thought for a long time that some of your pictures show a strong Abstract Expressionistic influence. Take that wonderful portrait of Barry Bingham that I saw in your exhibition at the Corcoran Gallery.*

G.C.   Did you like that one?

*The fiery background seemed very expressionistic. It gave the feeling of a man of force and of turmoil. When did you do that particular portrait?*

G.C.   I must have done that . . . it must have been done in the sixties, '65 or something like that.

*Were you painting particularly that way, then?*

G.C.   Yes, I've done a lot of pictures like that, although I haven't been painting that way recently. Recently, I've been more influenced by Japanese tones of black and gold.

*That's something we'll certainly return to; but for the moment, which other portraits would you say were influenced by Abstract Expressionism?*

G.C.   Well, the one of Robert Frost in the St. Botolph Club was done that way.

*And certainly the one of him you did for the Frost Library at Middlebury College . . .*

G.C.   Yes, that was done that way, the colors and so on. In fact, when you asked me who had influenced me and I said Pollock, I didn't really mean Pollock. I meant Abstract Expressionism. Oh yes, Abstract Expressionism was quite a good thing for me in many ways.

*I can see this in the Frost portraits certainly, and very clearly in that wonderful Bingham portrait. Wasn't that one of your most powerful periods?*

G.C.   Maybe. I know what you're talking about. It's exactly what I had in mind when I was doing those pictures. You see, I tried it another way with Bailey Aldrich by giving his portrait that thin, diaphanous stuff, so it had more atmosphere. It was an attempt to do the same thing another way.

*How about that portrait of Mrs. Schlesinger, in the Schlesinger Library at Radcliffe? Wasn't she done the same way?*

G.C.   No. She'd be more like Bingham. There wasn't much of the Bingham technique in the Corcoran show, though. Daggy had a little bit of it.

*Daggy's wasn't as strong.*

G.C.   That's right.

*To get back to Bailey Aldrich. How did you achieve the diaphanous quality?*

G.C.     In the background. With egg emulsion. Egg tempera emulsion, which is used in the Venetian technique with a little raw umber and a little raw sienna. You put it on first, then you cover it with oil. In Bailey's case, it is not covered with oil so you can see the white canvas through. This gives it depth. If that were oil paint, it would be flat. This is something that occurs to me all the time, one way or another. I do it in different ways. For a sharp person, I get little sharp things going around; or, for a calm person, you would do something a little bit different. With Barry, I used color quite a lot. Like fire. And I guess I did something of it with Goldberg. I certainly did quite a lot of it here and there. With Bailey, there's the judge's black robe . . . and the yellow . . . and a little bit of color. Japanese colors and a very dignified combination. Have I talked to you about the Japanese and where their taste came from?

*A little bit, but not on tape.*

G.C.     Well, one morning at the Holiday Inn, there were three Japanese having breakfast across the room from me, and they were quite beautiful leaning over this table. The sun was coming in, the morning light hitting them, and they were against the darker background of the restaurant. It suddenly occurred to me that the colors in their paintings, particularly the screens, are their own colors. Their golden skin, their coal-black, blue-black hair, their brown-black eyes, this is what they see in all their moments of great intimacy. Every morning when they look at themselves in the mirror, or at their wife across the table, at the kids, or when they're making love, they're looking at someone who's yellow and black. So here they were at this table at the Holiday Inn with the white china (the orange of the counter would be color a little bit), and it reminded me of their screens. You know, just a gold screen with a black rim. A lot of it is, in effect, yellow like the background in Bailey's portrait. I don't mean bright yellow, obviously, and not just like their skin; but black and yellow. And it occurred to me that it was in very good taste. It's strong. You know yellow and black are non-colors, and white.

*Yellow, a non-color?*

G.C.     That kind of yellow, yes. Yellow, if it is bright lemon and vivid, is color. But not gold. That's why they use gold frames because you can put any color with them. And the same with black. That's why dark-skinned people look so good in colors. You know, a black woman with a great turban on her head in a kind of neon-pink, or in a violent turquoise, looks all right, but on you it would look terrible. She can put on anything, because her black is a non-color. It sets everything else off. Now we have all kinds of complexions: ruddy, pale, with blue eyes, brown eyes, red hair, dark hair; we have to be careful how we dress, women particularly.

By this token, the Japanese taste, which I think is very great, is very dignified stuff. For instance, the background in Bailey's portrait is yellow. It's a Chinese kind of yellow. You can go up and down the scale with that quite a lot. The black judge's robe and the white shirt. There's no color there that anything can't go along with. There's a little blue in the tie, and his face has a little pink in it.

*The background is yellow?*

G.C.   Yes, as I told you. It's raw umber and a little raw sienna...egg emulsion. Part of the charm of that picture is the white canvas coming through, which gives it depth. But the gown is where the action is. I'd been doing gowns too smooth. Kissinger's suit is too smooth. I didn't like the way I did his clothes, but I let him have the portrait because I thought it was adequate...

*...and weren't you under pressure to finish it before the first of the year, Carter's deadline for the government picking up the tab for state portraits?*

G.C.   That was part of it, certainly. Anyway, as you know, he didn't like it. I might have changed the clothes and still might, because I suddenly realized I'd been making the gowns pretty plain with just a few lines in them. They were too much out of scale with the painting and the face. So with Bailey, I had the gown very rough. That was quite carefully thought through.

*How about Ammi's[15] portrait?*

G.C.   I used the same technique as Bailey's. It's got the same yellow background and his judge's robes are black, of course. The same so-called black-and-yellow scheme.

*Isn't what you've been talking about part of the interplay between artists and their influence on each other? Think of the interplay within your own originality: The Renaissance masters, Rembrandt, Velásquez and so on; the Abstract Expressionists; and the Japanese influence as a result of that breakfast epiphany at the Holiday Inn. Also, you've often mentioned Eakins and a Dutch picture of cows and trees at the M.F.A.*

G.C.   Maybe you're right. That's about right, although I don't reflect what's going on around me as quickly as that sounds. I'm steeped in the old masters, but even Rembrandt's not in my blood. Not as in some artists who spend years copying them. My mother did a lot of it; and Degas went out and copied Piero della Francesca for two or three years. That's really getting in there. I mean the actual copying. Probably it would have been better if I'd done more.

## 11

# Changes in the Arts (II)

*Do you wish to make any comments on the synopsis of last week's taping I sent you?*

G.C.   Well, these are like notes for a lot more, and I think I'll say more about this later on. But right now, as I said, I don't feel too smart this morning. One thing, though, I want to clear up a little bit. When you asked me what artists had influenced me, I said Pollock and Rembrandt. Pollock, as a matter of fact, influenced me practically none. There's probably fifty painters who've influenced me more. You know, we're all influenced by a great many people, and I wouldn't want to leave that statement at that. That would indicate Pollock was someone I paid attention to. I just used him as an example. From A to Z, he's Z. Way down the line. *Way* down the list. But the whole movement had some influence. That's the kind of thing I'd like to check this thing over for. It's what I said, but it doesn't indicate what I mean.

*I almost jumped out of my skin when you mentioned Pollock first, as the artist who had influenced your work. But now come to think of it, I can see his influence in some of your backgrounds.*

G.C.   You got what I said; but this, of course, just came out of my face. I think I know why I said Pollock. I was sure... I distinctly thought ... you'd expect me to say Sargent or someone like Velásquez. I'm sure the way my mind worked was that I'd start right off to show that Pollock was an example of the whole field of the many people who I'd be influenced by. He would not be what you expected.

*He certainly wasn't.*

G.C.   I wasn't thinking that hard, and it was a way of opening up the things right off the bat. He was just a symbol.

*As long as we're talking over last week's tapes, I'd like to tell you of a thought I had in connection with your contention that Abstract Expressionism was the result of Bauhaus architecture with its great white walls and its simplicity. I shouldn't interpose my thoughts, but I got this idea that when the guilds disappeared and skilled manual labor was replaced by machines, details in painting disappeared, too, in style and subject matter. Would it be possible that both the Bauhaus and the Abstract Expressionist movement were influenced by the fact that individual workmanship disappeared in favor of the machine?*

G.C.   I wouldn't know. I'd have to think that one over. I assume you're talking about furniture. I don't know. It's a good logical jump; but, if that hypothesis of yours is based on my remarks about abstract expressionism and the Bauhaus, I didn't explain that well enough.

There were painters at the Bauhaus . . . I think Kandinsky was there for a time . . . there were furniture-makers, of course, there were architects. I don't recollect any sculptor right now. There may have been some, but I don't recollect any. And they all worked together in this artistic community. I don't know how much they took from one another or got from one another. The point I was making about the Abstract Expressionists was that the Bauhaus architecture presented them with walls and places to put things . . . great white spaces to place their art where people could see it . . . The plainness of it asked for . . . was very receptive to that big, free stuff. So, it was more providing a space for their work to be seen than what you were suggesting. It's more that, I'd say. I used the example of the Victorian living room. Can you imagine a Pollock in a Victorian living room?

*I was thinking of music and writing, too.*

G.C.   To go on with furniture, I never thought of it as affecting painting, particularly. This is not to say there isn't some correlation there. After all, contemporary furniture has to do with Bauhaus plenty. Yeah. The boiling down . . . the analyzing . . . intellectualizing . . . as a man like Mondrian did. Some of the linear things would be reduced to very chaste and simple forms, as is the case in some contemporary rooms and in the work of a number of post abstract expressionistic painters. Mondrian was one of them. Barnett Newman,[1] even, would be an example of the very chaste, reducing it down to the barest thing. In furniture again, they'd take a chair and reduce it to a couple of pipes and put in an ash tray. This would fit your buttocks in just one position and so on. So, I suppose they were doing the same kind of thing in a different medium. But, more or less, the same kind of thing. The Bauhaus was a reduction of the complicated, getting to the bones of things as much as possible. This didn't apply to Abstract Expressionism. This didn't apply to Klee.[2] This didn't apply to Kandinsky, God knows. It didn't apply to the Abstract Expressionists at all. I'm just thinking of furniture in connection with painting, which I never thought of particularly before. It doesn't strike me off the bat as a very ... it would be straining a bit if you thought there was a connection.

*I shouldn't be wasting our time with my thinking but ...*

G.C.   You're not wasting time at all.

*... at least by throwing out ideas, you express your ideas in reacting to them. So, again this week, my mind went further to minimal art. Has that come along with the computer? Minimal art carried further is conceptual, which can be carried to the absurd, like that absolutely bare wall entitled,* Invisible! *Can this be connected with the computer and the Pill? Is this art responding to the take-over of human involvement by science? A minimal involvement?*

G.C.   I don't know. It doesn't happen to be my line of thinking, but you could certainly write a piece on it and get people to discuss it. I wouldn't say yes and I wouldn't say no. You see, the computer is coming in stronger and stronger all the time; and art is changing, getting away from that extreme simplicity. Like I said in that little piece in the 50th Harvard reunion program.* You know, every minute that's being borne out more and more. There is another wave coming that is anti the minimalist stuff. It's happening in architecture, too. It's happening across the board.

*Who are the leaders?*

G.C.   Oh ... er ... there hasn't been time to have any leaders, really. There are people who are fooling around. In architecture there's this fellow Bob Venturi ... and Mike Graves. Venturi was at the Academy of Arts and Letters. I saw quite a lot of him when I was a trustee there. Bob Venturi. He'd also been a fellow in Rome early; and Michael Graves was in Rome when I was there along with Musho.[3] Musho's in Pei now, and Graves is doing sort of experimental ... I'd say experi-

---

* G.C.'s speech in his Harvard Class's 50th reunion symposium, 1978, in Chapter 16.

ments. He's one of the leaders . . . one of the half-dozen names mentioned in N*ewsweek* as rejecting the Bauhaus, finding it dry and characterless, somewhat. This is the trend now.

The Bauhaus stuff was just beginning when I was at Tech in 1931. I remember it was 1931, and there was a fellow there named Sam McMurtry, who was an instructor. He'd been a student at Tech and he . . . he was a very charming little fellow. He was kind of a bald-headed fellow who was a very good designer and a very bright man. He went abroad for a semester, or a year. I don't know whether he got a prize to go or not. Anyway, when he came back, he produced a real Bauhaus answer to a problem. It was a room and I remember it was very very chaste in a great round circle. I've forgotten the details, but it was very chaste . . . a very Bauhaus answer to the problem. At that time, the rest of the department had been doing problems every week. They were doing buildings sort of early modernistic in style, like the Sears Roebuck building. There'd be pilasters . . . you know, a little relief in the brick . . . and, on top of them there'd be kind of a bunch of cancels . . . very stylized, very flat, just shapes . . . leaving the impression of a column with a cap, or a pilaster with a cap. The cap would be done with art deco forms. Things like that were being done a lot. I was in my third year, at that time, and the whole department was doing problems like that every week. So Sam put this, what was considered an extremely avant-garde thing up with the rest of them.

In those days they marked . . . I guess they still do . . . first place as eighteen. They had first medal and second medal; then they got down to the honorable mentions; and finally down to the X's. X was *Out!* And good old McMurtry got a big X over this thing! And he was mad as hell. You know, he'd gone abroad and this was the thing there, but it hadn't got here yet, quite. It had begun with Louis Henry Sullivan in this country; then Frank Lloyd Wright took it from him a little bit. Sullivan-Wright was kind of the beginning of some of this. They used a lot of glass in the structures; but it hadn't got to the architectural schools yet, though they greatly respected Sullivan. Not so much Wright. Bob Alles was out ahead in that style, too. A dry style. Wright was never dry, you know.

Well, the point I'm making is that it's about sixty-five years that styles tend to run through. Not sixty-five, obviously. I guess forty years or so, and architects are beginning to do things differently. If anybody should be a leader, I think it would be Venturi. He's a frightfully intellectual fellow. He went to Princeton and he was a cum laude student. His brain is a sensitive, quivering mass of powerful sensitivity. [*Chuckling*] He's not artistic, but he's intellectualized this whole business. He takes the strip outside Reno or Las Vegas ... er ... Las Vegas, that's it. That strip as you come in with the hamburger stands and the McDonald's and the gas stations and that stuff, with their signs and so on. And that's where he takes off from. He's taken that as ... er ... a merit in esthetic form. As a result, his buildings look very much like gas stations. On Long Island, there's a place where they sell duckling sandwiches ... or roasts ... just ducks; so he's made a building that looks like a duck.

*Like the cheese on the way to North Haven.*

G.C.   Right. Absolutely. Exactly. *Exactly.* [*Laughing*] He may have done that one.

*But I don't like that. Do you?*

G.C.   No. But this ... it's quite a change. He has a wife[4] and they're in this together. He wrote an article I read a couple of years ago, and you could see a lot of people could take off from this.

Now he proposed that buildings were just blocks to love in ... and to live in. This would be along the strip idea as you can see in a minute. They would have no individuality in themselves, but they'd have a sign on them that would clearly state what was going on in the building. Lily Saarinen would be a good one to put a ceramic ... a great ceramic over one side, like a piece of costume jewelry on a woman pinned to the corner of one of these white boxes ... say a beautiful blue. For instance, Symphony Hall is a box ... and a very good one acoustically. Just a good big brick-like rectangular block. It's not a cube. It's two cubes, actually, put together, as I think about it. Now Venturi would have had something on it to indicate what it did.

*You wouldn't do it with signs. You do it with ceramics or ...*

G.C.   Yes. You might do it by the old-fashioned signs. You'd maybe put a boot outside. Not as crude as that; but maybe even as crude as that, here and there.

Now, with this stuff in mind, if I were an architect, in the shopping centers and places of that sort, I'd be reminded of a Tunisian village or a Moroccan village. I say Tunis now, because I've been there and seen the white buildings ... white stucco or white plaster, or whatever it is ... they're very attractive. The point is with the white buildings and then just black doors, and then a color, you could make a helluva snappy-looking thing. And all around town you'd have quite a beautiful thing. Now that would be an idea you'd say that could have come from what Venturi is doing. They haven't done it this way, but some may well do it this way, someday.

So they've taken these ideas and they've started to dress things up and make things more interesting, instead of the very chaste, clinical things that Venturi was talking about when he said ... I think it was he who said ... "I'd rather be good than interesting." He'd rather be technically right, you know, than to have any interest. That was good enough for him, and that was the bible for a long while. It's changed. That's changed and it's changing all over.

But I don't see the connection between Abstract Expressionism or the Bauhaus movement with the computer. The computer's going pretty good. It's getting more ... more ... more. The arts are getting less, less. I don't think it had anything to do with those movements. I think the scientific inventions of the time got to the artists very quick. The scientific spirit ... the inventiveness that produced the computer ... that's had an effect all right. That's in that little piece I gave at Harvard in '78. I think it's in there. The inventions have made them begin to intellectualize ... intellectualize more; and there's all kinds of scope for this thing in our society today. This would be the great big buildings ... the shapes ... those great, chaste white walls. All kinds of things conspire to have a change. And there would have been a change anyway, probably.

Here's another thing about that. At least again ... I haven't read this, but I'm sure it's been written or should have been written ... there's nothing original about it. Maybe there is, but I don't know. I really don't know. But ... er ... the styles are always going to change after a while if there's any interplay. On the other hand, the style didn't change in Japan, apparently, for about three hundred years. That's when they developed so wonderfully, because the artists weren't concerned with being *original* except in the most subtle way. The West has never been isolated like that ... in recent history, that is. For several hundred years or more ... maybe a thousand years ... for a long time people have been moving back and forth. They've not been isolated, so there's been an interchange of ideas all the time ... and, of course increasingly so. So, the style changed in Japan very slowly. The artists' schemes and their approach to their paintings were the same ... different just in refinements which produced this very fine stuff they did. As I say, the artists weren't worrying about being inventive. What they were concerned with was to do it better or subtler. Whereas, in complete contrast, in the last fifty years and before ... probably since the industrial revolution, but particularly in the last fifty years of this century—in the West, where invention has piled on invention and ... er ... the media have produced (through the inventions) these magazines with color reproductions which, when we were small, we didn't have, you know. When we were young, we didn't have anything like that at all. It started off with the Hyperion Press books, then *Life* magazine. All these magazines ... art magazines ... could reproduce paintings. People could see them all over the place. Artists saw them and, of course, this changed their styles very rapidly. And then they began to try and be inventive. Even in talking about space ... space travel ... they started thinking about space. When you first start thinking about space, things get big. You have pictures ten feet ... twenty feet long. It's going to be spacious. The naturalists don't go for it; but you can give the illusion of space, obviously, by making a little picture this big [*Illustrating with his hands an area about a foot square*] and get a hell of a big feeling out of it if you want to. I did a picture like that, myself, once and I got a lot of space in it.

*How?*

Well, it had a great big ball about that big [*Illustrating*] which just hung there; and a horizon and a little pyramid in the distance; and an egg, an egg and a shell. It was very small but it did feel ...

*What happened to that picture?*

G.C. It went out to Chicago and won a prize. It was sold to somebody, and I don't know where it is now. But it was very small with a good feeling of space. But they did go for space also in a factual, actual way

*When did you do your series of spheres? Eggs and rocks and globes? I thought they were fantastic.*

G.C. They were done after I got out of the army. I even started doing them some while I was still in the army. Early in 1945. That winter of 1945-46.

*Did they reflect that sort of mystical experience you had during the last part of your time in the army and when you got out?*

G.C.   They certainly did indirectly. Directly. I just felt . . . I was in very good shape . . . uh . . . mentally and intellectually. It was a very productive and creative period in my life, as a matter of fact. Walter Lippmann expressed it as a "kind of explosion." I had a lot of ideas— when I say a lot of ideas . . . I felt for some reason or other . . . I can't explain just why I did those forms. But I liked the smooth shapes of the eggs; of course, a very basic shape. And the rocks were such a different texture and shape . . . jagged. And the broken eggshells. Distinctly, almost discord . . . struck a strong contrast . . . almost discord . . . a contrast with the smoothness of the unbroken egg. And so I took these very pure forms as counter opposed against the . . . uh . . . jaggedness of the rocks or the jaggedness of the broken shells, which also, however, were very delicate. And then I used to put big . . . uh . . . put sort of globes in the sky behind them. Sometimes there'd be only half of a very large globe . . . I can't think of the word right now . . . uh . . . large . . . celestial body. Just half of it would come down in the picture. It was so much bigger than the rocks and the eggs below. And there'd be little globes, too. It had a certain surrealistic quality. It wasn't exactly surrealist either, but they gave quite a feeling of space, too. It was basic forms— elementary forms. The eggs graced it particularly as, opposed to the globes . . . more boring shapes . . . and the egg is another kind of shape . . . and the broken eggs, as I say, were a very important part of it. And the rocks also. It didn't always happen in the same picture. Some of them would be just the eggs and the broken shells and the globes, but often the rocks were there, too, using some texture in them. Using a technique I'd learned before the war: the Venetian technique. And these pictures were very successful as far as people getting them were concerned. They were all bought very quickly. I haven't done them for years and years. I should probably go back and try to do a few, some time. The idea is still perfectly strong. Whether I will or not I don't know.

*Weren't they painted in . . . a . . . sort of a sand tone?*

G.C.   They were done with egg tempera and egg emulsion . . . part of the paint as a base. And then they were gone over with oil paint in certain areas, which is the Venetian technique. A lot of the egg emulsion . . . egg tempera, so to speak, has a certain diaphanous quality. You can

"The Serenity of the Eggs" is the title of this preliminary sketch
for painting, c. 1960. G.C. often resorted to scraps of paper
that came to hand for such sketches.

see through it a little bit, which made for a lot of good contrasting textures. Gave them depth, too. And they were all low-toned. They were low-toned. I mean they didn't have many colors. You see earth colors, and raw siennas and things like that. Then blacks and whites and a little blue . . . kind of subdued.

You know how our artists cross-pollinate. It's very important to them and cross-pollination is fast and furious today. So, if during these Japanese three hundred years they'd ever had our communications, in no time at all some fellow on Hobasaki . . . I don't know the names, but call it that . . . would decide to jazz up a monkey by putting an extra finger on it, maybe. Then, a fellow on the other end of the island would be adding another on; and pretty soon someone would be putting on another toe or another leg, and so on. They'd be going back and forth and that style would have changed in fifteen years. They'd have picked up this new thing right off and seen it had something to it. That continuity, that three hundred years would have been broken into and it would have busted up so fast. Of course as it has been busted up . . . now.

But on styles changing. There's a built-in thing to make them change: the metaphor gets worn out. The shock value gets worn out. Now this isn't quite right either, but it tends to do that, particularly if it's original. But the other thing that can't help but make a difference is one generation's association with another. New generations slowly begin to ask for something else.

Say there are two people: two sons of two families. Well, A. will revere his father, the tradition of the family and so on; and he will love the old things. B. can't stand his family. Don't like the old man. To hell with the lot! Phyllis's brother-in-law Ian Coving would be an extreme example of that kind of thing. B. doesn't necessarily have to hate his father, but he will want something new [*Chuckling*]. There's a lot of them and there's a call for this. At a certain point, the call gets pretty strong. Say you take the big body of Victorian painting, Edwardian painting, some of which is very good. This was out of style for a while; but it's now coming back again, because the generation association has gone out of it. So that factor in every generation is going to make a change somewhat.

*Isn't that healthy?*

G.C.   Yes, very. And the best artists of these times will last. You know Vose[5] . . .

*The head of the Vose Gallery?*

G.C.  Yes. Well, Vose has been in business long enough to understand this. He told somebody that . . . Well, A. was a painter, a very good painter in his day. He will go out of fashion for . . . er . . . twenty-five or thirty years. In about thirty years, if he's good enough, people will begin to get him again. Goya was out for three hundred years. No. Not Goya. I mean El Greco, you know. He was just forgotten. Then, about 1950, they began to dig him up . . . before then maybe, he became the patron saint of the avant-garde. It was before they hit Abstract Expressionism, maybe as early as 1930. Somewhere in there. Very recently, anyway. Somebody found him . . . looked him up, you know. He was in a museum in Toledo, where nobody paid any attention to him and they resurrected him as their patron saint. That's what they do. If they ever get back to worshipping the art of indication, for any reason, somebody will revive Sargent in the same way. Nobody's ever been defter than he was, but, of course, that went out of fashion.

Anyway, in about thirty years, the ones that are good, they come up.

*Do you think Modigliani[6] was influenced by El Greco?*

G.C.  No. I think it was the climate. A lot of people were doing distortions, in those days. They seized on El Greco to validate it early. There's a tradition here. They're moving . . . building on something. Modigliani may never have seen El Greco, but he was influenced by him . . . not imitating him.

*Do you remember the room of Modigliani in the east wing of the National Gallery in Washington? It's amazing how a whole room of his elongations seems to work.*

G.C.  Oh yeah. He's very good. The man can be copied, but it's never as good as he was, because what he did . . . er . . . he had a gift . . . you know these things are caricatures, but they feel like individuals.

*They feel perfect.*

G.C.  That's where he had a very unique gift. His elongated forms get across as types and you can feel them very strongly. He's been imitated many, many times and the people who imitate him don't have that gift so their things are nothin'. The style, itself, isn't much. Marie Ross imitated him. She derived from his styles and had certainly seen him and . . . er . . . she gave it a twist. There's nothing wrong with this. They all derive from something. Almost always, by this time, you can find some kind of precedent. Even with Mondrian there's a precedent there. There've been whole periods when they didn't have any geometric design. On the other hand, the Islamic people had *just* geometric designs. It was some kind of sacrilege to put a person in. They had filigrees and straight lines and curves . . . no objective stuff at all. It depends on who the person's being influenced by, and the good ones are never quite imitative.

I don't imitate anybody, you know. I'm influenced by others obviously, but it's an objective approach, and so on. But I could never really go into abstract expressionism because I was brought up . . . my whole being . . . it would have been a phony thing to do. I'd have been trying to follow somebody else's style, so, obviously, it would have been pretty imitative. But, if you go out and do your own thing . . . if you're good, you'll put your own thing into it finally.

*To me, you have a very original presentation. One can walk into a room anywhere and, if your portrait is hung one among many . . . like the one in the Countway Library[7] . . . you can identify yours immediately.*

G.C. The one you're speaking about in the Countway Library is of Howard Sprague[8] who was a lecturer in the Harvard Medical School. Maybe I have some originality, but not as much as Modigliani. He was more of an original. He was more so. And, obviously, Picasso was more so. But anyone who is any good has some of it.

*But how can you be really stylized if you're a portrait painter?*

G.C. I don't feel bad about this, mind you. It's just a fact. Some are more strikingly original. Mine are rather subtly original. But anybody who's any good is that. You can tell . . . I'm not the greatest admirer of Tarbell in the world, but you can tell a Tarbell.[9] But a lot of people paint like Tarbell and sometimes you can't tell it isn't one. A lot of people have tried to imitate Sargent in that way. László was really an imitator of Sargent, but he wasn't quite as good. Some are very slavishly imitative . . . imitating just the technique and not the general approach.

*How about this new portrait painter, Augusta . . . Augustus?*

G.C. George Augusta. He did one of George Widmer Thorn.

*And one of Franny Moore, too.*

G.C. I didn't know he'd done one of him. When did he do it?

*I don't know, but it's hanging in his house. I saw it when I went there to dinner. The thing that interested me about him was that he's damn good, but you wouldn't say if you saw one hanging on a wall, "That's an Augusta," the way one would with you.*

G.C.   I can usually tell them, but you couldn't. Now, funnily enough, he's been influenced by me a little bit. In his backgrounds and things like that; and the way he does it. I know this and others have mentioned it. He likes what I do and there's certain similarities in his work.

*That brings us back to cross-pollination. Does that happen to portrait-painters too?*

G.C.   Oh, God, yes! I was influenced by Augustus John.[10] Now here's a thing. I was influenced by Augustus John at the end, a little bit. I liked his freedom. I liked the scale of his paint ... brushed up if you like. I ... er ... was influenced by that. I didn't copy it. I didn't try to make it like John, but I liked his looseness in the background ... of leaving things sometimes. I leave more than he did. Now Augusta likes me. He's liked the same thing.

*How old a man is he?*

G.C.   Augusta? Oh, he's about ... oh, he must be about fifty-five now. He's a very nice fellow. He's rather a more phlegmatic person than I am. He ... er ... I think I carry things a little further than he does. He's a little looser than I am, and I don't think he goes in for things like two expressions, or anything like that. He just goes and does it. He kind of knocks 'em off. But he's got good taste. He gets nice effects. He's pretty good. I think he's one of the better ones ... best ones; but I do recognize my influence there. It has been mentioned not by me alone. Yes, I've had some influence on him, but there's no slavish imitation. He's about the only one I can think of that I've influenced. [*Chuckling*] My only one that I can think of.

Now Eakins has influenced me. He's influenced a lot of people. I don't paint like Eakins, but there's little approaches ... attitudes. Yes, cross-pollination is very marked. Sometimes it can be just the littlest bit of a thing taken from somebody else; and, sometimes, it isn't taken consciously at all. You can look at a thing and see just how it's done. In fact, it's very valuable to do that. That's how Renoir learned to paint, you know. When he was asked, "Where did you learn to paint? Where did you study?" he replied, "Au musée, parbleu." He just went and saw how they did it. And I've been told that is one of the very good ways to work . . . to do something yourself and then go out and see how somebody else did the same thing. Of course, this goes for anything. It goes for the Abstract Expressionists. There were plenty of people in Abstract Expressionism who imitated, believe me. In fact, that's almost entirely all it is.

But to illustrate how artists take things from one another and are influenced by them: Donatello, you know, traveled for miles to see how some other sculptor did something. They'd all go around and see how one another did. They'd hear that somebody or other was doing well, and they'd go and take some part of it. They'd take a piece of it. They'd have their own style; they'd have their own approach; but this fellow would have something that would help their approach. So pretty soon there'd be something in their work you could detect he'd seen in this thing . . . this other man's work. And that's all over all of them.

*Even from your very early training you must still have some of Hawthorne in your blood, whether it comes out or not.*

G.C.    Probably yes. Oh, yes.

*And didn't people—didn't Donatello work as an apprentice to some man and almost copy from him until he was on his own?*

G.C.    Sure. Oh, sure. That's the only way they studied, in those days. I haven't probably very much of Hawthorne now. I never painted like him when I studied under him; but, sure, I was certainly influenced by him at the time. In general. Yes, I think I was, because he was a wonderful colorist . . . a very subtle colorist. Oh, yes, there'd be some influence here still. You see, you take some things and you reject other things from the same man. As I've told you, he made his students paint with palette knives . . . putty knives so they'd get the color . . . "jooshy," he called it. He didn't paint that way in most of his paintings, but he had his students paint with putty knives so they couldn't start messing around. They couldn't blend . . . it was pure stuff. Very few people had the guts not to use palette knives.

*Would this be the place to go back a bit and talk about the factors of painting which you mentioned last week as something you'd like to talk about?*

G.C.    Well, sure. That analysis came in when I taught in the Museum

School in 1954 to '56. I took Karl Zerbe's place, when he went on a two-year sabbatical and I'd never taught before. Among other things I taught ... er ... I had to teach design. Color and design. And this I didn't know anything about. That is, I didn't know anything about it in a specific way. I'd taken a course in composition, for example, and gone to Tech and composed things, and so on; but I never took it ... studied composition *as* composition. And this design course ... I thought I was going to have a hell of a time with this. And ... er ... Actually, I did very well at it. It was one of the best things I did. It was even ... I got even better results out of them than Zerbe used to get out of them. I got very good results. I'll talk about that some other time. But the advantage of this was ... er ... it made me clarify my ideas a little bit. In other words, things I'd never put into words ... never thought of it that way much ... I had to begin to try and do this.

In the course of this, the business of "factors" came out, for example. You call it factors. The alphabet. The means. Maybe it would be a better word to say means; or maybe you can think of a better word than all those. But everything that's done ... every painting that's done ... every piece of visual graphic art that's done employs line ... and color ... and value (that's lightness and darkness) ... and texture. Now wait a minute, it employs one or more of these things. Every picture does not have all these things in it. All pictures are made from these things and only these things. Line, color, value, texture: means employed in conjunction or alone. And then here's some more. You say shape ... and size, which is a sense of composition and is, of course, done with those other things I mentioned. And you use the edge, disappearing and coming, softly ... hard ... a variety. On edge alone you could make a whole chapter with illustrations. I said shape and size ... edge. I think that's about it. Now as I say, those last three things you kind of do with the first four; but they're means. I might say the model form. Model form is really a variety of edges, very often. Then what one does, one employs combinations of these. Now if you draw, obviously you use just line. Then you shade the drawing or ... er ... you shade it at certain points and not at others. This, actually, is using edges. You may want to have a line or a part of a thing go into the background and come out again.

Color speaks for itself. And color will have edges, willy-nilly. It will end up someplace. The edge there is sort of a purely happening thing. It just happens. Cézanne made it quite clear. He put down little areas of color. They happened to have edges. It had quite a lot to do with what he did. And incidentally, when Picasso took his style . . . Picasso's a classic example of cross-pollination . . . he's pollinating all the time . . . he took those little squares of color of Cézanne's, and the step he took from them was cubism . . . in which he could get depth. He got depth through edges and value and no color, in many cases. There's a perfect example of cross-pollination. Picasso did a very original thing out of another person's idea carried in another direction. Lugged it off and did something else entirely with it.

Well, you can go on endlessly about this. The way to talk about it so you can really communicate needs to have pictures seen with it. I've made quite a number of lectures . . . talks, in the past, using slides; and they say they've been quite successful. I don't like to do it much because it's terrific . . . you get bored with it. I've been asked to do it recently again . . . in the last two or three years, off and on. The way I've done it has been a popularizing thing. I did it with the students when I was at the Museum School. Every week I had to talk to the whole damn school, and I did this with the design class, too. Using slides, you can talk about line, edge. You can talk about line and edge and pick out slides that illustrate that kind of thing. For the students I did a different kind of talk than I did, say, to the Examiner Club. I had to give a talk at the Examiner Club every three years for years, and some of the talks were quite good. I mean they got quite a hand. The point was to make it interesting to people like Wyzanski and . . . er . . . Aldrich and . . . oh hell! I forget all the people in there. Billy Morris. I can't remember names now, but they were highly intelligent men who weren't painters. So, it was a kind of popularizing thing; or, at least, something they could grasp.

*To interrupt a minute with something along this line . . .*

G.C.    You can go on endlessly . . .

*You know I had a nice talk with Dave McCord recently.*

G.C.    You were nice. You wrote about it.

*. . . and he is so admiring of you. He thinks you are one of the greats and a genius. His evaluation of your painting is much what you've said to me: That you've done many good ones ("excellent," his word); but, sometimes . . . and this is a quote, "A portrait doesn't come off." Your good ones, according to him, are the best.*

G.C.  That's right.

*And David McCord said to me, "What are you going to do with all this?" And I said, "At the moment, nothing except as planned: to give it to the Smithsonian archives; and to put it in some kind of form for Gardner's children." And he said, "There's a gold mine for a book if it were done with illustrations. Take the Acheson or Frankfurter portraits . . . Robert Frost . . . illustrated, and add the fly-on-the-wall sketches to see how they were built up." And what we've been talking about today—factors of painting, cross-pollination, line, edge —really should have those slides with them. Even in the book for your children. Dave added another dimension to my thinking.*

G.C.  Illustrations would be very important with what I've been talking about this morning. You probably wouldn't have to have too many. There's two kinds of talks: There's the one of practical value to the painter; then there's the talk for the average person . . . the intelligent person, helping him to look at a painting and adding interest for him in the picture. These are two kinds of things, both of which I've done; but they both need slides, particularly the one that will give the intelligent people . . . the non-painters other ways of looking at pictures.

*The idea of cross-pollination is extremely interesting to me.*

G.C.  That's certainly true and it gets us back to what true criticism is. The important criticism is what's going on in that cross-pollination. Taking the check and taking the check all the time.

*What would be metaphor in portrait-painting and how would it be arrived at?*

G.C.  Well . . . uh . . . the word "metaphor" is a confusing word. "Saying one thing and meaning another" is probably as good a definition as any. However, if you want to make a metaphoric statement, portrait-painting is not the best way to do it. You are limited to getting the feeling of a person. You aren't as free as Pollock to do just one thing, nor de Kooning, nor any other abstract painter. Or like the young man, Forsyth, I told you about who responded to one impulse after another. That's why portrait-painting is looked down on.

Take a man like Albert Pinkham Ryder. In those dark pictures of his, he puts in a boat, and a moon, and a cloud with a nimbus over it; and they are very mysterious and very, very metaphoric. Mondrian gets a metaphor: his plus and minus, good and evil, directly opposed at right angles. Those kinds of pictures, not portraits, are easy to get a metaphor in.

How do you get a metaphor in a portrait? Well, for that you have to go back to the factors used. You get it in color, particularly in color. You get it in texture. You get it in the way the lines are drawn. You can get it in motion like this [*With a swirl of the left hand*]. The way the paint is handled a little bit. The way the edges come and go. A great portrait would have all these factors used.

That business of the test of a picture being how it affects you after you come back from an experience of great tragedy: now a good portrait would be such a thing that is *not* offensive; or another could be very offensive if it didn't have any metaphor at all, like the picture of a little child on a candy box. That would be very unmetaphoric as far as feelings are concerned or the important things of life.

The impulse to put in metaphor is when you scumble over the background and leave stuff coming through. In Rembrandt, it's the way the things loom out of the canvas, the very soft edges around the hat that come and go and stay in the canvas and don't jump out at you. Take another example: in a Titian portrait, the use of edge is subtle and would be used in different kinds of ways, and the use of texture would be subtle too. In El Greco, (maybe in all the great ones) there would be examples of the factors throughout the picture to give it mystery, to give it accent, to give it force, to give it different qualities which you could connect with life or expressing the person. To repeat: this is done through the factors used, particularly in color, particularly in texture, and particularly in the handling of edges and line. These all can be used to express a feeling.

*But isn't metaphor in portraits connected with the characteristics of a person?*

G.C.   No. I think the metaphor is feeling. I think you feel it.

*But aren't such characteristics as humor, cruelty, kindness, et cetera, part of the universal? Part of the metaphor?*

G.C.   Also. Not part of, also. The main object is to get the feeling of the person.

*And the factors? Aren't they only the technique that creates the metaphor?*

G.C.   No. They are the metaphor itself. You are not right that the person is the main thing. He's a part of it, but maybe the metaphor will be in the drawing. Edges, particularly, are the metaphor itself. You see, it's not done consciously. Even in the drawing, the way it's done is instinctive.

Now take that portrait of Charlie's father there [*Gesturing*]. I guess it looks like Charlie's father and it's a man. Where Hopkinson, as an artist, comes in—and there's nothing unique or original about this, Rembrandt probably did it better, and Titian, they're all doing the same thing you see in there—is the way the picture's done and the colors used. The suit. You don't see much of the suit. You see just enough of the arm going off there, so it's a little mysterious. Hopkinson was a man of good taste, and he appreciated good things in painting. That portrait reflects this, but it's not one of his great pictures, you know.

*But it's an awfully good likeness, and he caught my father-in-law's humor and his almost conscious charm, which he turned on and off. To me, it's a metaphor of him.*

G.C.   Not knowing the man, that doesn't make much difference to me. I repeat, the person is not the main thing. That portrait up there now is just a decoration on the wall which is in rather nice proportion of rather somber, quiet colors with that little bit of light; and it's a pleasant thing that wouldn't be offensive if you came back from some terrible tragedy.

As I say, the metaphor is very subdued in these things; but it is capable of being done all over, although it seldom is. This has to be in the hands of someone good. And I think how the consciousness comes in, how it is very often arrived at.

Well, I'll use myself as an example, because I have some sense this way. I've boiled it down now; but before I thought this through, I used to do it instinctively. Say you do a picture and it doesn't feel just right. It feels too pretty, so you smudge it over, smutty it up. Or you want to blur the edges a little bit. There are a lot of successful portrait painters who have little instinct along this line. Their pictures aren't interesting in that way at all. They don't feel quite right. They feel kind of cheap.

So, the answer to your question of metaphor in portrait-painting is: Yes, you can get it in there, but it's far subtler, it's less compelling than it is in many other kinds of painting.

*How about architecture? What is its metaphor and how is it arrived at?*

G.C. Before we think about metaphor in architecture and how it is arrived at, it is necessary to start with those elements that all the arts have in common.

Step one: The most common denominator is that art, in its various fields, creates order out of chaos. In the tremendous confusion of things, artists pick out what they want to make their accent about. The very able people, the creative people in any field, will have this quality of going for the jugular and of keeping things in proportion: subordinate things, subordinate; main points, main points. A great business man has that sense in his medium of affairs and money. A great lawyer will have it in his field. Certainly, it is one of the common denominators of the arts. I have always known this. I knew this in my teens.

For step two, we must go to Robert Frost's statement that all poetry is metaphor. He went further and said every poem is one. I could take that one apart. If this is true of the greatest of the arts (and, in my opinion, poetry is the greatest of them all, the most trenchant form of human expression), it is reasonable to expect it to be true of the other arts too. So, how does it express itself? Theoretically, each art has something to say that others cannot; and each art has its own thing it can do better than any other. Music tries to be descriptive; painting tries to be musical; or writing tries to be something it isn't. But, basically, each arrives at its own thing through the limited (and unique to each) factors it works with. Music through instruments; literature through words, clauses, and sentences; and painting through the seven or eight factors I've talked about. Start looking around and see how the different arts are expressed and what each does the others can't. I think it's pretty obvious they do different things. Therefore, the metaphor would be different in each. Art, when it is good, says more than it's saying. That is the metaphor. So, in starting with Frost's statement that all poetry is metaphor, and later he went further by saying it is the only art that has metaphor. I can take that one apart: music is pure metaphor; writing is self-evident: the novel says more than the story; and it is there in all the other arts, surely it must be found in as great an art as architecture. In great architecture, I mean. Boy! do architects think they're great! [*Laughing*] The so-called mother of them all. But where is its metaphor? I couldn't figure it out. It didn't come readily. And then in a taxicab in New York, ten, fifteen years ago, for some reason it suddenly occurred to me.

New York City has every type of architecture. It's got mosques, synagogues and cathedrals. It's got skyscrapers and old buildings. Looking at them it began to occur to me that, designwise, the architect has definite factors he works with analogous to the factors used by the painter. Throughout the ages he has used the tower, the column, the dome, the arch, the lintel. That's about it. It's these things combined he works with and it's proportion that makes them work. So proportion is another factor, and size. Size is very important. Sculpture gets pretty big, but nothing like architecture. Architecture can go up and it can surround you, like the cathedrals in France soaring up, and interiors as big as the Parthenon. No art has anything else like it.

Now what comes readily to mind here is that these elements reflect the masculine and feminine quality in us. The tower and the column are phallic . . . and the obelisk. In early times that's certainly what they were. The dome is a feminine thing, kind of a breast, I suppose. It's a feminine shape. It's also a masculine shape in a way, from the end of the penis we'll say. It's masculine and feminine. And the lintel is primarily masculine.

*And the arch?*

G.C.    The arch is feminine, and masculine, like the dome. Of course, since Freud, we've all been aware that no human being is all masculine or all feminine. It would be a deformity. Related to my theory, any building that is all masculine or all feminine is terrible. Anything that is all masculine, like the big office buildings that go straight up, or the Tomb of the Unknown Soldier, in Berlin, are too overpowering. Office buildings are essentially towers—phallic. What makes the John Hancock building in Boston so good is that it is a tower, but its walls of mirror reflect the sky, a sunset, clouds. This is a feminine quality which makes it quite beautiful. The Taj Mahal is primarily feminine, but not all. Any building, like any woman who is all feminine, would be "schleep." Have you ever seen the Taj?

*Yes. I saw it by moonlight, but I've never seen the Tomb of the Unknown Soldier in Berlin.*

G.C.    Well, it's very Germanic, as opposed to the Taj Mahal. It's very masculine. When I saw it, in 1936, two soldiers were standing outside in full field equipment, helmets on, bayonets at the ready, rigid. It's a little dark-brown, stone temple about as big as this room, a little higher. Inside there's a small, temple-shaped pediment with two dark columns, no entasis. You go down two steps and there's the tomb. A big block of black basalt under an opening in the roof; and, on top of it, there's what looks like a Mack truck tire which turns out to be a very Germanic, bronze oak wreath. No softening tendrils. Unlike the tombs in other capitals, it's too masculine.

You might say the inside of St. Peter's in Rome is the grandfather and the grandmother of them all. Take the columns. The thrust obviously is masculine, but the flutes and the entasis are a mixture. The caps are a mixture. The Parthenon also is a very good example of a well-balanced building. The delicacy of the entasis in the hall ... those steps you look across to, with the little rise ... and the flutes and the pediments. There's the feminine all through it, and the masculine.

Now architecture can express this and speak to this feeling as no other art can; because it does, in fact, do masculine and feminine things. A house. It has a mother and a father quality, as does a well-proportioned room. Strong, protective, comforting. You say you come into this house and you love it. All art can do that. So that's where the metaphor is, I would say, and it is a very great one, which is one of the reasons this is such a great art. It's great, even with all the haggling over prices, and the architect often not as good as his drawings. It's always contended to be the mother and the father of the arts; and as I've said before, Boy! do the architects preen themselves on that. "Painters can decorate; sculptors can decorate a little bit; but the real fellow is *ME!*"

# 12

# Kingman Brewster of Yale

G.C.   I've done quite a lot of judges, and we have pretty much done the Supreme Court, haven't we?

*Not all the judges . . .*

G.C.   Because there are quite a lot of judges, a lot more than the Supreme Court. Judges and lawyers. Chafee[1] and Seavey[2] of the Harvard Law School . . . law school professors, several of them. William Hastie, the Pennsylvania judge.

*Hastie would be one of the good ones.*

G.C.   Well, he's not quite as interesting as, say, Chafee or some of the others. Seavey's a great teacher at the law school and Reed Powell.[3] It might be a good thing to have a bunch of doctors there's quite a bunch of lawyers, not too many doctors; have 'em all in one area, they might feed on one another—all in the same category.

*Do you want to start on Brewster?[4]*

G.C.   Yeah. Sure. I'm ready to talk about Brewster and Levi.[5] But there are some other presidents. Have we got Conant and Mildred Horton[6] of Wellesley?

*Yeah.*

G.C.   And we've done Gettell[7] of Holyoke?

*And Hatch of Michigan.*

G.C.   Hatcher.[8] We've done almost all of them, haven't we?

*I think we've done all but Brewster and Levi. Just to start the ball rolling on Brewster, when did you paint him?*

G.C.   I must have painted him about 1967 . . . started him then. It took about two years. It was finished in '69, I think. I haven't got the figures here, but it took a couple of years. Those were the furious sixties, when student unrest was building up. It was all through that period. I was painting him through the period of highest unrest in New Haven . . . the time they were trying Bobby Seale for murder there. It was May . . . the end of May of that year that the hippies and young people and protesters got together and concentrated on New Haven. This was the time . . . that weekend at the beginning of the trial, that Brewster made the remark that dogged him quite a bit. He said he was skeptical whether a black man could get a fair trial in this country. This was used against him. He didn't say legally he couldn't get it. He said he was skeptical whether, with all the publicity and brouhaha and so on, the emotions of the jury or any group wouldn't be influenced somewhat. I was just finishing him then so it would date from that. It was a bad time for them. I went down a lot over the two years. I used to stay with them in their house on Hillhouse Avenue . . . the president's house. I'll go into things that happened there later.

At this particular time of the trial . . . at the beginning of the trial . . . they were barricaded in the house. I wasn't there. I came down a couple of days after that. But they had sandbags, they had buckets of water at the windows. They were virtually in a situation in preparation for a siege. And Cyrus Vance[9] came down as a man they counted on in trouble. He was one of the corporation fellows and . . . uh . . . he came as a pacifier, as a decent influence and as an adviser at that time. He stayed with them in the house. This was long before there was any question of his being Secretary of State, but it is a good example of the faith people have in him.

*For the record, Gardner, who was Bobby Seale and what was he being tried for?*

G.C.   Well, he was a Black Panther . . . head of the Black Panthers,[10] and he shot a woman in San Francisco. They claimed he had. She was a whore, you know, and some pimp was mixed up in this thing. I just saw in the paper the other day that he had been exonerated. The trial in New Haven was a mistrial, I guess. I forget what happened there, but he wasn't convicted at that time. He was tried again in California and . . . uh . . . just this week he was declared innocent. In the beginning, it was a frame-up I guess, apparently, he was innocent.

*Except for the remark Brewster made, why should the president of Yale have to barricade himself inside his house during a public trial?*

G.C.   Oh, this was because, at that time, there was unrest all over the place. They'd carried Skiddy von Stade[11] out of University Hall and then occupied it. That had happened only a month or so before. They had occupied the building at the University of Chicago where I painted Levi. He'd had to leave. Brewster had the best record of any college president. He'd never had to use the police, never had any buildings taken over, and they were concentrating on him. This was a cause. This was the focal point of the next trouble in the college communities. There'd been all sorts of trouble for the three years before that, but he'd always been . . . uh . . . I'll go back a little bit.

As I say, I'd been down there a lot over those three years. Every few weeks or every couple of months I kept going down and a lot of things happened while I was there. It got to be kind of joke that, when I turned up, there'd be some trouble. What Brewster did was to anticipate possible results of the student unrest that was building up in the early sixties. When it first began, he went around to the houses . . . kept rotating around . . . and he'd spend the evening answering questions and beefs and complaints. In other words, feeling the pulse and giving the students a chance to express themselves. He'd done that over all the university. He anticipated trouble by several years . . . had been doing this so that, when it came, he had an extremely good relationship with the students. He had high visibility. He had accessibility. They knew they could get to him and that he'd talk reason. He had a natural . . . uh . . . a discussion and argument. This came naturally to him, I think. I won't say it was easy. It took a lot out of him, of course, but he did it well and, as I say, I think he enjoyed it. I went with him several times and listened to him talking to the students. You could see he enjoyed it and could take care of himself. They'd ask questions. They'd ask quite insulting questions. Certainly they'd ask very direct questions.

*Do you remember any of them?*

G.C.   Not right at this moment. Later on I think I may. I don't want to go into that right at this moment. So he was ready for them. By the time of the Seale trial, things were so hot they finally had to do something about it. They had to get into this state of almost siege. And it passed. Probably it passed because of the remark he made about being skeptical about a fair trial. In other words, he didn't take a hard line on

Seale. If he'd taken a hard line on Seale, they'd probably've come in and taken the place apart, or tried to. This is speculation now, but this was held against him by many of the alumni and the corporation fellows. They thought he was knuckling under, when he wasn't knuckling under at all. It was quite a fair remark, as a matter of fact. He stood by it. I talked to him about it afterwards and he said he wouldn't change a word of it; so he never backed down on that statement at all. He's got a lot of guts. He's got a lot of courage. He's a wonderful fellow, I think, and very bright. He's got the common touch and he's fun. No pomposity whatsoever.

His oldest daughter was a great friend of my youngest daughter Poppy—Constance Brewster—and she used to be around the house when he was a professor at the Harvard Law School. She used to be around the house quite a lot. And Poppy would go down and visit them at Martha's Vineyard. They were very very close. So I've known them for a long time. When he was at the law school the little girls... they had quite a big family... the little girls went to Buckingham School. They'd have a Fun Fair early in the spring. They'd pretend it was a circus, and I can remember him putting on a silk hat and dressing up like a buffoon and running around trying to sell things like a barker. No false modesty and no pomposity whatever. And he had the same quality right along... straight through.

There were a great many interesting things in connection with this in painting him. This lack of pomposity, this availability to discuss situations as, of course, a good lawyer should... this showed up in lots of incidents in little ways. There's one that comes to mind right off.

One time I went down and I got there on a Sunday night. It must have been... uh... let us say, 1967, about in there, before things reached their height; but they had been boiling along all the time on the campuses. I was a little late. It was about eight o'clock and I got out of the car and there was a young fellow walking up and down in front of the Brewsters' house. I had a bag... a very heavy bag... and the fellow said, "Would you like me to give you a hand?"

I said, "Sure, oh, sure."

So he picked up the bag and we walked up the front steps to the house and rang the bell. Constance—his daughter—opened it and the fellow pushed right in to the hall and said, "May I see your father?"

She said, "Wait a minute. I'll see."

He wasn't rough at all. He was just insinuating himself. I left her talking to him and went through to the back of the house where the dining room was. They were having Sunday-night supper. It was just his wife, Mary Louise, and Kingman, and a young man named Chauncey who was assistant to the president. He's a provost now, I think. Young Henry Chauncey, son of Henry Chauncey[12] of Harvard. Very much like him and a very nice fellow. He was there, as he often was; and a very bright young student who was living in the house. They always had a student living in, one following another. And he was there at the table. Constance had already eaten. And Kingman said, "What's the trouble out there? Should I go out?"

And I said, "Maybe you'd better.

So he went out and he came back with the fellow and sat him at the table. And Kingman said, "Would you like some supper?"

No, he'd had supper.

And then they went on talking about things. Brewster was sitting at the end of the table. I happened to be on his right and the fellow sat down on my right. Things were very easy. People would go out to the kitchen and get food and bring it back and sit down any old place. So this boy sat down and was just included. Nothing was made of him at all.

"Would you like this?"

"No."

"Would you like a glass of wine?"

"No."

And then they went on talking about things and he was fairly quiet. Finally, Brewster said to him very easy, "By the way, what's on your mind?"

And the fellow said, "Well, I've been wondering..." He was getting kind of nervous. It was all very well done.

Brewster prodded him a little bit, "What's on your mind?"

And the boy said, "I've come because I was wondering about your accessibility."

Apparently he'd been playing softball on a playing field, that afternoon, when Brewster and Mary Louise had walked by.

"We were wondering why you didn't come over and speak to us."

Brewster said, "I'm a little shy about that sort of thing."

And then the fellow went on to say that, a little later in the afternoon, he'd gone out to a town playground and tried to play with some little black children. This had a kind of eerie sound. And he had other criticisms ... I don't remember exactly what ... about the establishment as opposed to the undergraduates, rather vague and disordered.

Chauncey was getting a bit angry and spoke up, "You've come in here," he said, "with a lot of criticisms and I think you ought to come up with some suggestions. I think you ought to come up with something concrete."

And Brewster said, "No, no. Don't force him like that. He doesn't have to do that."

The fellow started a sentence but didn't finish it. Then he blurted out, "I'm ashamed. I'm terribly ashamed. I just got over an LSD trip."

Brewster didn't pay much attention to this and the conversation became general again. The boy just shut up and sat there. Nobody chastened him. Nobody was snotty to him. Nobody paid any more attention to him than they had before. It was the damnedest thing! [*Laughing*] If he wanted to chip in, he could. If he wanted to cool off, he could. It was a wonderful piece of work. Just natural humanity, as a matter of fact.

Afterwards in the living room ...

*Was the boy still there?*

G.C. [*Laughing*] He didn't know how to get away. We were sitting around the fire and Brewster said to him, "You say your name is Johanson. By the way, is So-and-So Johanson your uncle."

The boy said, "Yes, he is."

"Well," said Brewster, "I remember a letter I got from him recommending you. I better write your uncle and let him know how you are getting on." [*Laughing*]

He said it pleasantly. He made it as kind of a joke. It was kind of funny. Then he let the boy stew around a little bit. General conversation went on. The fellow was getting more and more uncomfortable and it was beginning to make me uncomfortable. This guy was having a worse time every minute, and I couldn't stand much more of it myself.

So I said ... I painted down in Woodbridge Hall ... I was painting the picture there in the big room where the corporation meets and where they have the portraits around like in Harvard's University Hall. I wanted to go down anyway and get the things set up for the next day. I thought I'd give this bird a chance to get out and, also, get out myself. So, I said, "I'm going to Woodbridge Hall to stretch my canvas." And, turning to the fellow, I said, "Would you like a lift?"

Well! He couldn't get out of his chair fast enough; and on the way down he told me he thought Brewster was wonderful. It was wonderfully done. There isn't one college president in a thousand who would have done that.

Another time I came back . . . it was after a football game around Halloween. And there was this little fellow waiting at the front door, a little bit of a guy. He hadn't got up nerve enough to press the bell.

*Was this at the president's house?*

G.C.   Yup. This was another time during this period. So I rang the bell and this time a servant . . . Jason, I think, was his name . . . answered the bell. The young man wanted to come in with me. He had a little orange in his hand and they'd carved a face on it like a jack-o'-lantern. Constance and her friends, boys and girls, were in the parlor, or room next to the front door. They were sitting around in front of the fireplace after the game. So this little fellow and I stood in the hall and Kingman came out. This fellow screwed up courage and said to him, "I've come here on behalf of the freshman dining hall and I want to present you with this token." And he held out the orange made into a jack-o'-lantern. [*Laughing*]

Brewster said, "Well, thanks very much." Then he said, "I'd like to give you a glass of sherry, but I can't because they've just passed a rule I can't give anyone under twenty-one anything to drink. But you come back after three years and I'd be delighted to. I'd be delighted to. Why don't you go in and have a good time with everybody."

And the kid said, "You mean you're not going to ask who I am?" [*Laughing*]

"No, no, of course not." Brewster didn't need to know his name.

His friends were all hiding in the bushes outside watching to see what was happening to him. They'd sent him off with a pat on the back and here he was taking a terrible beating for his impertinence. . . . "Come back in three years and you can have a glass of sherry when you're old enough . . . I don't need to know your name."

The kid said, "Aren't you going to ask me why I'm here?"

"No. No."

It was nice, because it was supposed to be a fresh, sassy gesture to give him this thing as an indication the food wasn't what it might have been. It was intended to be sarcastic. The boy expected to get a rating. He obviously thought it was a very courageous thing to do with his friends in the bushes outside, wondering what was happening to him. So he was totally disarmed and just left. Pusey's[13] a nice fellow, but he could no more do that than the man in the moon. Well, not many could, you know.

*I wonder if Bok could.*

G.C.   I don't think he could. Brewster's awfully free and lively. I remember going down there one time. I was looking over a book of heraldry that they had in their house. Yale goes in for that kind of stuff, like that fellow "Tubby" Sizer, the father of Ted Sizer,[14] headmaster of Andover. He used to crochet; or what is it you do very fine?

*Needlepoint?*

G.C.   Needlepoint's another one. What's the other one?

*Crewel?*

G.C.   Crewelwork. He did a rug for his house with a crest. They had a whole bunch of crests written up in this book and a whole bunch of funny terms like, "Fitchey Gules." This made a great curse word: "Fitchey Gules!" you can say. Or, "You Fitchey Gules, you!" It's a pretty insulting remark you know, and he thought it was funny, too. So, we were driving down to the Bowl, one Saturday, for a football game. Brewster was driving and he'd stick his head out the window and say to a cop, "Fitchey Gules!!" [*Laughing*] This was in the middle of a pretty good crowd. Most college presidents wouldn't do that. Yup. He had a very light touch.

*Did you keep your own room in their house, like you did at the Harrimans'?*

G.C.   No. I used the guest room when I was there and, as I say, I painted him in Woodbridge Hall in the big room where the Fellows of the Corporation meet. This is the room where the portraits of all the presidents are, like its counterpart in University Hall at Harvard. There are some very good ones painted by well-known people. There the best of them is a Stiles.[15] This room has big tall windows and a great long table where the Fellows sit. Vance was a Fellow while I was there. Scranton[16] was one. Lefty Lewis was one. Robert Taft[17] was one. Acheson had been one. That kind of stuff. I had done the fly-on-the-wall sketches of Brewster in his office across the hall, but I painted him in the corporation room because it wasn't used very much.

Sketch of Kingman Brewster in his study at Yale, 1966

*How was the light?*

G.C.   The light was good. As I said, there were big tall windows—a high room . . . and, on the north, I put brown paper across the lower half of the windows and drew the curtains across, so there was a high light. It made a very good studio light. He'd put on his robes and pose there and again, as he posed, I had a good example of how he handled the students . . . met them halfway. His office was across the hall from this room; the top administration offices were in that building . . . and he'd walk across, take his robes off the table, put 'em on and stand there. I had the easel set up and the painting tables . . . it made a little studio at that end of the room. He'd stand there . . . he'd stand there with his arms folded . . . pose . . . and talk to a committee of dissatisfied students. There're not many college presidents who could do that. They'd want to take their robes off or apologize. They'd be too self-conscious. Almost any of 'em. But not him. Now and again, when things got hot, he'd sit down and talk. But he didn't mind looking ridiculous standing there with his robes on and a medal.

There were lots of groups who came in, both black and white. I remember several times the blacks came in. There was one group . . . very impressive . . . very big. They were an imposing bunch.

*This was while you were painting him?*

G.C.   Yup. He'd stand there and I'd go on painting.

*Were they belligerent?*

G.C.   Well, they were there to complain. They weren't there as friends. They were there as people who wanted improvements; but they were intelligent and controlled. There wasn't any loud screeching or anything like that; but they were hostile. They were there to see if anything could be done about some things. Some of the things they wanted, he could do; and some of the things, he couldn't. But he'd talk to them. And he made friends with them. So much so that later on . . . but they differed. He didn't . . . it wasn't all sweetness and light, that kind of thing. He'd say to them, "We can't do this. This is just something that can't be done for you." To other things he'd say, "We'll see what can be done about this." The talk was full of character on both sides and he respected them and liked them.

A lot of groups came in like this, both white and black. And in the end, oh, months later (this was the advantage of having gone there over such a long period of time) . . . I had an opportunity to see how things worked out. Oh, months later . . . half a year or more . . . there was going to be an SDS[18] demonstration against the ROTC. Do you remember that Reserve Officers Training Corps? The ROTC was meeting and they anticipated trouble. And this black group came in to see him . . . into his office about two o'clock the afternoon of the meeting and said . . .

*The same black group?*

G.C. Yeah. The same black group or their representatives. A couple of them came in and said, "We'd like to help you out on this. If you want to quiet this down, we can take care of some of these people."

And he said, "No, no. They have a right to do this, but thanks very much."

They had wanted to go up and help him. There were a lot of students like that. They so outnumbered the SDS that it never got off the ground. That's the kind of thing that kept him out of real trouble. He had the great body of students behind him. There were other examples of this, many of them.

*You once told me that, while you were painting him, you could hear crowds of students shouting from outside.*

G.C. Oh, yes. Everybody roaring, "Mother-fuckers!" All that kind of thing. Woodbridge Hall is on a sort of plaza. Across from it is the Beinecke Rare Book Library; and then there's Woolsey . . . the enormous hall with colonnades where the students eat and they have dances there after the football games. You probably remember it when you were a kid. Well, there's this great space of pavement between them all and that's where the students gathered and where the shouts were coming from. Right outside the window. "Mother-fucker!" and one thing and another. "Brewster is a . . ." The administration is a . . ." I remember these words floating right in as we were working away and nobody paid any attention to them. [*Laughing*]

One time when I was painting him there was a terrible screaming downstairs. Screeching!

*Women or men?*

G.C. You couldn't tell. [*Laughing*] It was just a helluva scream. Quite a lot of it for a short time . . . probably a minute. There was obviously a terrific ruckus going on. I went right on painting and he went right on posing. He was cool as a cucumber. [*Here G.C. lets out a blood-curdling scream*] *SCREEEEEE!* You couldn't tell whether it was a man or a woman

*You certainly can with you.*

G.C.    It turned out to be a great big black woman, actually. It was all aimed at Tracey Barnes, who was one of their public relations men. I don't know what his title is, but he's way up in the administration. It was in his office, one floor below, that this was going on. This big black woman had come in, thrown an inkwell at him, and generally tore the place apart before they could stop her. She had some kind of complaint about housing ... a town-and-gown affair of some sort. Nothing to do with the students. Brewster never batted an eye. He didn't even send to find out what it was all about [*Laughing*] ....

And another time ... remember he had an untarnished record as far as any of the buildings being occupied were concerned ... Henry Chauncey rushed upstairs and said, "They've taken over University Hall at Harvard!"

You couldn't help seeing they were kind of amused ... smiling a little bit.

"Oh, that's terrible, terrible! Ha ha . . . ."

There was another incident when I think I had some influence the way it was handled. The art department had commissioned Claes Oldenburg to do a statue. To do a piece of sculpture rather. He did an enormous lipstick on the top of a tank.

*I've seen some of his things so I know what you're talking about.*

G.C.    They're kind of amusing, as a matter of fact. This thing was a lipstick ... uh ... a little higher than this room. It was on a base that suggested a tank and it was tapered off with a little red thing on top. Very phallic-looking. The base was of black ... black plywood. The whole thing wasn't made of very permanent stuff.

*You mean to say the art department could order this without the approval of the administration or the corporation?*

G.C.    Apparently, because the first time anyone in the administration saw it was when they lugged it out to the plaza between Woodbridge and the Beinecke Library on a huge trailer. The art department at Yale is fairly advanced ... Scully's[19] the head of it ... and they raised five thousand dollars for Oldenburg, who is one of their alumni, to do this very avant-garde, rather outrageous thing. When they put it up, the metal for the red tip wasn't ready, so, as a substitute, Oldenburg had a little sort of plastic bag which had to be blown up. [*Laughing*] The result looked like a contraceptive device. It was blown up, and the air would come out of it a little bit and it would flop down. You'd see this thing hanging down... this rubber-like thing... and it was obscene and very funny. [*Laughing*] The art department didn't like it at all. It made them look ridiculous.

Actually, it was a gesture of a type of defiance. They were doing their thing the way they wanted to do it. There was a lot of debate whether it should be taken down, and Brewster asked me what I would do. I strongly advised him not to have it removed, because it would have been interpreted as an act of intolerance and would have started a storm of protest all over the place. A lot of people would have written in; artists would get all steamed up and there would have been quite a brouhaha over that one. I did have a little effect on that decision. Brewster admitted it.

*Is it still there?*

G.C.   No. Of course it fell apart. It couldn't have lasted more than two or three years anyway. With the weather and everything, it went to pieces, and they finally took it away. There were a lot of SDS people mixed up in the fine-arts department unrest. This was a spot where they felt they could make trouble because artists can be very unreasonable, and they were just waiting to get Brewster on something. I went with him to one of the meetings he had with them.

He went to this meeting with Howard Sayre Weaver, who was a provost, I think; and I went too. They went over from the administration to listen to their demands. As I say, artists can be very unreasonable; more so than blacks, who are rational enough, when you get down to certain things, I remember one demand that was made. It was a question of subsidizing artists throughout the department. The university had a policy of subsidizing only those who really needed the money. The fine-arts people were now demanding that every artist in the department be subsidized whether he drove a Porsche or not, their argument being why should you discriminate in favor of Joe just because he didn't have any money? Or against Dick because he did?

Brewster said, "We just haven't got the money for this kind of thing." And then he said, "I hate to say this . . . I am sorry to have to say that, in this day and age, you aren't going to get the support for the fine arts that you will for the sciences. People aren't going to pay for some guy's abstraction they don't like when they can give it to cancer or energy research, and I don't blame them." Then he said, "I cannot get you money for this."

Well, they were pretty sore about this. When artists get together, they work on one another badly and are not very logical. They think they are great; and they think that people don't understand them enough. And, of course, they don't often. But they get quite a chip on their shoulder about the bourgeois and the philistine and so on. I remember the point Brewster made was you could get this kind of money for the sciences quite easily, but you couldn't get it, when the pinch is on, for this. They'll give you eight million dollars for cancer research before they'll give it to subsidize artists. So, "I can't do anything for you."

The meeting ended on a bitter note. They were very ominous, talking as though he were the enemy . . . a bad man and a son of a bitch. How he kept his cool I'll never know. Afterwards they had a meeting to see what they would do about it.

*They weren't all SDS members, were they?*

G.C.    Well, they were mixed up in the same sort of thing. It was that kind of a group. When I say SDS, I'm being a little bit loose; but this was a hostile group. I wandered into their meeting almost by mistake. I wasn't spying or anything. I passed by and went in out of idle curiosity; but I suddenly realized I was among the enemy, so to speak. I was representing the enemy—or it might be interpreted so. The point they were making was, here is this fellow Brewster, with an unblemished record, and the one thing he's scared of is trouble. They were trying to work out how they could get him. Get him by embarrassing him. And then they got talking about how the rest of the college wouldn't go along. It wasn't going to work. You see, all this work he'd done with the students was paying off. Even with this group, he'd faced them honestly. That's the thing he was respected for. Well, they came to the conclusion not to do anything because they knew they couldn't quite get away with it.

*Did he ever indicate to you he was having trouble with the Corporation or the alumni? He certainly was not popular with the rich alumni.*

G.C.     He was all right with the Fellows of the Corporation. It was the alumni he had trouble with.

*Donations fell off tremendously, didn't they.*

G.C.     Yeah, and he knew it. Oh sure, he knew that. They say now he wasn't particularly good at that sort of thing. Personally, I think he is a great fellow.

*Gardner, why did it take you so long to do that portrait?*

G.C.     Oh, I guess I liked going down there and doing it. I liked being there. He was interrupted a lot, so that made it easy for him, too. Sometimes I wouldn't go down for weeks. I went to a lot of football games. God! I had fun! I got wonderful seats. I'll never have them again like that. Right next to the president. Right in the middle of the Bowl, just over where the team comes out. The one Harvard man in miles. [*Laughing*] Once I took Poppy down to a Harvard-Yale game and we were sitting next to Charlie O'Hearn, the famous Yale football star. Boy! We cheered our heads off. Poppy was going *Rrrhhhaaa!* Things were going badly for Yale, and I could see Charlie O'Hearn wanted to tear her to ribbons.

It took me a couple of years to do Levi, too . . . the same kind of thing. He'd go off out of town sometimes; and sometimes I wouldn't go out to Chicago for months. The actual sitting time for both pictures didn't take that long.

*How about Mrs. Brewster? Did you see much of her?*

G.C.     Mary Louise? She's very nice. She's attractive . . . warm. I like her. She was a great horsewoman. She's a strong, attractive woman and a very good wife to him . . . very. It's a good couple. She told me a lot of things about his early life. She said he had a sister and there were just the two of them and their parents were divorced. Brewster's father had been married five times. He was a very charming fellow, apparently, and when he died, all five of his wives came to the funeral and cried! [*Laughing*] He wasn't a very good guy to be married to, but he was a very charming fellow.

*A little like Robert Lowell's two wives driving in the same car to New Hampshire for his burial after the funeral in Boston.*

G.C.   Somewhat, I suppose. But this guy had *five* wives and they *all* cried! [*Laughing*] Also, he was a very, very reactionary Republican with strong opinions. Naturally, Kingman was a Republican too, but a very liberal one. About this time, there was a Reston article in the *New York Times* about the Republican party not... uh... this was when Eisenhower was President and it was a question who was to succeed him. Of course Nixon was moving forward... Rockefeller was moving forward. At any rate, Reston wrote this article saying it was too bad the Republicans didn't dig down to some of the very able young men they had. Mac Bundy[20] was a Republican; Brewster was a Republican, and there were a couple more he mentioned as possible presidential candidates. I would have voted for him myself. I remember calling up saying I was coming down or something or other. Mary Louise answered the telephone and I mentioned the article to her. She said, "Oh yes. They're calling him Woodrow now. Woodrow Brewster." [*Laughing*]

Again, I got this from Mary Louise, I think. When Brewster was an undergraduate... it must have been around 1941... he was a big America First-er. Very active politically and strong against our getting into the war. I guess it was Angell who was president and he... just a college boy... persuaded him to get Lindbergh to come and speak on campus. He did a lot of negotiating with the president... talking and persuading and so forth. It just shows how active he was. He had enough force to do this. Of course, as soon as war was declared, he went right in as a navy flyer and did patrol flying up and down the coast looking for enemy submarines.

*In this country?*

G.C.   He may have gone overseas later. I don't know; but this is just an interesting little war story he told me. He said they went out on patrol and got lost in the fog. They were running out of gas; everything was going wrong and they were lost. It was a question of whether they'd make it back. Well, Brewster had done a great deal of sailing... he was a great fellow for sailing and he'd cruised a lot. He'd done a lot of cruising around Long Island. But now they were running out of fuel in a thick fog and they were a couple of hundred miles out. Lost. They didn't know where the hell they were when, suddenly, out of the mists he saw these cliffs. They'd happened to hit a place on Long Island he knew well from cruising, and *then* they knew they'd make it. But it had been very tense. He's got enough to handle that... cool with the heat.

Other things stand out in my mind. One particularly when it came to tap day for those secret, senior societies . . . you know, Bones, and so on. He didn't go out and stand waiting to be tapped the way you do, so Mac Bundy came to his room . . . looked him up to tap him for Bones. Brewster said he'd have to know first what they expected of him . . . what were the conditions of joining. And Mac said, "I can't tell you. It's terribly secret stuff." And Brewster said, "Unless I know what I'm in for . . . what Bones stands for . . . I can't join it."

And he didn't. For an undergraduate at that time it was a very courageous thing to do. So he never joined any senior society because of the secrecy connected with all of them. That showed a very independent fellow. It's one of the things that's interesting about him. Nowadays, joining clubs and societies in college is not all that important. Turning them down is done all the time . . . or more so anyway. But they took clubs very seriously then.

Yes, I like him very much. I like Mary Louise too. I'm very fond of the whole family.

*They must be fond of you too. You seem to be welcome any time. Do you remember the time when you were painting Kissinger . . . after Brewster had resigned from Yale and had been appointed ambassador to the Court of St. James's . . . and you arrived on the wrong night?*

G.C. Oh God yes! I remember that. Oh sure. I was bringing a picture down. I did a number of pictures while I was painting him . . . sketches and stuff . . . and I was going to give him a charcoal sketch . . . a pretty good one . . . that had been hanging around the studio for a long time. They asked me down for the night, and they were having Bill Scranton to dinner . . . just the four of us. That was really something, four of us. And I got the wrong night! That was something I would have liked to do.

*When did you realize it was the wrong night?*

G.C. It didn't take long. I arrived in the middle of a big reception . . . their last commencement reception for students and their families. There was a line a block and a half long, and three deep outside their house. [*Chuckling*] I realized pretty soon something was wrong. But with all that crowd and so on it was about half-past seven he came out of the house and crossed the street to help me with my bags.

*Brewster did?*

G.C. He did. Come to think of it, it couldn't have been my bags, because obviously I wasn't staying; and the picture was light. Oh I remember now what it was. I was bringing back ... Josef Albers[21] had given them a big bunch of books of his works and I'd borrowed them from him. I'd had them for a long time and was finally bringing them back. That's what he was helping me with. That's what it was.

*Did you ever get to the Scranton dinner?*

G.C. No. I was a week late for that, but I came down the next week with the charcoal sketch and I can remember it was Chester Kerr,[22] instead of Scranton, who was there for dinner. Not quite the same thing.

Actually, at the time, I was just starting to paint Kissinger and was dropping the picture off on my way down to Pocantico Hills ... you know the Rockefeller estate on the Hudson ... where I was painting him. Phyllis called to say the secret service men were trying to get hold of me to tell me not to come down until the next day, because President Ford was visiting Rockefeller and security was tight. That's why I stayed over

*While you were painting Brewster, I know you were painting a lot of other people at the same time. Someday we ought to take time out to synchronize in point of time your other portraits. Like today, you have five or six in your studio in different stages of completion. Right there is shown the scope of your work and your life; also, so it would reveal a lot about those Brewster years if we knew who you were painting besides him.*

# 13

# "On Human Nature"

G.C.  Thanks for your letter. I got it yesterday afternoon. You have things in there . . . that are very helpful. I'm very glad you sent it. Very much. And then you had this question about some of those questions I ask the people I paint: What would you endow a child with and what motivates us. That's something I can make a stab at today. Obviously these are questions you can think about a long time.

*And you can change your mind about them.*

G.C.  I've kept changing my mind all my life a little bit, you know. My ideas now aren't the same they were when I was younger. Even this book[1] . . . this book of E.O. Wilson's—*On Human Nature*—is just a collaboration, an elaboration and so on. In general the way both of us think. As a matter of fact, we rather think the same in many ways. For me, these views are subject to change, from time to time. A new idea can be a little reinforcement to something I think or feel . . . or what seems good to me. And others may reverse things a little bit. So, I haven't any *one* thing I've been goin' on. I've thought I had it . . . found it . . . several times in my life, as I've told you. And that was all right, but it wasn't the whole thing. Yes, the Wilson book has had an effect.

*I must get it.*

G.C.  Well, I don't know whether you'd like it. Some of it I don't like. I haven't quite finished it. I've read a great deal . . . enough of it. I'm down to the last two chapters, "Religion" and "Hope" . . . halfway through "Religion." In there, he's trying to show you that . . . I always have to stop and think of this word. I know it perfectly well. You know it. Darwin's . . . uh . . . Evolution.

*Survival of the fittest?*

G.C.   Well, that's it, but I think there's a better word than that. In other words, the genes are what give you the stuff to survive. He thinks that we have no moral purpose, particularly. Our purpose is to ensure the perpetuation of the genes. The moral purpose comes in, of course. We've got it and we think we've got it; but, actually, what makes civilizations do what they do, races do what they do . . . wars and so on . . . everything we do really is for that one purpose: the perpetuation of the genes.

Now this does not take away the idea of religion. Right in the beginning of the chapter on religion, he says it is *the* thing that every race has always had. There are something like a hundred thousand religions. It's a very deep, genetically-ingrained thing, as a matter of fact. It's as deep as anything. Altruism is another genetic characteristic. Aggression is and sex is. Language is another one. That's a unique gene we've got that animals don't have. We are genetically programmed to grasp syntax and words; and language is always growing, and so on. Other than that, we share many genes with the animals. Even altruism. Wilson goes into that at some length. That's an interesting chapter, as a matter of fact. The ants . . . the social insects . . . they're the ones that *really* are altruistic. They die for the race. Bees die for the hive without a thought.

He divides altruism into what he calls hard-core and soft-core. He can be good and dogmatic. He'll say this is so, or something like that, now and then; and, once in a while, he can irritate you with this. But it is interesting stuff. He makes a good straight division between hard-core and soft-core. Hard-core we always admire a great deal: the Medal of Honor winners and people who do absolutely selfless acts such as throwing themselves on hand grenades to keep other people from being blown up. Well, the ants and bees . . . the social insects . . . do this all the time. They don't have any soft-core altruism. That's what we have when we stand up for the family. That's where it shows the most, in the family relationship. Then the kin relationship. Then the clan relationship. It's gotten spread out as we've gone along because of communications, and so on. But many times, what you see in soft-core, according to him, is really hypocrisy. [*Chuckling*] There's no hypocrisy among the ants. They just go out and die, but they don't claim they're being good. They don't get any pleasure out of being holier-than-thou or anything like that at all; whereas, we get quite a lot of that. Of course, that's what makes us tick. That makes the whole world get on and makes civilizations possible.

So, these are the things I hadn't thought about quite like this before. They enrich things for me. And with this in mind as a recent thing, I looked back over Lewis Thomas's[2] essays last night. They're brilliant and lovely and interesting ... very; but they're not the whole thing like Wilson's book is. Wilson explores whole areas in more depth than Thomas does. But Thomas writes a terrific advertisement for this book. And I guess you'd better read it.

To get back to the religious business. Wilson says the more you know, the greater your belief in some great force or plan. Before, I'd always thought of God as someone very intimate who sent the rain and brought the thunder ... right down to the old man with the whiskers, and so on. That's all gone. It's getting moved over a little bit. In Wilson's opinion, genetics and their effect on our thinking don't seem to negate religion at all.

*In other words ...*

G.C. In other words, the more the truth is known, the more the myths are being exploded a little bit. It isn't just the soul that makes us so special. It's something else. Maybe it's bigger than that. He thinks our brain ... he says this categorically (and he may be wrong, as a matter of fact) ... that our brain is the most complicated machine ever made in the world. What is it? Something like ten billion little neurons going on in there and ... uh ... two hundred thousand genes. Wilson would claim that the human brain is the most complicated machine in existence.

*Has this influenced your basic thinking?*

G.C. Not much, no. I'd say it hasn't. It makes it clearer to me. At least I can grasp it a little bit. One of the things he says early ... and I've heard it said before . . . that we aren't genetically composed to understand God. Like the bullfrog, you know. He sees only four things. He has only four, five things he is genetically set up to grasp, and nothing else.

And there's light. Light apparently has vibrations or a spectrum that are one hundred or a thousand meters long ... I don't know how many ... but we are only constituted to see something like a millionth or a billionth of this. A very small amount. Everything we see is in our limited range of vision and all those other rays outside it we can't see at all. Aren't constituted to see. Machines can measure them, but this is not for us. With this kind of thing in mind . . . and he suggests this, we probably aren't programmed, aren't genetically constituted to understand what the score is. We kind of feel some of it, but it's just something we may never be able to grasp. That's an interesting thought. But again, it doesn't throw religion out.

Going back to religion, he says it is the common denominator of *all* civilizations since the cavemen made their little altars with sets of herbs and flowers and so on. So, I was thinking I have changed over the years. I've changed since the experience I had in the war, when I had what I thought was an insight. Which was an insight, a very valuable one. It's still all right, but it's limited.

*Was it a spiritual insight?*

G.C.   Yes, but there I felt this thing about the soul. I was thinking about God as quite a clear force that went through us. That still holds. I still think of myself as an instrument, just as you think, too.

*Very, very much.*

G.C.   I think there are waves going through the air even, that come in through us like a radio which kind of wears out and dies. Then the music goes through some other instrument, like in that little poem of Wheelock's. Well, that's all right; but after reading Wilson's book, it takes a little different turn. I get down to genes a little bit more. My ideas change a little, but it doesn't alter the general idea of the bigness of this force going through us.

*As you know, opening the door to that force has got me through many a bad time.*

G.C.   Now there's where Wilson, probably, would say something like this: Your constitution enables you genetically to feel this way more than others would. They might feel it in another way, but still it's a kindred thought. It's a kindred idea, in a way. But, obviously, a spiritual person is a person so genetically constituted as to grasp and feel a sensitive something more than the average. More than the average a great deal. The greatest man that ever lived, you know.

Well, with all this as background, you asked me what I'd endow a child with . . . what quality above all others? I think the best answer is the capacity to love. After all, the Bible says in II Corinthians, Chapter

13: "The greatest of these (beyond gold!) is love." You know the passage. All things come along with that. I'd hope a child would be bright; I'd hope he'd have good looks, that he'd be charming. I'd hope he or she would have a good sense of humor and so on. No. I wouldn't want them to be too good-looking . . . man or woman.

*I wouldn't mind it.*

G.C.   You don't need it. If you'd been beautiful [*Chuckling*] you might have gotten into a lot of trouble. [*Laughing*] You don't think of looks with you. Oh, I put that *way* down the list. I only put it in because you'd like to have them have everything. Being pretty didn't help Kate, you know. No, it's not the best thing in the world. In fact, it can be quite a hazard.

*Was Kate pretty?*

G.C.   Very. Oh, God, yes! She was awful pretty. Yes she was. She was a beauty. Didn't you ever see her?

*I saw her once walking down the main street of North Haven, but never to speak to.*

G.C.   She was very good-looking indeed. She had everything.

*Was she bright?*

G.C.   She was bright, but she had a block. She pretended not to be bright, but she was bright about some things. She wasn't good in mathematics and things like that, but she did all right in school. Well, this is another story. She had a will to fail. A real destructive thing in there that kept blocking her. As an example: she was a very good athlete. She played a very good game of tennis, but she never wanted to go on and try to be a champion or really good. She was very well coordinated, but she'd get just so far on a thing and then wouldn't go any further, because she didn't *dare* to succeed. She could be very charming, and all kinds of times she'd be great fun, but she had this destructive quality about her. It was too strong . . . just too strong. . . .

I'd give it love. And I mean by love something wider. It might even extend to what your grandson has. His love of prints. That's love. I don't mean sexual love. When I say "love," I also mean the capacity to be enthusiastic about something. I'd like to look up the word altruism.

Of course, I know what it means, kind of, but Wilson uses the word for that whole area. Does it mean love of man? Does it mean love generally? Is it unselfishness? Posty Riley, would say that unselfishness may be negative and isn't necessarily desirable, unless you feel holier-than-thou in being it, which of course people do. Wilson points out that even the great heroes expect to go on and have afterlife. [*Laughing*] They have strong self-interest in self-sacrifice. There's nothing bad about that. It just isn't hard-core. Hard-core is when you go out and die for king and queen and nothing could stop you.

*Are you still doing T.M. How does it come into all this?*

G.C.     Yes. I'm still doing it. I don't do it quite so regularly as I did, but I do it pretty regularly. You're supposed to do it twice a day, and sometimes I don't do it twice. I almost always do it once. It's a calming thing for me. In a good big depression it wouldn't do any good at all. I look back on the depression I had last time and know it could have been much worse as they go, but it seemed terrible, as far as I was concerned. It was crippling for the moment and T.M. didn't help. I didn't do it then. I haven't been depressed that much in my life. It's just a little recurring thing, but most of the time I've been fine. I've had my highs too, you know. I may never have another depression or, again, I may. But I'll never wait so long to get help as I did last time. Let the thing get away with a life of its own.

To go back to T.M. historically, it has its counterpart in the Catholics' saying beads, chants, and repetitions, like that thing at Mt. Athos in the eleventh century. The monks there repeated what they called the Jesus prayer.

*What was that?*

G.C.     Well, it's "Christ have mercy on my soul. Christ have mercy on my soul." They'd say this for four hours. It was meaningless. It was like a mantra; and, of course, T.M.[3] is based on a mantra. Repeating meaningless sound which distracts you in the repetition of it. Tennyson did it, only he used his own name: "Tennyson, Tennyson, Tennyson." he'd say it to himself. And what it does... uh... it kind of clears your mind and refreshes you. So, if you have a problem that is bothering you, a little bit... beginning to get into you so that you can't quite get rid of it... T.M. has a tendency to break the rhythm so, for a while, you're thinking of nothing. Then when you stop, after twenty minutes, you have a little respite. It gives you a little chance, as I see it, to get your haunches under you. Indeed it does. At least it helps me and I think it helps everyone. That's the point of it. It's a crude way of going down and examining yourself. There are levels of consciousness, and I remember now that they claim that this goes down, deeper down. What it does do, is in that little book, *The Relaxation Response* written by a Harvard professor named Herbert Benson. I guess you've seen it, haven't you?

*No, I haven't seen it, but I've heard about it. Doesn't it use "one one one" as a mantra?*

G.C. They did an experiment with that at the Harvard Medical School. This was a team there under this fellow who is an associate professor. They went to the maharishi, who's a teacher of T.M. and asked him if he'd mind cooperating and letting some of his students, who'd been at it for quite a while and were thoroughly imbued with it, let themselves be treated with electrodes and all that kind of stuff, to see what their physiological reactions were, if any, during T.M. Greatly to the maharishi's credit, he was most delighted and offered any assistance they wanted as long as they took these tests over a period of six years. They found out a whole lot of things: heartbeat slowed, blood pressure went down, and breathing slowed down a lot. They also found that when stress comes, the lactic acid increases in you greatly. No question about it. And after T.M. it drops way down. T.M. definitely breaks this churning, this going around, for a little while, and it's very good indeed. Everyone has this churning somewhat and T.M. is a little refresher. You feel a little better, not a helluva lot, but just a little, and it makes a lot of difference. I wouldn't have started it if I hadn't been subject to those depressions, now and then, and I've talked it over with the psychiatrist, Dr. Stanley Howard Cath. He thought it was very beneficial. They use it quite a lot. They use it in hospitals sometimes. Churches, plenty of them have it. At King's Chapel[4] they have a little group. And the church in Cambridge ... The Unitarian Church.

It isn't a religion at all. It makes no difference what you are. You could be a Jew or a Muslim or a high-church Episcopalian. It has nothing to do with it at all.

But to go back to the "one one one" mantra ... or "Tennyson Tennyson Tennyson" ... I find I get distracted by associations. When I think of one, I think of two, or one *of* something. That's why the impersonal mantra ... which does, in fact, have an ancient source ... is best for me. I'm really thinking of nothing.

To get back ... way back to this theory of force flowing through you as an instrument. This applies to Christ on the cross, too, in my opinion. I never understood his cry, "My God, My God, Why hast thou forsaken me?" until I thought of his body as a damaged instrument. I've been thinking about this, during this Holy Week.

# 14

# Levi of the University of Chicago

*To start us off, do you remember the date you painted Edward Levi?*

G.C.   Yeah. I don't right this minute. I'm so bad about numbers. I can easily find out, but I don't know just now. It would be seventy-one, or -two, or -three, some place in there. It was probably five or six years before he was . . . er . . . before he was Attorney General. It was finished about a year before that.

*Whose cabinet was he in?*

G.C.   He was in Ford's, yeah. Why do you want to know?

*Because there's an interesting comparison here. You did President Conant of Harvard in the fifties . . .*

G.C.   Forty-seven.

*. . . when the campuses were more or less stable and quiet; and you did Brewster of Yale in those terrible sixties . . .*

G.C.   Sixty-nine.

*. . . when the campuses were erupting in confrontations; so, if you did Levi of Chicago in point of time in the seventies . . . .*

G.C.   I did Levi in point of time . . . as our old friend[1] used to say when that expression first came in. Was it Watergate when they first used it? [*Chuckling*] It was after Brewster. It was very shortly after Brewster, I'd say about seventy, seventy-one. Probably nearer seventy. It was just after the worst campus troubles had happened in Chicago, and I remember talking to Brewster about Levi before I painted him. The reason, also it's hard to pinpoint the time . . . but this is part of the story a little bit . . .

Studies for portrait of Edward Levi of the University of Chicago, 1973

I was asked to paint him, and the commission went through Portraits Inc.,[2] long before I did it. It must have been several years before I got to it. I said I'd do it and never got to it. In fact, it was commissioned to be done for the law school, of which he was the dean, and which he'd greatly built up into a first-class law school. It's one of the very best, you know, very good. And . . . he was responsible for enlisting and getting people to come in there who were very red-hot stuff; and he had the law school building built by Eero Saarinen who came down and spent a lot of time on it. First-class building. First-class piece of Saarinen design. It was very good and the picture was to be done for that when he was dean of the law school. But I put off doing it for so long . . . which I've done before and since . . . that he became president of the university. So, by the time I had painted him, he was president of the university and had been through the campus troubles for a couple of years. As so often happens with these busy birds, they don't care at all, you know. They've got so much to do they're actually relieved, almost, that they don't have to do it. They have no trouble filling their time. I wrote him after a couple of years of this . . . Portraits Inc., of course, had been on my tail a little bit . . . I wrote him and said I'd put him off so long that, although I was interested in painting him, if he wanted to drop me . . . leave me . . . he had every right to do so and it was all right with me. He wrote back. I think all he said was, "Of course not." It was as brief as that. I think that's what he said: "Of course not. Yours sincerely, Levi."

*That shows what kind of a guy he is. Delightful.*

G.C. So I went out and this must have been, as I say, about '70, '71. The wave of campus riots had broken. It was a little bit less tense, you know. Harvard had been taken over, as you know, and Levi had had one of his buildings taken over. The crest had peaked and was dropping off, but there was still plenty of . . . er . . . of ferment. The fire had gone down, but it was still there ready to spout if the wrong move was made.

The thing I remember very distinctly . . . and it is pertinent to all that. When I went out to meet him, it must have been in late June of the eventful year. It was a Sunday night, I think, and I met him at a place called the Tavern Club which is on top of a skyscraper. Very nice. A very pleasant place to have dinner. Very quiet. And . . . er . . . almost the very first thing he said, as I sat down with his wife . . . who turned out to be a very nice woman indeed . . . one of the first things he said was,

"I'm going to go through with it," in a defiant way.

You know, he knew he was going to be criticized for having his portrait painted. For spending the money on it. He realized this was going to be possible trouble for him, but he was damned if he wasn't going to do it! [*Laughing*] This was so unlike what would have been said fifty years before. Sargent painted Lowell and that portrait was in the college yearbook. College presidents were honored to be painted and expected to be painted and liked to be painted. But now, here was one gritting his teeth and, Jesus! he was going to do it. [*Laughing*] That's about what it amounted to. [*Both laughing*]

*It was a turnaround.*

G.C.   It was a turnaround. It would not have been approached like that at all, in the early 1900's. And so I went to work. Actually I was looking around as I always do . . . had been for a long time, even then.

*Fly-on-the-wall stuff?*

G.C.   Yeah. Sure. I'd been doing that for a long time, by that time. I would go to his office, and I stayed at the house, so I saw a little bit of him. That whole university was built with a tremendous lot of Rockefeller money, apparently, on the site of the . . . er . . . I guess it was the 1893 World's Fair. The World's Fair brought in McKim, White, Burnham and Saint-Gaudens and Frank Moore. All those fellows got together there. The renaissance in this country started from them. And Bertram Goodhue, a very good architect, did a lot about the University of Chicago, particularly the chapel. Did you ever see it?

*No.*

G.C.   The university was built on the site of the fair, so, where the lagoon had been, is now a long, greensward whose sides are about six feet down. It's part of the landscaping of the place. The buildings were put up then . . . a lot of them . . . the main bunch. Later, they had the law school and another building Saarinen did, which was never quite finished. They never finished the tower because they ran out of money.

I'll just digress on this architectural problem of running out of money. [*Chuckling*] They get a damn good building and Saarinen wanted another thirty-five feet, but it was terminated. It's like a statue with its head off. [*Laughing*] That happens a lot, but it doesn't happen often when they get to that point. They usually go through with it.

Anyway, the Levis had a nice, big house that looks over the old lagoon that is now grass.

*On the lake, I assume.*

G.C.   Near the lake. The lake is probably a half a mile beyond. The greensward is flanked by the college buildings on one side... the main college, so to speak, his house, and the chapel. And, on the other side, are buildings like the law school. It's surrounded by buildings on both sides, the contemporary ones on the far side from the college. It's big, you know, spreading over several blocks.

Their house is a big, gray, stone house. Stone, plain and sharp. No rough-hewn. A presidential house of large rooms for entertaining and then intimate rooms. A very pleasant house. It had one fault: it was totally air-conditioned. Right around the year. I went there a great deal, off and on, and it was very depressing living in a totally air-conditioned house. Office buildings you go in, you don't think much about it; but, in a house, you want a little bit of fresh air. You want to raise the window at night so you can see all the green things under the trees waving a little bit; but, with air-conditioning, you're not getting anything. It was all very nice and so on; but by God! it was so sanitary, so antiseptic that it began to get on my nerves. I couldn't put the window up and let the breeze come in, and that can get you down, almost. I remember that very strongly.

So, when I began to do him, I went there off and on over a couple of years. Sometimes six months would pass, a month would pass, two months would pass. I'd work mostly weekends in the house on him. He'd pose for me in one of the rooms upstairs. And he had some very brilliant sons, one with a terrific, real brain. A very bright bunch. And the experience was a nice one. I got very fond of him. I'll never see him again, I suppose now. They came to the show in Washington (in the Corcoran Gallery), that opening night. But I don't write much and they didn't. They liked me all right. I'm sure of that. I know that. And I liked her. She was a little difficult, not unpleasant; but she used to argue a little bit. But I liked her very much. She was a very, very nice woman.

*What did she argue about?*

G.C.   About the picture, really. She thought she knew a lot about pictures and she'd slip in an idea. Would discuss it a little bit. She didn't see the final thing for quite a while, but she couldn't help getting glimpses of it, once in a while. She would come in and try to make little hints, suggest how I should do something, and we used to have little arguments about this. [*Laughing*] But I liked her very much, so we had a good time. I got a very good picture of him in the end. Pretty good. Pretty good.

*What kind of a man is he?*

G.C. Obviously, he is a very intellectual man. He's lean. He's fairly slight, medium-sized, with a long face and a long nose. A rather sardonic, pleasant . . .he has kind of an archaic smile all the time. An archaic smile, an ancient smile. He's an ancient . . . er . . . an ancient, Jewish type. He'd come from three generations of rabbis, all intellectual as hell. He's an intellectual man with a nice, sardonic sense of humor. Various people would come to the house. Almost all his intimate friends were Jewish. He wasn't limited in this way, but they just naturally were. There was a Russian woman who was the wife of a professor at the university law school. I can't remember her name now, but she was a very able woman. Afterwards, she went some place, I think it was Columbia. And then there was a professor who had written a biography of Frankfurter, who he had clerked for. A big, fat, very nice fellow; and my picture of Frankfurter was in the frontispiece of his book. It was because of this portrait of Frankfurter that I was doing this one of Levi. They all knew it; and that was why he waited so long and that kind of stuff.

Well, to go back to what he was like: he was this lean man with an archaic smile, very hard-working but not tense. Very relaxed, but steady-working. Tremendous capacity to go on and on and on. He was rather sad-looking. I don't think he was particularly happy. To illustrate this, he told me a story of a young girl who came to his office one day. She was president of the student council and this was just before or during the campus troubles. And he said,

"What's the matter?"

And she said, "I'm not happy here. I'm not happy."

And he said, "Nobody's happy, so let's talk about something serious."

And he said this did her a lot of good. It made her feel much better. And then they got down to certain situations among the students and what to do about it. "Nobody's happy" he said. Nobody's happy and he meant it. He wasn't unhappy particularly, but he certainly wasn't happy. He worked like hell because of it. He was busy all the time doing things for the college. Worked on Sundays. He'd come in and pose for me on Sundays. And he smoked cigars. By God, he smoked cigars all the time! He had his weaknesses. Drank a cocktail . . . two cocktails every night, which he measured out. They were mild ones, but he had two. So he wasn't a rigid, puritanical type. He didn't overdo it, of course, because he didn't want to stir things up out of the side of his mouth.

To illustrate how he handled the campus troubles: Now, next to Brewster, he did about the best of any of the college presidents; but they did take over his administration building. This building was one of the ones added on later and, as he described it, it was "penitentiary modern." It was a terrible-looking building. Really modern, rigid. Well, the students took it over, and he told me the trustees wanted him to call in the police to throw 'em out. And he refused to do it, wanted to think about it. Said he'd think about it over night. And he told me he didn't sleep all night long. He walked up and down the library all night long. He said he'd come from three generations of educators, as rabbis are, you know. His father had been at the University of Chicago before him, not as president, but as one of the professors. And he said this was not the reason alone, but it was in his blood not to allow police interference in this area. So he told the trustees in the morning that if it came to it, if they had to do it, he'd call the police in; but with him calling the police in, they would receive his resignation. They never did call them in, so he stayed.

He was a high-minded man, a gentle man. A gentle man. Reserved, no back-slapping, *"hey-hey!"* stuff at all. Rather formidable, in his reserved, sardonic way, but very kindly and very realistic.

So, to continue the story, they didn't call the police. They eventually solved the problem. One of the ways they solved it . . . in fact, the way they solved it . . . was that he went into the building to see them. About five hundred students were occupying it, and he went in and addressed them. It was a terrible building, he told them, and they could have it. He'd moved all the records out and said, "You can have it. I've never liked it." And left them there. They'd had food brought in; they were lying all over the floor, and an lot of 'em got sick of it and began to dwindle off. At the end of two weeks, there were only about fifty left. The hard core. The rest of 'em had left. Nothing done to any of them.

*They didn't vandalize the building at all?*

G.C. No. No. No. If they'd vandalized it, they would have lost their case. They came into occupy it, not to trash it. So . . . er . . . at about the end of two weeks, the fifty sent representatives to him and said they wanted to leave. "We want to get out of this," they said, "and we want you to give us a face-saving way of doing it."

And he said, "No. You wrote the first act, you finish the play."

So they crept out, and he fired the last fifty. He suspended the ring leaders for a long time. I think that was a pretty good way of handling it, because he didn't let 'em get away with it, but he didn't fire everybody. He didn't let the police in and I admired this in him. Oh, he's tough enough. He's tough enough, sure. That was all very like him. Very.

*And that was before you started to paint him?*

G.C.   Oh, yes. That was before. That was about the time that Harvard...that University Hall was taken over. You see, Pusey didn't handle it quite as well. He was not a man to get mad and blow his top at all, you know. It was typical the way he handled it.

Well, those are the things I remember very distinctly. There are lots of little things, too. Levi used to teach classes. He loved to teach. He didn't have much time to do that kind of thing with all his administration duties. He did teach one class a week. I remember going to that class. He'd bring the students out very well indeed, asking the questions that would lead them on. He was extremely good at it.

*What did he teach?*

G.C.   He taught, I think it was, history and government.

*Did you paint him in his study?*

G.C.   No. I painted him in the upstairs sitting room.

*Was he standing or sitting?*

G.C.   He was sitting. He was sitting in a very good light. He could be very Mephisthophelean, with his long face and archaic smile. It was good enough. It was good enough. I did a little piece at a time. I went out there a long time, every little while for a couple of years. I said I didn't like the house, but it was actually, quite comfortable. I'd go out there for the weekend. I'd get around a little bit, but it was way out of town, you know, so I didn't go to town much. Oh, I went in to see what artists were doing and so on.

*The portrait's in the law school out there, isn't it?*

SKETCHES FROM LIFE 255

G.C.   Yes. It was commissioned for that. A very good building. A very nice building. A very elegant building. Incidentally, before we leave the University of Chicago: Ed Barnes... he's a very good architect ... was doing a great art complex at that time including a library. It's this huge library ... modern building ... It's so arranged, with little rooms like this as they seem to be, with a couch like this and a couch like that, and soft chairs over here and there all around in different places, making it very conducive to study. And it is open twenty-four hours a day! People can study there all night long if they want to. It was the most conducive place to study I ever saw. It invited you to sit down. You could sit there all day. All over it. All over it. And, of course, stacks of thousands of books. A great big library. Very famous, you know. You wanted to go in and spend all day there. It was very, very, very attractive indeed and ... er ... exciting. It was so inviting.

*Before we begin on Lefty Lewis as we planned to do, do you remember you talked about the Harold Talbott[3] portrait, Eisenhower's Secretary of the Air Force, and said that he had a hard, disagreeable expression which you got and his wife loved it? In Arthur Schlesinger's biography of Bobby Kennedy,[4] which I have been reading, he said that Talbott came up before Bobby Kennedy's crime committee [The Senate subcommittee on Investigations, John McClellan, chairman, Robert Kennedy, chief counsel]. The charges were that he was using his office as Secretary of the Air Force to get contracts for a building concern he was connected with; but that he, Talbott, was so respected that when his case came up before the committee, and he told his story in a straightforward way, he was just about to get off free, when Bobby Kennedy ripped into him and Eisenhower had to fire him. Did you realize that Bobby Kennedy nailed the accusation to him? If it hadn't been for Bobby Kennedy, Eisenhower wouldn't have fired him.*

G.C.   Was Bobby Kennedy vindictive?

*Well, Talbott was about to be whitewashed ...*

G.C.   Was Bobby Kennedy doing the right thing?

*I'll read from the biography:*

>   The committee dropped out of the headlines. One 1956 investigation did, however, attract attention. Harold Talbott, Eisenhower's Secretary of the

Air Force, had retained half-ownership in Paul B. Mulligan & Co., the firm of so-called efficiency engineers. John F. Kennedy's friend, Charles Bartlett 3rd, heard that Talbott had been hustling business for the firm out of his Pentagon office.

G.C. Bartlett exposed this?

*Bartlett exposed this. Probably what he was doing was, as you have said, using Air Force letterhead paper for business.*

G.C. He certainly did that. I know that.

*Well, to continue:*

Bartlett then proposed a joint inquiry to Robert Kennedy, an alliance of the newspaperman and the senate investigator, each tapping his own resources and pooling the results. Talbott was a genial fellow [*That fits your description.*] His vivacious wife [*You thought she was great.*] was even more popular.

They were Palm Beach acquaintances of the elder Kennedys and had many friends in the Senate. But Bartlett soon published letters by Talbott on Air Force stationery soliciting contracts for Mulligan from firms doing business with the Pentagon. [*That's pretty bad.*] Called before the committee, Talbott denied wrong-doing. Committee members responded admiringly. Joe McCarthy said virtuously that he deemed it extremely important to make sure that, by innuendo or otherwise, the Secretary doesn't get an unfair deal or a smear.'

*That's pretty funny coming from McCarthy.*

G.C. It is pretty funny all right.

*The biography continues:*

None of the members of the McClellan Committee, Bartlett wrote later, would give Kennedy support and the young counsel had to pursue the case in hearings in which he was the only one asking questions. Kennedy, age thirty, began a tough cross-examination. He asked Talbott, age about sixty-seven, whether he had instructed anyone in the Air Force to make representations to RCA for not renewing a Mulligan contract. Talbott said, 'Absolutely not!' Kennedy broke down his story. 'Talbott,' wrote Krock, 'was not a crook, but rather a man whose excessive egotism led him to suppose that no one could question his motives.' Eisenhower now requested his resignation. Bartlett won a Pulitzer Prize and Robert Kennedy confirmed a reputation as a relentless prosecutor.

G.C. That's very interesting. The fact that Krock said anything is interesting, too. Did I ever tell you things pertinent to this about Talbott that I learned from a Yale man I painted?

*No you didn't. We haven't got it on tape anyway.*

G.C.  It's just an interesting thing about Talbott as a prelude to all this. Of course, Talbott was genial enough. He was a man of the world, but he wasn't what you'd call a jolly good fellow. Oh, I can see him back-slapping and all that kind of stuff, but that's not how you'd describe him, exactly. It isn't the outstanding thing about him.

What was outstanding about him, he worked his head off and he'd had a heart attack, a bad one.

*When he was Secretary of the Air Force?*

G.C.  Either when he was or before. I think it was before. I'm not just sure when it was, but the point is he'd had one and he didn't spare himself in the slightest. He was always taking little antacid pills and things like that. And he had a little scare at the Y. A little scare of some kind. But ... er ... he gave his all, and he was very instrumental in building the "West Point of the Air" in Colorado, where I think that picture may be now. He worked tirelessly and gave everything he had, and he was a patriot from way back in this thing. He was very admirable in his efforts, regardless of his health. He didn't seem as old as sixty-seven, though; but he blotted his copybook.

Sometime afterwards, I painted a man ... er ... I can't remember his name. I liked him very much. I remember him personally very well. A person who had gone to Yale with Talbott. I think they both went to Hill School. They got out of Hill School and he and Talbott had gone to Yale. This fellow I painted comes from Pennsylvania. A very nice guy, who as I say, went to Yale the year Talbott did. He was tapped for Bones by Averell Harriman. He was a lawyer ....

*I wish you could remember his name.*

G.C.  Oh, I'll think of his name. It's just a boring thing not to remember it. Alex Tener[5] it was. He was one of the nicest men I ever ran into. A very nice man.

*From where?*

G.C.  Well, he was brought up in Philadelphia, I think it was. The interesting part of his life was that he was living in Kennebunkport and he had a lovely schooner. A lovely schooner. A black schooner. Very smart, nice. He sailed it by himself a lot, up and down the coast. He loved to sail along the coast. He was being painted because...and this is very rare: he had brought up his son since he was four years old, after the mother died, and this son wanted him painted. The son was forty-five years old who had a family down in Virginia, or wherever it was. He had a nice big house and he was a successful man. And he wanted a picture of his father right up there in the middle of the living room. Apparently, they wanted the old man about the house. This is very rare. Sons get 'em for the banks, they get 'em for this and that; but very few want them right about the house. This fellow loved his father, no question about it. He initiated the portrait, paid the money and everything.

Well, if you knew Tener, you'd know why. Nobody could be better-living than him. Oh, he's a beaut! But...er...at any rate, he was married to somebody he loved very much. I remember it was a lovely thing. He was devoted to this woman. They were down in Washington ...after Yale, after the Harvard Law School, very young, and they had a child, this little boy. And then the terrible flu epidemic of 1918 during the first war and people died like flies. Do you remember it?

*Oh, I do. I remember it very well.*

G.C.   She died, and he couldn't get her body out of Washington. He finally got her onto a train and took her up to some place in western New York where she'd come from and buried her. But he hadn't been able to get her out of Washington for quite a while. Very bad, it was. It was very bad. And he had this little boy, and so he took care of him. He had a sister and family who wanted to do it, but he was the one who brought him up. He eventually married again. So that he's a very nice man, that's all I can say.

*Where did you paint him?*

G.C.   I painted him in the studio in Boston, and then he'd sail into North Haven and come ashore and I painted him there.

*In the boathouse?*

G.C.   No. In the big studio down by the shore. He was a very touching, sweet, sad man. I liked him very much. The last time I saw him was years later...a couple of years later. I hadn't met the son. I was in the Oak Room of the Plaza having dinner by myself, and, by God, there was Alex and his son! And Alex came over and put his arms around my neck and hugged me cheek to cheek. It was the damndest, you know... it was a sweet thing to do. He was a much older man, in his later seventies then. He was a very warm fellow, but a very reserved fellow, too. Then he introduced me to his son.

While I was painting him, we talked about Talbott and he finished his story. Tener said they were in the same class at Hill School and that Talbott was a big shot there. He was a very good athlete. Muscular, coordinated, a very good athlete and he was bright. On the student council. I'm not sure he wasn't head of the school. Two weeks before graduation, at chapel, the headmaster got up and said that Harold Talbott had been fired. And nobody ever knew why. It was never explained what he did. Maybe it was the kind of thing he did in Washington. In those days, it wasn't ruinous to get fired, you know. People got fired and got into college anyway. So he went on to Yale and, again, he was in the same class as Tener. And, by God, the same thing happened there! He was as big as he had been at the Hill... and he performed very well. And then, just before the end of his last year, he was fired from there too.

*What for?*

G.C. Some little irregularity. Could have been cheating or something like that.

*He must have had a terrible flaw in his character.*

G.C. Either that or he'd get to a certain point and then he'd go and do something to ruin it all. There was something destructive in him. That's the reason I talked about how well he did as Secretary of the Air Force... and he did do awfully well. He expended himself. I told you, in the face of death he was very patriotic. He could have died any minute, the way he was going. And then he had to wallow it up in the end. He had to screw it up. Which he didn't really need to do. He didn't need to do anything at school either. He was doing fine. Isn't that interesting? Sort of a Greek tragedy. It was very interesting to come on that other man later on and have him finish the story.

*You mean Tener?*

G.C. Yes. Tener. One last thing about him. He used to quote *The Wind in the Willows,* I think it was. Some animal... I think it was Toad

... says to another, "There's something awfully comforting about messing around with boats." This was like him. He loved to mess around and paint his boat.

*Speaking of quotes. You gave one a while back. What was that quote of A.E. Housman's?*

G.C.  Housman said, "Luck's chance, but trouble's for sure." [*Laughing*]

# 15

# Wilmarth Sheldon Lewis

*Didn't Lefty[1] Lewis go to Yale and wasn't he a great friend of Dean Acheson's?*

G.C.   They were very close. He, Dean Acheson, and Archie MacLeish were very close friends through college and always kept in touch. Lewis and Acheson were in Key;[2] but I'm not sure whether they were classmates or not.

*Wasn't Lefty Lewis a lawyer in Hartford?*

G.C.   No. He wasn't a lawyer. No. He was a scholar. Actually, he was a collector. That's what he is. He's still alive. He lives in Farmington, Connecticut, where he has his famous Horace Walpole collection, which he is leaving to Yale. It's all in this lovely old house ... very attractive indeed ... which he has also left to Yale. Scholars will be able to go there and study his extraordinary collection of seventeenth-century books and prints.

*Where did he get his money?*

G.C.   Well, his wife had a lot of money. He married an Auchincloss ... Jackie Kennedy Onassis's mother married Hugh Auchincloss. Mrs. Lewis was his sister and they had wads of money ... a great deal of money. Lefty came from California and went to some well-known school out there like Cate, before going to Yale. So he was well-off, but she was the one who had the money. We ought to talk about him now. As a personality, he is something! Judge Hand was another one who was a great friend of his. This is turning into a gossip column here, but Lefty Lewis is full of that kind of thing, too.

*How did the Lefty Lewis commission come to you?*

G.C. His name was Wilmarth Sheldon Lewis and they called him "Lefty." The article in the *Smithsonian* said he was named after a gangster.[3] I've always thought it was after a football or baseball player. Maybe I'm wrong, but I think it was a baseball player. At any rate, he was called "Lefty."

*How did the commission come to you?*

G.C. Well, it came to me through Kingman Brewster, who I had painted. I think he was the initiator here. Lewis was a fellow of the Yale Corporation. He was a very prominent... er... major member of the board for quite a long time. A very long time. Ten years, I guess. This was because of his Horace Walpole collection, which was housed at his place in Farmington which he was going to donate to Yale. He was going to give the whole thing to the university with the collection remaining at his place. Which he did. The portrait was put in the Beineke Library because of this collection and his donations and services to Yale, but primarily for the collection. He said himself that he identified himself with Walpole. He was almost a re-creation of Walpole. He's still like that. I did him after I did Kingman Brewster. I can't remember the date, but I can figure it out.

*It was the year Kate died.*

G.C. That's right, 1969. Ten years seems long and short. It's only ten years ago. Yes. It was '69.

He tells about himself in a book he wrote called... er... *One Man's Education*,* which I've got a copy of. He also wrote a book about collecting. There were others. There was another one about himself that tells about how he liked to go to galleries all over the world, wherever he was. If he liked a picture very much he would... er... think of it as his own. His picture. So he had a collection of pictures like this in his mind that he had selected as his pictures. A museum in his head. In his book he took fifteen, sixteen pictures that he liked and talked about 'em. It was quite a nice little book.

*Can you remember some of the pictures?*

G.C. I remember one. It was the... er... *The Horse Race*. A small picture and I think it's in the Boston Museum. By Degas. Just a little one, a twenty-inch-long picture and probably eight inches high or less. Smaller than that. Jockeys and horses. You know the picture?

---

* New York, Knopf, 1967

Oh, yes, I used to hang a reproduction of it in patients' rooms around the Brigham Hospital. One man said all those horses' rear ends gave him ideas.

G.C.   Well, it's a good one, and there's a carriage. He didn't describe it from a painter's point of view, but he goes into speculations about the ... er ... nobleman with his daughter on his lap in the carriage. And there's a few things that made this picture listen to his imagination. It was a charming little book. He may have written more than that, but I know there's those three.

*Did he write an books on Walpole?*

G.C.   He must have written in countless pamphlets. He may have written one, for all I know.* I don't remember. I never saw one, but he knew more about Horace Walpole than anyone else in the world.

*When did he become interested in Walpole?*

G.C.   He went to college at Yale. First, he went to a fashionable school out West...in California. The Cate School, I think. It wasn't Cate. A similar one. He went there and ... er ... he went to Yale. He was very fortunate, he felt, that he had gone to Yale. If he had gone to Harvard, he said, he'd have kind of gotten lost. But he went out for things at Yale. He was very active and made Key, the secret society. That and Bones are supposed to be the best. They certainly were then and I guess they are now. It meant a lot to him. He told me that if he'd gone to Harvard, he'd have just disappeared into the college. Not coming from the East and so on, and people aren't as interested there in activities. You well know how Harvard is. So he was very devoted to Yale. After he graduated, he hung around and did some postgraduate stuff, but for a while he didn't quite find himself. And then, at a fairly young age, he came across Horace Walpole and felt this affinity. From then on it was just ... er ... straight going. He made a life of collecting and studying Walpole ... made a career of it, and, as a result, made himself a very eminent man. A great performance. At the same time, he became a member of the governing board at Yale.

*Where did you paint him?*

G.C.   In the big room where the Yale corporation meets. Yale's corporation is much larger than Harvard's thing. In numbers more like Harvard's board of overseers. I'd say Yale's board has twenty people.

---

* Lewis wrote over fifteen books on Walpole

There's a room with a big table . . . a big, long table with their names on their chairs. Little brass tabs with their names, you know. I remember Scranton, Vance, people like that. That's where I painted Brewster and Lewis. In that room.

*Let's go back to Lewis as a collector.*

G.C.    Well, that article in the *Smithsonian* tells it well. He collected anything connected with Walpole. Anything at all. Even cigar butts.

*One of the things in that article that fascinated me was that bit about Louis XVI. He translated Walpole's book on Richard III into French while he was waiting to be guillotined. Weren't you fascinated by that? It was an insight to that king. I always thought he was a lightweight, but he did have enough intellect to spend his last days doing this translation. Lewis has it.*

G.C.    I certainly admire that, but I don't think I'd be able to keep my mind on that sort of thing if I were sitting around waiting to be guillotined.

*I've gotten us off our subject. But to get back to Lewis: Did you go down to Farmington to do your fly-on-the-wall stuff?*

G.C.    Oh, yes. Oh, yes.

*Where did you do it?*

G.C.    He's got a very nice house down there. He's got an old Federal house . . . 1780, 90, somewhere around there. And . . . he had a big library put on it by Billy Delano.[4] It's a very attractive room. A great big room. Delano was a New York architect in a very well-known firm at that time: Delano and Aldrich. He was a very distinguished architect. Very good taste and so on. It was a very lovely, big room filled with books. I did a lot of him there sitting around; and I did a lot in another room built on, where he kept his steel files and that kind of thing. Actually I did his portrait in that room, too. The rarer stuff was in there. Kind of a vaultish section of the house where his office was, and stacks, too. Oh, he had Walpole diaries . . . deep little things . . . little personal things that Walpole had.

But I went down once in a while . . . every little while and did fly-on-the-wall stuff . . . and it was a very nice place to stay. He had two old servitors; the cook and the housemaid. The housemaid's name was Bridie, I think, and she had a very *very* jarring voice. Good as gold, but harsh as you could imagine. A lot of good will, but, unfortunately, it was seated in her head or her chest or someplace. They'd been with him for years and years and years, and they waited on him hand and foot. They knew just how to do everything. It was a very, very, *very* tight ship. A very well-run ship. I used to look at books in the library myself, you know, and it was very nice, very good. It was very high off the hog. But there wasn't anything particularly that I can think of now.

*Weren't there any anecdotes?*

G.C.    Lewis was always interesting, especially when he talked about collecting. The experiences he had had. Well, one, particularly comes to mind. There was this dealer whose name was Hogg. It wasn't Hogg. It was one of those very simple, blunt English names, undistinguished-sounding. This dealer was very high-class, as were all the dealers he dealt with; and because of his great interest in Walpole, they would save the best things for him. After a while, it began to have a life of its own. Lefty was the great market for that stuff. He had kind of a corner on it. The dealers were all very knowledgeable and they'd get these things for him.

Among the things he particularly wanted to get of Walpole's were a series of sketches that were made by ... er ... Lady Berkeley. I'm not sure of her name, but it doesn't matter whether I'm right or wrong about that. She was a neighbor of Walpole's and an old woman. Anyway, she had done a number ... about twelve ... sketches for scenes for a masque which Walpole was putting on at Strawberry Hill. Lewis was quite sure these existed. He knew they'd been done and he was trying to get them. He'd put out feelers and the dealers all knew he wanted them. I think it was the prime thing he wanted to get at that time. Now he used to go over to England every spring, in April, to see what was up. If the dealers had anything for him they usually let him know. This was an annual thing. Well, he'd been in the market for these sketches for some time. And one spring when he went over, he hadn't heard from Hogg for a long time. Let's call him Hogg. It was that kind of a name, and he was red-hot. So, Lewis called him up when he got to London and said he'd like to see him. And the dealer said,

"Why don't you come to lunch?"

Remember, Lewis hadn't heard from this dealer for a long time. So he dropped around to this fellow's shop and was taken upstairs to a little room where the dealer crouched in his own little area. A private room, of course. He looked around and saw on the table the drawings.

Bottom up! He knew right off that that was what they were. Mr. Hogg didn't say anything about them at all. He just said:

"I've got to do something downstairs. I'll be back in a minute. Wait for me here."

So, Hogg left him alone in the room. Lewis, of course, confirmed right away that these were the sketches, by the watermarks, things on the paper, you know, and the size. Up to this time nobody'd said a word. The sketches were just lying there. So, when the dealer came back, Lewis was in such a sweat to get these things, he got so excited, he said,

"How much do you want for them?"

They both knew what he was talking about. And then Lefty said that Hogg dropped a bomb naming a terrific price.

"I'll take them," Lewis said,

And the deal was done. This fellow, he said, named a helluva price. A real bomb. Then they went out to lunch. A nice lunch. And at the end of it, Lewis said he just had to ask him, "What did I do wrong?"

And the fellow said, "You were a little too eager." [*Laughing*]

*Do you suppose the dealer'd had these things for a long time?*

G.C.   Of course. Of course. He'd had these things many months and was just waiting for the spring visit. And he'd laid them out there deliberately. He had it all set up. Lunch, but no word of anything else. Got Lewis all steamed up and then hit him with this terrific price. By this time Lewis could not afford *not* to get them. Oh, Hogg played him like a fish with the greatest of artistry. As I say, all during lunch Lewis was squirming around wondering how he'd got so took . . . There wasn't any question of coming down. He was stuck. Apparently that's the way they do business. Good finesse. And that amused me.

*Did you see the sketches when you were down there?*

G.C.   No. They were in a file someplace. He told me another time when he was very young, before he began to collect Walpole, he collected other things a bit. I think he went to Oxford a little time after Yale. He was in England, anyway, and he heard about this poor old widow who had an attic full of old books. He figured she didn't know the score. He bought a whole lot of them. Screwed her terribly.

*Did he?*

G.C.    Well, he certainly wasn't trying to do the right thing by her. The great thing is to get a thing for nothing if you can. It's a real game, apparently. Anything's fair.

Another story that sticks out in my mind . . . a collector's story . . . is the one about the early Anglo-Saxon weight. Lewis told me this, and it shows what collectors are willing to do to get something. It's rather long one. I'm not going to use the real name of the chief actor in this story; but he was a doctor in Boston. A very respectable and respected one. I happen to have known this doctor and his daughter. I knew his background, because I knew him myself. He was a highly-regarded gentleman, in the old sense of the word: social, urbane, charming fellow who, I say, was respected. He'd gone to Yale and he'd been in Key, before Lewis. He was an older man than Lewis and he'd married a very rich woman. He went to medical school after he got out of Yale, but then he married this rich woman and he never practiced medicine. But he did become a great collector of medical books. He had a great medical library. And then the Depression came along. At this point, I'm going to give a name to this doctor just so it's easier to handle. Say, Dr. Tompkins. Well, Dr. Tompkins had amassed this terrific library . . . very extensive one . . . and then the Depression came along, his wife lost a lot of money, and he had to sell it. Which was a tragic thing to have had to do; but he did it.

Then things got a little better and, like a collector, he had to collect something, so he started collecting weights. He got a terrific collection of weights. And so, like Lewis about those sketches for the masque by Lady Berkeley, this Dr. Tompkins had his eye out—or knew about—or found out about as they do . . . it must be one of the pleasures of collecting . . . that there was this ancient Anglo-Saxon weight. The oldest weight in all England. He traced it down and found out that a vicar in a small English village owned it. I don't know how he tracked it down, but he did. He found this clergyman had it and he went to see him. Well, the clergyman wouldn't sell it; wouldn't sell it for anything. Out of the question. He wasn't a big shot, this cleric, but a nice cultivated Englishman. And, somehow or other, he had inherited or owned this weight.

So, every year, Dr. Tompkins cultivated this fellow. Sent him Christmas cards, you know. When he went over to England, he'd drop in and see him . . . have tea. They wouldn't discuss the weight at all. Just friends. Nobody shoving anybody or pushing anybody. Just friends, you know. Very genteel. And this went on for years. This went on for a very, very long time. And then, one year, one spring, Dr. Tompkins heard that this clergyman had come on hard times.

Now I'm going to stop this story right here for a moment and put another angle on it. Remember this is all part of a story Lefty told me, but this is where he comes into the story. He and his old friend, Dr. Tompkins, were returning from England on the same boat, the good old *S.S. Champlain*, and Tompkins told him the story I've been telling you. He told Lewis he was on his way home from seeing this clergyman.

Remember, it's Lewis telling me the story, but it's also my assessment of the doctor because I knew him. Well, the clergyman, his old friend, had lost a lot of money and ... er ... his wife was sick. He'd had various doctors and they hadn't been able to diagnose what the trouble was. Or just what to do and he was at his wit's end. Then, he thought suddenly,

"You're a doctor. Would you look at her?"

Well, Dr. Tompkins hadn't practiced medicine for thirty years, forty years, maybe; [*Laughing*] but he allowed he would. So he looked her all over and the upshot was that he prescribed that what she needed was a trip to a southern climate, some place in Spain or Italy. He was pretty sure that would fix her. But there wasn't any money. So, he got the weight. It was sold to him for the money to pay for the trip. [*Laughing*]

And, when Tompkins met Lewis on the boat, he couldn't resist telling him this. This reminded me of the collectors' game: the long playing of the fish. This was a terrible thing to have done. His diagnosis wasn't worth a damn! [*Laughing*] It was nothing but to get the weight out of the fellow. And Tompkins took Lewis down to his cabin and undid this little thing from tissue paper. It looked like a burnt, old-brown sweet potato, about that big, this weight used by King Alfred. There it was. He had it.

The story goes on. There's a sequel, where Tompkins, you might say, was the acquisitor's victim.

Here's Tompkins with his collection fleshed out, filled out with this thing he'd acquired, along with the rest of it: Egyptian and early Italian weights and so on. About this time, Lewis was trying to get ... was instrumental in promoting ... a library at Yale to house Harvey Cushing's[5] medical collection. A medical library which was very extensive, and he was very instrumental in putting this through. They raised the money to build the library. Cushing was also in Key, and he was also a friend of Tompkins. They were all friends through this Key business. Different years, but they were all members. Knew one another. And ... er ... Lewis and Cushing got talking it over and Lewis said,

"How about getting Tompkins's collection of weights to go in the library?"

They had medical significance, were appropriate; and it was a very distinguished collection indeed. And Cushing thought it would be a great idea. The question was how to loosen Tompkins up. And ... er ... Lewis said,

"I'll go down and see him in Stonington and I'll feel him out."

Lewis told me he went down and had luncheon with Tompkins and he said ... here again is this thing [*Laughing*] ... he said they had lunch, and they took a little stroll, and they were walking around, and Lewis said to me,

"I remember right where it was. Right behind the barn where I put it to him. Put the first little flea in his ear."

All, again, very elegant you know, very delicate. "The possibility and so forth. His weights would be appropriate." He just sowed the seed. I guess he tried to sow it pretty well; but it wasn't anything: no direct or rough approach at all. Just sowed the seed. And then he said to him,

"Well now," he said to the unsuspecting fellow, "How about having lunch with Cushing and me in a couple of weeks at the Lawn Club" (or someplace like that in New Haven)?

And Tompkins was delighted. The thing was settled ... the little idea that had been put in his ear. [*Laughing*] The deed was done. Right behind the barn it had started. [*Laughing*] A couple of weeks later, Cushing and Lewis set up the dinner. The way they set it up was ... er ... they were going to have a dinner with cocktails and stuff before. Just Lewis and Cushing and Tompkins at, say, Cushing's house. A good dinner, a nice dinner, and afterwards they were to go out into the other room and have a brandy. Cushing was going to get up and excuse himself and say he had some business with the architect who had come up from New York, and he wanted to look at the plans, which were about done. The architect was going to spread the plans out on the dining room table and he and Cushing could talk about them. Meanwhile, Lewis stayed and continued the brandy with Tompkins. Lewis said everything was set up in the other room with the plans on the table with the architect and Cushing leaning over the table looking at them. And Lewis said ... er ... to Tompkins,

"Let's go in and see what they are doing."

So they got up and went in. And Tompkins had to look over their shoulders to see the plans. There, on the second-floor plan, was printed out: "Dr. George Tompkins Weight Collection." Lewis said, "He had to lean way over to see it—and they got the collection." [*Laughing*] They got it, and it's in the library, but that's not quite the end of it.

Well, the library was built, and they had a great celebration to inaugurate it. Librarians and doctors came from all over the place. A lot of people were gathered there. It was a first-class dinner with a dais for the principal contributors and people and the rest of them around a large dining area. Naturally, Tompkins was there. Second-biggest contributor. When they went in to sit down to dinner, nobody could find Tompkins. They couldn't find him anywhere. It began to be embarrassing. Suddenly Lewis had an idea. He had a hunch, he said. He raced up the stairs to the second floor into the Tompkins's Collection room, [*Laughing*] with all those glass cases around. And there was Tompkins. He'd opened up the case and he'd gotten out the Anglo-Saxon weight. And he was standing there with it in his hand just looking at it. The Anglo-Saxon weight.

That is the story that stands out in my mind particularly. There were a lot of little anecdotes, little items, you know. Lewis was a funny fellow. But the ones I've told you were the best.

*That's lovely story, but rather sad, really. While you were staying with Lewis, did he have people in to dine? Did you go out? I know you went to John Parsons's for lunch.*

G.C. The Alsops lived in Farmington. We saw them quite a lot. Joe[6] would come over and help Lefty catalogue his library, and we saw John and Mrs. Alsop.

And I remember there was something in Hartford called the Monday Night Club. I realize now it was an honor to be taken there. Lefty wanted to have me see him in other surroundings. John Parsons belongs to it, as a matter of fact. It's an old club that I think Mark Twain belonged to and so on. It meets once a month on a Monday night and, apparently it's quite a special little club. I went there and it was very good fun. Pleasant. Jolly. Black tie. They didn't have much to drink and they were all very respectable, but it was jolly.

*Is it anything like the Tavern?*

G.C.    That kind of thing. Yes. The same kind of people. But not quite, because it's just a monthly club. More like the little dining clubs in Boston. That kind of thing because it was all men. I was the only guest they had for dinner for I don't know how many years. I didn't think much of it at the time, but I found out from Lewis later that it was very special. I suppose because he was an honored member. He wanted me to see the different aspects of his life.

Farmington's a nice little town. It's a pretty little town. Do you know it?

*I've been there several times. Have you been back to see Lefty?*

G.C.    I'd like to, but it's just out of the way. Actually, I don't know what he thinks of me now, because the last time I heard from him . . . When I did that picture of him, I did a first one that I wasn't satisfied with so I did another one. Which is the one, actually, that's at Yale. But the one I did and discarded was pretty good too, as it turns out. He wrote me several years ago and said he would . . . er . . . he remembered the picture I'd done, and there was some question of getting something for the Farmington Foundation, and how about letting him have that one? And I . . . er . . . I didn't want to . . . er . . . I could fix it up some. There were some parts that would have to be changed . . . worked over some . . . in which case it would be pretty good. I wrote back, "Ten thousand dollars." Which is what they'd paid for the other one.

*He paid ten thousand dollars for the one at Yale?*

G.C.    I don't know who paid it. They paid it. Lewis was pretty sharp on money, as I guess collectors are inclined to be. Except when they want something. And he had had a very rich wife. He was married to Hugh Auchincloss's sister. Apparently she was very nice. I never saw her.

*Annie. Her name was Annie and she died in 1959.*

G.C.    That's right.

*And, according to that article . . . I don't know why I'm telling you all this. You read it yourself . . . he wanted to involve her in his Walpoleana, so he got her interested in collecting prints.*

G.C.    Which she did very well. The prints are very good. That's right, and I saw some of them.

*Were they up?*

G.C.   They're in long drawers, you know; but you get 'em out and see them. Eighteenth-century prints, Walpole's century, you know. And there are all kinds of artists in it... Rowlandsons and English cartoons. It's a very handsome collection of English cartoons.

I don't know who paid for his picture, but there's plenty of money there. I didn't want to give him a bargain, so I said ten thousand dollars. He didn't understand this and wrote me back that, as I hadn't thought the first picture was as good as the second, he didn't see why he should pay as much for it. I never answered that letter. I'm not pleased with what I did. I don't like this story about myself; but, with all his money, I didn't want him starting to chop away. I really didn't want to give him a bargain.

*Was the first one a good portrait?*

G.C.   Not too bad. He has kind of sprouting hair that shoots up in the air. He's kind of sassy-looking, rather tough-looking, too. He can be very imperious. I know you said that Lombard didn't like him.

*No. He said he was too arrogant.*

G.C.   He could be quite arrogant. Yeah. He could be arrogant. And he could be imperious. He looks imperious in this portrait.

*What was the pose?*

G.C.   He's sitting looking right at yer.

*Where's the second one now? Gardner, what do you do with portraits like that?*

G.C.   Oh, I don't know. There was some question of that portrait going to the National Portrait Gallery. I don't know if there's much demand for it. It's hanging around, and when I get old, I might give it to him in the end, or I might burn it. It's got some virtue. It's an honest head of him, and what I'd have to do would be to bring the rest up to it. Then it would be a pretty good picture. It would be worth ten then, for sure.

Well, he's getting old now, and Farmington is just enough out of the way so I don't go down there. I'm bad about that, but you can't go tearing around everywhere, you know. To go there is a day and a night's stay, and we weren't that close. But we got along very well indeed. God, we spent a lot of time together! Sitting around and having drinks. I've seen him couple of times since. At the Tavern Club, lot of fun together, and in Washington.

G.C. captures a moment of bewilderment—and frustration in this 1965 self-portrait while he was trying to paint the late John F. Kennedy from a photograph (see introduction). "I've never been able to get the feel of a person from photographs . . . I tried for a year on that Kennedy thing, but it was no use."

# 16

# At the Harvard Fiftieth

Included in "A Symposium by Members of the Harvard Class of 1928 on the Occasion of their Fiftieth Reunion" were these remarks by Gardner Cox:

I shall talk about the present and the future of the visual arts, hereafter referred to as the arts. To begin with, the progress of the arts is linear—that is, they progress in a long undulating, horizontal line. We don't write better than Shakespeare; we don't sculpt better than Michelangelo; we just do differently. Science, on the other hand, is vertical—brick upon brick of discovery creating an ever-rising edifice of knowledge.

If I had a brain tumor and Hippocrates was around, I would walk right by him and go to our classmate, Dr. Lawrence Pool. On the other hand, if I was going to have my portrait painted and Rembrandt was available, I certainly wouldn't hesitate to go to him.

Will Durant, the historian, when asked to sum up the history of mankind in one sentence, said:

> Order leads to Freedom,
> Freedom leads to Chaos,
> Chaos leads to Order.

This is wholly applicable to the fine arts, and never more so than during our lifetime.

When we left college in 1928, there was comparative *order*—that is, there were traditional and recognized standards, largely based on skill, and in some ways rather confining. There was ferment in the air, reflecting the questionings, theorizing, and inventive spirit of our scientific age. It led finally, in the 1950s, to the flowering of abstract expressionism as typified by Pollock in painting ("Paint is Beautiful" was the cry) and by Calder in sculpture. This period was original and experimental. An undulating line of lasting value.

It was a period of *freedom*
which led,
about 1965, to minimal art,
exemplified in painting by the all-black canvas (one color) and in sculpture by the formica box placed on the floor. The slogan "Less is more" was borrowed from the architects and confidently proclaimed.

There followed a kaleidoscopic descent through many short-lived movements and to conceptual art. An illustration of the latter was the inclusion in the Venice Biennale (it was 1972, as I remember it) of an "artist" who sent in (and he was invited to do so) ten thousand butterfly eggs that were supposed to hatch in the middle of the exhibition. They didn't.

Conceptual art went even further, in its final development, to the point where the "artists" just used *words* to describe *acts*. And this brings us to a man named Robert Morris, who had been an initiator and in the vanguard of five movements within five years. He was a great manifesto writer, and he came up with this statement a few years ago:

"I propose to establish an art which anyone can do and does not need to be seen to be appreciated."

No standards whatever! This was *chaos*.

### THE PRESENT

A new undulation is beginning in the long horizontal line. Critics, who have long promoted the avant-garde, in its various manifestations, are agreed that it has now lost its force and that a historic change is occurring. The modern movement is changing to the postmodern; and an appreciation of *order,* a re-establishing of standards, seems to be asserting itself.

Originality as an end in itself eventually appears ridiculous; people are no longer much amused by novelty for novelty's sake. "Less" is not proving to be "more." "Less" is proving to be a "bore."

Realism, representation, and objectivity generally are coming back into favor with increasing numbers of the young.

The ablest no longer are content to get their inspiration from the subjective thinking and inventions of other artists. They want to go back to nature—to the horse's mouth! They are becoming aware that the objective world provides a far richer source of inspiration.

Museums, reflecting society's mood, have in increasing numbers been staging large exhibitions of traditional classics. For example:

Ancient Chinese Art and Tutankhamen's Treasures, traveling shows, originating at the National Gallery in Washington, that went around the country this past year.

Cézanne, this last year at the Museum of Modern Art in New York; Pompeian art, currently at Boston's Museum of Fine Arts.

In London: in 1975, Turner; in 1976, Constable.
All the above have drawn huge crowds daily. Today, museums all over report the largest attendance ever. In short, never before have so many people shown so much interest in the arts.

The arts, of course, reflect the changing moods of society. They do not initiate change, whatever artists may sometimes think. What are they reflecting?

 A conventional trend?
 A nostalgia for the reliable nourishment of the classics?
 A return to basic things?
 The security of order? You can answer as well as I.

### THE FUTURE

I find myself perforce in the position of the little girl who, when her mother asked her what she was drawing said: "God." "Why, you can't do that," her mother remonstrated, "nobody knows what God looks like." To which the little girl replied: "Well, they will when I get through!"

I expect that the present post-modern movement will continue, with growing interest in representative and recognizable work as noted in the last paragraph. And here I would like to emphasize that this does not mean reactionary stuffiness, nostalgia, or a slavish return to former styles.

It does mean a return to original sources, to the wide world about us with its myriad ramifications which are subject to infinite interpretation and reaction. It has through history inspired the most diverse responses. One has only to compare the Altamira cave drawings, Hokusai, Leonardo DaVinci, El Greco, Rubens, Milton Avery, Rodin and Brancusi—to name a few at random.

Many paths have been cut up the mountain. Many young people are now preparing to cut new ones.

This is about as far as I dare go. I just haven't got the assurance of that little girl.

# Chapter Notes

## Chapter 1

1. Aldro Thompson Hibbard (1886-1972) landscape painter; G.C. teacher-Rockport.
2. George B. Bridgman (1864-1943) G.C. teacher of anatomy in New York.
3. Alfred Easton Poor (1899-1988) architect.
4. John William Taylor, painter at Provincetown.
5. Mary Marvin Heaton Vorse (1888-1966) author and a guiding spirit of the Provincetown art colony.
6. Frank Shay (1888-1954) editor, publisher; founder of Provincetown Playhouse.
7. Peter Hunt (1896-1967) Provincetown painter.
8. Charles Hawthorne (1872-1930) Provincetown painter; G.C. early teacher.
9. George Elmer Brown (1871-1946) painter at Provincetown.
10. James Frederick Hopkins (1868-1931) painter at Provincetown.
11. Willard Leroy Metcalf (1858-1925) American Impressionist painter.
12. George Lyman Kittredge (1860-1924) Harvard professor; authority on Shakespeare.
13. John Livingston Lowes (1867-1945) Harvard professor.
14. Richardson White, sculptor.
15. Joseph Arthur Coletti (1898-1973) Boston sculptor.
16. Mrs. Thomas Stillwell Lamont.
17. Cornelia White (Mrs. Richardson White).
18. Later, Mrs. Charles C. Cunningham.
19. Arthur Boylston Nichols Sr. (1869-1955) investment counselor.
20. Nathaniel Saltonstall (1903-1971) architect; G.C. partner.
21. Undergraduate social club.
22. Philip Hale (1854-1931) painter; music and drama critic.

23 Frederick McCurdy Eaton (1905-1984), lawyer; diplomat.
24 Mrs. Frederick M. Eaton.
25 Bailey Aldrich, Chief Judge, U.S. Court of Appeals.
26 Margaret Homer Shurcliff (Mrs. Arthur Shurcliff) (1879-1959).
27 Among the others were McKim, Mead & White, Carrère & Hastings; Cass Gilbert, and Charles A. Platt. Their average age at the time was 45; Allen Cox was only 29.
28 Octavia Hill (1828-1912) English pioneer in housing reform.
29 W. Lincoln Boyden Jr., architect.
30 Cecil I. Wylde, architect.
31 Oliver Perry Morton, architect.
32 Angela Forbes Winthrop (Mrs. Frederic Winthrop).
33 Douglas Swain Byers, anthropologist; archaeologist.
34 Robert Giffen Stewart (1892-1948) early G.C. friend.
35 James Rowland Angell (1869-1949) president of Yale, 1921-1937.
36 Kenneth W. Pendar (1906-1972) diplomat; administrator, Daniel Chester French Museum.

# Chapter 2

1 James Hampden Robb, architect.
2 John Lavalle (1896-1971) painter and architect.
3 Donald Mitchell Oenslager (1902-1975) scene designer.
4 Jo Mielziner (1901-1976) stage designer.
5 Thomas I. Laughlin (1906-1965) painter.
6 John Erskine (1879-1951) author.
7 Harry Emerson Fosdick (1878-1969) clergyman and popular author.
8 Asa Gray (1810-1888) botanist, taxonomist; Harvard professor.
9 Hamilton Fish Armstrong (1893-1973) editor.
10 Walter Lippmann (1889-1974) journalist; writer.
11 Alfred E. Smith (1873-1944) Governor of New York, Democratic presidential nominee, 1928.
12 Felix Frankfurter (1882-1965) Harvard professor, 1914-1939; Associate Justice of the Supreme Court, 1939-1962.
13 Ferdinand Pecora (1882-1971) jurist.
14 J. Pierpoint Morgan Jr. (1867-1943) financier.
15 William Orville Douglas (1898-1980) Associate Justice of the Supreme Court, 1939-1975.
16 Thomas Carlyle (1795-1881) English historian and essayist.
17 Robert Frost (1874-1963) was 80 at the time of the first portrait.
18 David Thomson Watson McCord, poet.
19 Lilian Swann Saarinen, sculptor.

20 Mrs. John P. Marquand.
21 Charles Woolsey Cole (1906-1978) president of Amherst, 1946-1960.
22 Wendell Willkie (1892-1944) industrialist; GOP presidential nominee, 1940.
23 Walter Paul Paepcke (1896-1960) businessman; founder of Colorado's Aspen Institute.
24 Charles E. Wyzanski Jr., Federal judge.
25 Arthur Lee Kinsolving (1899-1977) Episcopal clergyman.

# Chapter 3

1 William Ernest Hocking (1873-1966) philosopher; Harvard professor.
2 John Kenneth Galbraith, economist; Harvard professor.
3 Arthur M. Schlesinger (1885-1965) historian; Harvard professor.
4 Alfred North Whitehead (1861-1947) philosopher; mathematician.
5 Ralph Barton Perry (1876-1957) philosopher; educator.
6 Lucien Price (1883-1964) writer; columnist *Boston Globe*.
7 Henry Copley Greene (1871-1951) author.
8 Bertrand Russell (1872-1970) British mathematician and philosopher.
9 T. North Whitehead (1892-1969) industrial psychologist.
10 Edward Waldo Forbes (1873-1969) director of the Fogg Museum, 1909-1944.
11 John Singer Sargent (1856-1925) celebrated American portraitist.
12 Cambridge literary and professional society.
13 James Byrne (1857-1942) lawyer; Harvard overseer; G.C.'s father-in-law.
14 Abbott Lawrence Lowell (1856-1942) president of Harvard, 1909-1933.
15 William Lawrence (1850-1941) Episcopal bishop of Massachusetts, 1893-1926.
16 Long-running Olsen and Johnson Broadway revue, with many audience "plants."
17 Lee McCanliss (1883-1968) lawyer.
18 Austin Lamont (1905-1969) physician; son of Thomas W. Lamont.
19 Mrs. Geoffrey Platt.
20 Priscilla Choate Hallowell (Mrs. Norwood Penrose Hallowell Jr.).
21 N. Penrose Hallowell Jr., master at Andover.
22 Lea Barnes Iselin (Mrs. John Jay Iselin).

## Chapter 4

1. Thomas William Lamont (1870-1948) banker.
2. Charles Sidney Hopkinson (1869-1962) painter.
3. Thomas Stillwell Lamont (1899-1967) banker.
4. Charles Crehore Cunningham (1910-1979) director, Wadsworth Atheneum, 1946-1966.
5. Russell Cornell Leffingwell (1878-1960) banker
6. Charles Gates Dawes (1865-1951) and Owen D. Young (1875-1962) promoted plans—1924 and 1930 respectively—to stabilize Germany's economy. Dawes was Coolidge's vice president 1925-1929.
7. John P. Marquand (1893-1960) noted novelist.
8. Robert A. Lovett, Secretary of Defense, 1951-1953.
9. John Carroll (1892-1959) New York painter.
10. Thomas Hart Benton (1889-1975) artist and muralist.
11. Reginald Marsh (1898-1954) painter.
12. John Hay Whitney (1904-1982) ambassador; publisher.
13. Skull & Bones, undergraduate social club at Yale.

## Chapter 5

1. Dean Gooderham Acheson (1893-1971) Truman's Secretary of State, 1949-1953.
2. John Lord O'Brian (1874-1973) lawyer.
3. Saul Steinberg, *New Yorker* artist; cartoonist.
4. James Bryant Conant (1893-1978) president of Harvard, 1933-1953.
5. Martina Brandegee Lawrence (Mrs. James Lawrence Jr.).
6. Joseph R. McCarthy (1908-1957) demagogic anti-communist; U.S. senator.
7. Katherine Cox, G.C.'s daughter.
8. Low-lying area near the Potomac; metaphor for "State's" miasmic attitude.
9. Dean Rusk, Secretary of State, 1961-1969.
10. Archibald MacLeish (1892-1982) poet; playwright; Harvard professor.
11. Jesse Holman Jones (1874-1956) banker; Secretary of Commerce, 1940-1945.
12. Harold L. Ickes (1874-1952) curmudgeonly Secretary of the Interior, 1933-1945.
13. Cordell Hull (1871-1955) Secretary of State, 1933-1944.

14 Lloyd Embry (1913-1979) portraitist.
15 William E. Jenner (1908-1985) right-wing Republican U.S. senator.
16 Tom Connally (1877-1963) majority leader of the U.S. senate.
17 Elihu Root (1845-1937) Secretary of War, 1899-1904; of State, 1905-1909.
18 James Reston, journalist, pundit, editor—all with the *New York Times*.
19 William S. Knudsen (1879-1948) industrialist, World War II production "czar."
20 Laurence Manuel Lombard, lawyer; philanthropist.
21 John Marshall Harlan (1899-1971) Associate Justice of the Supreme Court, 1955-1971.
22 Arthur Joseph Goldberg (1908-1990) diplomat; Associate Justice of the Supreme Court, 1962-1965.
23 Byron Raymond White, Associate Justice of the Supreme Court, 1962-1993.
24 John Singleton Copley (1738-1815) self-taught as a painter; loyalist.
25 Paul Mellon, philanthropist; art patron; trustee, National Gallery of Art.
26 Barry Bingham, publisher, *Louisville Courier-Journal*, trustee, National Gallery of Art.
27 John Nicholas Brown (1900-1979) educator; real estate executive.
28 Marvin Sherwood Sadik, director, National Portrait Gallery, 1969-1981.

## Chapter 6

1 George Catlett Marshall (1880-1959) World War II army Chief of Staff, and later Truman's Secretary of State, 1947-1948; and Defense, 1950-1951.
2 Anthony Eden (1897-1977) British Foreign Secretary; Prime Minister.
3 Brehon Burke Somervell (1892-1955) soldier; engineer.
4 Douglas MacArthur (1880-1964) General of the Army, 1944-1952; presidential aspirant.
5 W. Averell Harriman (1891-1986) diplomat; financier; Governor of New York, 1955-1959.
6 William Walton, architect; painter.
7 Jo Davidson (1883-1953) sculptor.
8 Paul Henry Nitze, Secretary of the Navy, 1963-1967; presidential advisor.

9 Anatoli F. Dobrynin, Soviet ambassador to the U.S., 1952-1955.
10 Philip C. Johnson, architect.
11 Arthur Judd, sculptor; artist.

## Chapter 7

1 Eero Saarinen (1910-1961) architect.
2 William Hayes Fogg Art Museum at Harvard.
3 Roger Merriman (1876-1945) historian; Harvard professor.
4 Alexandre Iacovleff (1887-1938) French painter.
5 William James Jr. (1882-1961) artist son of the psychologist; director, School of the Boston Museum of Fine Arts, 1913-1925.
6 John Franklin Enders, biologist.
7 Robert Strange McNamara, Secretary of Defense, 1961-1968; president of the World Bank.
8 International Bank for Reconstruction and Development.
9 Edward Sagendorph Mason, economist; Harvard professor.
10 Lucius Nathaniel Littauer legacy, accommodates Harvard's Economics Department.
11 Paul Freund (1909-1992) professor at Harvard Law School.
12 George F. Kennan, historian; diplomat; educator.
13 Bronson Alcott (1799-1888) educational and social reformer; transcendentalist.
14 Herbert Croly (1869-1930) journalist; *New Republic* editor, 1914-1930.
15 Marion A. Denman Frankfurter (Mrs. Felix Frankfurter) edited husband's non-judicial papers.
16 *Roosevelt and Frankfurter: Their Correspondence, 1928-45.* Boston: Little, Brown, 1968.
17 Louis Adelbert Toepfer, president Case Western Reserve University, 1970-1981.
18 Potter Stewart (1915-1985) Associate Justice of the Supreme Court, 1958-1981.
19 William Morris Hunt (1824-1879) influential U.S. Barbizon painter.
20 Louis Agassiz (1807-1873) geologist; zoologist; Harvard professor.
21 Archibald Cox, Solicitor General, 1961-1965; professor at Harvard Law School.
22 John Huston Finley (1863-1940) classicist; Harvard professor.
23 Daniel Patrick Moynihan, educator, U.S. Senator.
24 Elliot Lee Richardson, Nixon appointed him to several cabinet posts in the early 1970s, as Attorney General, Secretary of H.E.W., and Defense. He resigned as Attorney General over Watergate in the 1973

"Saturday Night Massacre." He was Ford's Secretary of Commerce, 1976-1977.
25  Robert R. Bowie, Harvard Law School professor, 1945-1955.
26  Julius Adams Stratton, president of M.I.T., 1959-1966.
27  Jerome Bert Wiesner, president of M.I.T., 1971-1980.
28  Howard Wesley Johnson, president of M.I.T., 1966-1971; of the M.I.T. Corporation, 1971-1983.
29  Derek Curtis Bok, president of Harvard, 1971-1991.
30  Francis Daniels Moore, physician; Harvard Medical School professor; Chief Surgeon at Peter Bent Brigham.
31  William Henry Claflin III, securities executive.

## Chapter 8

1  Earl Warren (1891-1974) Governor of California, 1943-1953; Chief Justice of the United States, 1953-1969.
2  Henry A. Kissinger, presidential advisor; Secretary of State, 1973-1977.
3  Hugh Doggett Scott (1900-1994) U.S. senator.
4  William Thaddeus Coleman Jr., lawyer; Secretary of Transportation, 1975-1977.
5  William Henry Hastie (1904-1976) Federal judge.
6  Robert Francis Seybolt (1888-1951) author.
7  C. Douglas Dillon, Secretary of the Treasury, 1961-1965.
8  Fred Lawrence Whipple, astro-physicist; Harvard professor.
9  Donald Howard Menzel, astronomer; Harvard professor.

## Chapter 9

1  Sons Benjamin and James.
2  Learned Hand (1872-1961) jurist, 1909-1951.
3  Thomas Walter Swan (1877-1948) Federal judge.
4  Mrs. Geoffrey Platt.
5  Classic burlesque and vaudeville house in Boston's Scollay Square.
6  Originally, a fraudulent brokerage.
7  Augustus Noble Hand (1869-1954) jurist.
8  Undergraduate social club at Harvard.
9  Hasty Pudding, undergraduate drama and social club at Harvard.
10  Francis Joseph Kernan (1859-1945) financier.
11  Oliver Wendell Holmes Jr. (1841-1935) Associate Justice of the Supreme Court, 1902-1932.
12  Wife of Arthur M. Schlesinger.

13 Sarita Choate Kellogg (Mrs. Frederic Kellogg).
14 Daughter-in-law Dagmar Henry Cox (Mrs. Benjamin Cox).

## Chapter 10

1 Rufino Tamayo, Mexican painter.
2 Roberto Matta Echaurren, Chilean painter.
3 Arshile Gorky (1904-1948) Russian Surrealist and Abstract Expressionist.
4 Joan Miró (1893-1983) Spaniard, whose lively and intricate fantasies are reminiscent of Klee.
5 Jackson Pollock (1912-1956) pioneer post-war Abstract Expressionist.
6 Willem deKooning, dynamic leader of post-war Abstract Expressionist movement.
7 Wassily Kandinsky (1866-1944) Russian painter, often called "the father of Abstract Expressionism."
8 Thomas Eakins (1844-1916) great Philadephia figural painter and teacher.
9 Robert Clarke Morris, art theorist.
10 Piet Mondrian (1872-1944) Dutch painter known for abstract geometric forms.
11 Claes Thure Oldenburg, sculptor.
12 Gabriella DeFarrari Jeppson, administrator, Institute for Contemporary Art.
13 Alfred Hamilton Barr Jr., art historian; since 1929 a force in New York's M.O.M.A.
14 Robert Motherwell, painter; writer and exponent of "automatic abstract art."
15 Richard Ammi Cutter, Associate Justice, Massachusetts Supreme Judicial Court.

## Chapter 11

1 Barnett Newman (1905-1970) painter known for "lyrical" abstraction.
2 Paul Klee (1879-1940) Swiss painter who refined Cubism into playful but highly disciplined compositions.
3 Theodore John Musho, painter as well as architect.
4 Denise Scott Brown.
5 Robert C. Vose (1873-1965) proprietor of venerable Boston art gallery.

6 Amedeo Modigliani (1884-1920) came to Paris from his native Italy early 1900s; died young.
 7 Francis A. Countway Memorial Library, at Harvard Medical School.
 8 Howard Bennet Sprague (1895-1970) heart specialist at Harvard Medical School and Massachusetts General Hospital.
 9 Edmund C. Tarbell (1862-1938) American Impressionist painter.
10 Augustus John (1878-1961) British portrait painter.

## Chapter 12

 1 Zechariah Chafee Jr. (1885-1957) professor at Harvard Law School.
 2 Warren Abner Seavey (1880-1966) professor at Harvard Law School.
 3 Reed Powell (1880-1955) professor at Harvard Law School.
 4 Kingman Brewster Jr., professor at Harvard Law School, 1950-1960; president of Yale, 1963-1977.
 5 Edward Hirsch Levi, president, University of Chicago, 1968-1975; Attorney General, 1975-1977.
 6 Mildred Helen McAfee Horton, president of Wellesley, 1936-1949.
 7 Richard Glenn Gettell, president of Mount Holyoke, 1957-1968.
 8 Harlan Henthorne Hatcher, president, University of Michigan 1951-1967.
 9 Cyrus Roberts Vance, Secretary of State, 1977-1980.
10 Militant African-American party of the 1960's.
11 F. Skiddy Von Stade Jr., dean of freshmen at Harvard, 1952-1976.
12 Henry Chauncey, assistant dean at Harvard, 1929-1943.
13 Nathan Marsh Pusey, president of Harvard, 1953-1971.
14 Theodore Ryland Sizer, headmaster at Andover, 1972-1981; educator at Brown University.
15 George William Stiles (1887-1949) portraitist.
16 William Warren Scranton, Governor of Pennsylvania, 1962-1967; presidential advisor.
17 Robert Alphonso Taft (1889-1953) U.S. senator; G.O.P. presidential candidate, 1982.
18 Students for a Democratic Society, an organization for protest in the 1960's.
19 Vincent Joseph Scully Jr., professor of art and architecture at Yale, now retired.
20 McGeorge Bundy, dean of Arts and Sciences at Harvard, 1953-1961; presidential advisor, 1961-1966.
21 Josef Albers (1888-1976) painter.
22 Chester Brooks Kerr, director of Yale University Press, 1959-1979.

## Chapter 13

1. *On Human Nature*, by Harvard social anthropologist Edward Osborne Wilson, Harvard University Press, 1978.
2. Lewis Thomas (1913-1993) author, educator, physician; director, Sloan-Kettering Cancer Center.
3. Transcendental Meditation. Hindu-inspired relaxation and meditation via a mantra initially conducted by an authorized maharishi.
4. Birthplace, in 1785, of Unitarianism in America.

## Chapter 14

1. G.C. is referring to Richard Nixon here.
2. New York agency for commissioning portrait art.
3. Harold Elstner Talbott (1888-1957) Secretary of the Air Force, 1953-1955.
4. Arthur Schlesinger, Jr., *Robert Kennedy and His Times*, Houghton Mifflin Co., 1978
5. Alexander Campbell Tener (1888-1965) judge.

## Chapter 15

1. Wilmarth Sheldon Lewis (1895-1979) editor, writer, and authority on Horace Walpole
2. Scroll & Key, undergraduate social club
3. "Lefty Louis" Rosenberg, one of the infamous "Four Gunmen" of a gangland homicide.
4. William Adams Delano (1874-1960) architect.
5. Harvey Williams Cushing (1869-1939) neurologist; neurosurgical pioneer.
6. Joseph Wright Alsop Jr. (1910-1989) journalist; columnist.

# Chronology

| | |
|---|---|
| 1906 | Born January 22 in Holyoke, Massachusetts, the son of Allen Howard and Katherine Gilbert Abbott Cox. The family moved to Boston two weeks later. |
| 1910 | Father bought Asa Gray house in Cambridge. |
| 1920 | Attended Cambridge High and Latin School; began study with Charles Hawthorne at Provincetown, Massachusetts. |
| 1923 | Attended Country Day School, Newton. |
| 1924 | Entered Harvard. |
| 1925 | Studied at Art Students League, New York with George Bridgman. |
| 1927 | Left Harvard at the end of his junior year. $1500 Harvard *Lampoon* art award for travel. |
| 1928–30 | Attended Boston Museum School. |
| 1929–31 | Attended MIT Architectural School. |
| 1931–36 | Practiced architecture with his father's firm of Putnam & Cox in Boston. Also painted some portrait commissions, travelled to Europe and studied briefly in Paris. Left architecture for full-time painting in 1936. |
| 1937 | Trip to Europe.<br>Married Phyllis Moira Byrne of New York City. |
| 1939 | Birth of Benjamin Cox. Exhibited "Portrait of a Boy", Boston Institute of Modern Art. |
| 1941 | Birth of Katherine Gilbert Abbott Cox (deceased). Exhibited at Carnegie International, Pittsburgh. "Directions in Painting." |

Portraits, Inc. gallery exhibition, New York City.
"Portrait Painters," *Life* magazine, February 3.

1942-45 Served as camouflage officer in Army Engineer Corps; left with rank of captain.

1942 Exhibited portrait of "My Wife, Phyllis" at first members' show, Boston Institute of Modern Art.

1943 Birth of James Byrne Cox.

1945 Margaret Brown Gallery, Boston, portrait exhibition.

1946 Birth of Phyllis (Poppy) Byrne Cox.
1st prize, members' show, Boston Institute of Modern Art for "Study Interior."
Exhibited at Addison Gallery, Andover, Mass: "Prize Winners, 1946"; and at Biennial of Virginia Museum of Fine Arts, Richmond, with "Basic #5."

1947 One-man show, St. Botolph Club, Boston.

1948 Exhibited at Art Institute of Chicago, and Virginia Museum of Fine Arts, biennial: "Basic #7."

1949 One-man show, Mount Holyoke Friends of Art, South Hadley, Mass.

M.V. Kohnstamm Prize, American Exhibition of Watercolors, Art Institute of Chicago for "Basic Forms."

1950 Exhibited "Maine Study" at Metropolitan Museum of Art, New York City "American Painting Today" exhibition.
Submitted "Crab" in show of contemporary artists at Springfield (Mass.) Museum of Fine Arts.

1951 Norman Wait Harris Bronze medal at 60th American Exhibition, Art Institute of Chicago for "Maine Study."
Exhibited "Basic #12" in "Contemporary American Painting," University of Illinois.

1952 Exhibited portrait of Phyllis Cox at first Boston Arts Festival.
One-man show, Margaret Brown Gallery.
Boston Society for Independent Artists at Museum of Fine Arts, Boston: "Dew."
*Time* Magazine, July 21: "Portraits by Cox."

1954 Cambridge Art Association, "Exhibition by Invitation."
Elected honorary member, Harvard chapter, Phi Beta Kappa.
Acting chairman, Department of Painting, Boston Museum School, to 1956.

*Art in America* Winter: "Three New England Artists" by Bartlett H. Hayes.

1955 Elected to American Academy of Arts and Sciences.
Executive Committee, Boston Arts Festival, through 1965 when elected president.
Pittsburgh International, Carnegie Institute: "Dr. William Weir."

1956 One-man show, Farnsworth Museum, Rockland, Maine.
Elected associate, National Academy of Design.

1957 Elected to National Institute of Arts and Letters.

1958 Farnsworth Art Museum, Tenth anniversary exhibition.

1959 Chairman, Jury Committee, Blanche E. Colman Awards, through 1983.
Popular prize, Boston Arts Festival for portrait of Robert Frost (Middlebury College).
*Time* Magazine, September 14, "Summer Prizewinners."

1961 Artist in residence, American Academy in Rome.
Exhibited at Corcoran Gallery of Art, Washington, D.C., 27th Biennial with portrait of Justice Felix Frankfurter.

1962 Received Signet medal, Harvard.
Named trustee, Saint-Gaudens Memorial, Cornish N.H.
Exhibited Justice Frankfurter's portrait at "American Painting 1962," Virginia Museum of Fine Arts.
*The New Republic,* April 16, "The Painting of the Sixties."

1963 Elected trustee, American Academy in Rome.
One-man show, Saint-Gaudens Memorial Museum.

1965 Appointed member of Massachusetts Art Commission. Served until 1980.

1966 One-man show, Newport Art Association, R.I.

1968 One-man show, Marion Arts Center, Cape Cod, Mass.
Century Association medal for portrait of Douglas Dillon.

1970 Elected Academician, National Academy of Design.
Cambridge Art Association exhibition: "Lily Saarinen and Gardner Cox."

1971 Cambridge Art Association exhibition: "Six Cambridge Artists."

1975 One-man show, Corcoran Gallery of Art: "Portraits by Gardner Cox."

| | |
|---|---|
| 1978 | Boston Athenaeum, in exhibit of "Boston Draughtsmen." August *Yankee* Magazine, "Oh My God, Do I Look Like That?" by Austin Stevens, photograph by Herbert Randle. National Portrait Gallery medal presented for service to the arts. |
| 1980 | Cambridge Art Association: "Art Week 1980." Copley Society of Boston Centennial exhibition: portrait of Prof. William E. Hocking. |
| 1981 | One-man show, Boston Athenaeum: "Portraits, Working Drawings and Bird Studies." Bicentennial exhibition, American Academy of Arts and Sciences, Cambridge: "Dr. John F. Enders" portrait. |
| 1984 | Francesca Anderson Gallery, Boston, "Drawing" exhibition. Publication of "Lawyers Painted by Gardner Cox" Harvard Law Library, Bernice Loss, editor. |
| 1987 | Cambridge Art Association fall exhibit: "Basic #7." Exhibited portrait of Robert Frost (Amherst College Library) at National Institute of Arts and Letters portrait show, New York City. |
| 1988 | Died January 14 in Cambridge. May 22 awarded honorary Doctorate in Fine Arts degree from Tufts University, received by Phyllis B. Cox. July *Smithsonian* magazine: "For a Portraitist, Making of Faces is a Hard Day's Fight" by Doug Stewart. Photographs by Richard Howard. September 29 – November 10, Memorial exhibition at St. Botolph Club. |
| 1989 | National Portrait Gallery Jurists Exhibition with portraits shown of Justice Felix Frankfurter, Chief Justice Earl Warren, Judge William Hastie, Judge Learned Hand, and Professor Zechariah Chafee. |

# Sources

Although this book required no formal bibliography, the following partial list of published sources may be useful to the reader. It begins with a *Life* magazine article in 1941, ends in 1989 with "Portrait of the American Law", by Frederick Voss, and includes the Memorial Exibition at the St. Botolph Club in 1988. With the latter notable exceptions, it does not include the many exhibition catalogues featuring Gardner Cox's work.

*Art in America,* Winter 1954. "Three New England Artists" by Bartlett H. Hayes

*Harvard Law School Bulletin,* Fall 1980. "Portrait of the Artist."

*Life,* "Portrait Painters" February 3, 1941.

*Maine Times,* November 15, 1985. "The Portrait Painters."

*New Republic,* April 16, 1952. "The Painting of the Sixties."

*Newsweek,* June 15, 1953. "Portraits by Cox."

*People,* April 10, 1978. "Kissinger excercises a veto on his portrait."

*Smithsonian,* July, 1988. "For a Portraitist, Making a Face Is a Hard Day's Fight" by Doug Stewart. Photographs by Richard Howard.

*Time,* July 21, 1952. "Experiments in New England."

*Time,* September 14, 1954. "Summer Prizewinners."

*Yankee,* August 1978. "Oh My God, Do I Look Like That?" by Austin Stevens, photographs by Herbert Randle.

"Gardner Cox In Memoriam: 1906-1988." Exhibition catalogue September 29-November 10, 1988. St. Botolph Club, Boston. With essays by Robert Taylor and David McCord.

"Lawyers Painted by Gardner Cox", Bernice Loss, editor. Harvard Law Library, 1984.

"Portrait of the American Law." Frederick S, Voss. National Portrait Gallery, 1989.

# Index

Abbott, Dora  18
Acheson, Dean Gooderham  41,
   60, 90-3, 94-103, 120, 127,
   138-9, 153-4, 164, 215
Aldrich, Bailey  15, 60, 128-9,
   132-3, 166, 169, 195-7, 214
Angell, James Rowland  24, 236
Armstrong, Hamilton  39, 64
Augusta, George  210-1
Avery, Milton  277

Barnes, A. Edward  255
Bingham, Barry  109, 194-5
Bok, Derek Curtis  147
Bowie, Robert R.  146
Boyden, W. Lincoln, Jr.  21
Brancusi, Constantin  277
Brewster, Constance  224-5, 227
Brewster, Kingman, Jr.  xvi, 158,
   221-36, 247, 253, 262
Brewster, Marie Louise  225,
   235-6
Bridgman, George B.  3
Brown, Denise Scott  203
Brown, George Elmer  5
Brown, John Nicholas  109
Brown, Robert  xv, xvi
Bryce, Ivor  26, 64
Bryce, Sheila Byrne (Mrs. Ivor)
   26, 64, 74

Burlingham, Charles  65
Byers, Douglas Swain  23
Byrne, Beatrice  64
Byrne, James  62-3, 65-71, 73-4
Byrne, Mrs. James  63-4, 66-7,
   73-4
Byrne, Jimmy and June,  74-5,
   132

Cabot, Maude  127
Calder, Alexander  160, 276
Caner, Johnny  13-4
Carrère & Hastings  16
Carroll, John  85
Carter, Jimmy  xiii, 154, 161,
   163-5, 197
Cézanne, Paul  33, 98, 194, 214,
   277
Chafee, Zechariah, Jr.  221
Chaplin, Oona O'Neill (Mrs.
   Charlie)  4, 9
Christo  189
Churchill, John  14
Claflin, William H.  147
Cole, Charles W.  44-5
Coleman, William Thaddeus, Jr.
   154, 165-6
Conant, James Bryant  92, 94,
   221, 247
Constable, John  277

Coving, Ian 208
Cox, Allen Howard xiii-iv, 11, 16, 18, 20, 35, 38, 39-40, 46
Cox, Archibald 146-7
Cox, Benjamin xi, xiv-v, 33-5, 37, 74, 85, 87-8, 170, 182, 184
Cox, [Children] 128, 215
Cox, Dagmar Henry (Mrs. Benjamin) 181, 195
Cox, Danny 14
Cox, Gardner *passim*
Cox, [Grandfather], xiv, 18-20, 38
Cox, James xi, xiv-v, 35, 87-8, 170, 181-4
Cox, Kate 33, 35, 85, 94, 181, 242, 262
Cox, Katherine Gilbert Abbott (Mrs. Allen Howard) xiii-iv, 11, 17, 18, 38-9, 53-4, 198
Cox, Phyllis Byrne (Mrs. Gardner) 23-4, 26-7, 31, 33-6, 38-40, 44, 62-4, 66-8, 70, 75, 82-5, 158, 170, 181, 184, 208, 238
Cox, Poppy (Koch) xi, 76, 85, 181, 183, 193, 224, 235
Cunningham, Charles Crehore 79
Cushing, Harvey Williams 268-9
Cutter, Richard Ammi 197

Dalton, Fratty 12
Dalton, Kay 12
Deering, Joseph 47
Degas, Edgar 198, 262
de Kooning, Willem 186, 191, 215
Delano & Aldrich 264
Donatello 212
Douglas, William Orville 42, 133
Driver, Phoebe Barnes *passim*

Eakins, Thomas 198, 211
Eaton, Frederick McCurdy 15, 89, 104
Eaton, Justine (Mrs. Frederick M.) 15
Eden, Anthony 113-4, 119
Eisenhower, Dwight D. 130, 184, 236, 255-6
El Greco 188, 209, 216, 277
Embry, Lloyd 97-8, 102, 104-5
Enders, John Franklin 131, 147
Erskine, Graham 31
Erskine, John 31

Ferguson, Marian 18
Fink, Reggie 176
Finley, John Huston 146
Fleming, Ian 26
Forbes, Waldo 59
Ford, Gerald R. 158, 162-3, 169*n*, 238, 247
Fosdick, Harry Emerson 35
Frankfurter, Felix 41-3, 60, 63, 90, 108, 133-45, 193, 215, 252
Frankfurter, Marion A. Denman (Mrs. Felix) 136-41
French, Daniel Chester 5, 279*n*
Frost, Robert 43-53, 57-8, 195, 215, 218

Galbraith, John Kenneth 53, 132, 146, 152
Gettell, Richard Glenn 221
Gilbert, Cass 16-8
Giotto 188
Goldberg, Arthur 108, 144, 196
Goodhue, Bertram 250
Gorky, Arshile 186
Goya 188, 209
Graves, Michael 201
Graves, Phil 14

Greene, Copley  57

Hale, Nancy  14-5
Hale, Philip  15
Hallowell, Norwood Penrose, Jr.
    76-7, 177
Hallowell, Priscilla Choate (Mrs.
    Norwood Penrose, Jr.)  75-6,
    177
Hand, Augustus Noble, 175-6
Hand, Learned  62, 135, 138,
    150, 172-9, 261
Harlan, John  108
Harriman, Pamela  120, 123-6
Harriman, William Averell  45,
    87, 89, 95, 98, 109, 120-6,
    153-4, 257
Hastie, William Henry  166, 221
Hatcher, Harlan Henthorne  221
Hawthorne, Charles  5-6, 212
Hibbard, Aldro Thompson  3, 7
Hocking, Agnes Boyle O'Reilly
    (Mrs. William E.)  53-6
Hocking, William Ernest  53-7, 60
Hokusai  277
Hopkins, James Frederick  5
Hopkinson, Charles Sidney  78,
    146, 174, 217
Horton, Mildred Helen McAfee
    221
Hunt, Peter  4-5
Hunt, William Morris  146

Ickes, Harold L.  97-8
Iselin, John Jay  153
Iselin, Lea Barnes  76

Jaegel, John  185-7, 193-4
John, Augustus  211
Johnson, Howard  146
Johnson, Philip  125-6
Judd, Arthur  126

Kandinsky, Wassily  186, 200
Kellogg, Sarita Choate
    (Mrs. Frederic)  180-1
Kennan, George  134
Kennedy, John F.  xiii, 138-9, 274
Kennedy, Robert  xiii, 165, 255-7
Kernan, Francis Joseph  177
Kernan, Maude (Mrs. Francis J.)
    177
Kinsolving, Arthur Lee  52
Kissinger, Henry A.  xiii, xvi, 59,
    94, 109, 129, 133, 148, 151-
    68, 237-8
Kissinger, Nancy  129, 153,
    156-7, 160, 163-5, 197
Kittredge, George Lyman  12
Klee, Paul  201
Koch, Poppy  (see Cox)

Lamont, Austin  75, 78, 84, 87-8
Lamont, Ellie
    (Mrs. Thomas Stillwell)  12
Lamont, Ellie (later, Mrs. Charles
    C. Cunningham)  13
Lamont, Lansing  13, 75
Lamont, Teddy  13
Lamont, Thomas Stillwell  79
Lamont, Thomas William  78-9,
    80-4, 171, 177
Laughlin, Thomas I.  29
Lavalle, John  28-9
Lawrence, Martina Brandegee
    (Mrs. James, Jr.)  92, 180-1
László, Moholy-Nagy  210
Leonardo da Vinci  277
Levi, Edward Hirsch  xvi, 144,
    221, 223, 235, 247-54
Lewis, Ann Auchincloss
    (Mrs. Sheldon W.)  271
Lewis, Dudley  75
Lewis, Wilmarth Sheldon  94-5,
    139-40, 228, 255, 261-71

Lipchitz, Jacques  160
Lippmann, Faye Albertson
  (Mrs. Walter)  81, 135
Lippmann, Helen Byrne
  (Mrs. Walter)  39-40, 64, 74,
  76, 135-6
Lippmann, Walter  39-42, 64, 80,
  133-6, 139, 152, 176, 178,
  206
Lombard, Laurence Manuel
  104, 107, 272
Lovett, Robert A.  85-9, 94, 117,
  119
Lowell, Amy  17
Lowell, Guy  16
Lowes, John L.  12

Marquand, Adelaide  44, 83
Marquand, John P.  83
Marshall, George Catlett  85, 87,
  89-90, 94, 99, 110-5, 116-21
Mason, Edward Sagendorph
  132, 167, 171
Matta Echaurren, Roberto  186
McAlpin, Molly Angell
  (Mrs. Ronnie)  24
McAlpin, Ronnie  24
McCanliss, Lee  71, 73
McCord, David  43, 48, 145,
  214-5
McKim, Mead & White  16
McKim, White & Burnham  250
McMurtry, Sam  202
McNamara, Robert Strange  121,
  131-2, 171
Merriman, Roger  129-30
Metcalf, Willard Leroy  7
Michelangelo  3, 274
Mielziner, Jo  28, 31
Miró, Joan  186-7, 194
Modigliani, Amedeo  209-10
Mondrian, Piet  189, 193-4, 200,
  210, 216

Moore, Francis Daniels  147,
  210-11
Moore, Frank  250
Moore, Henry  160
Morris, Robert  188, 276
Morton, Oliver  21-2
Motherwell, Robert  191
Moynihan, Daniel Patrick  146
Murchie, Aggie  15
Musho, Theodore John  201

Newman, Barnett  200
Nichols, Arthur Boylston, Sr.  13
Nichols, Rose  17

O'Brian, John Lord  90-1, 103-7
Oenslager, Donald Mitchell  28
Oldenburg, Claes  189-90, 232-3
O'Neill, Eugene  4, 8-9
O'Neill, Irene (Mrs. Eugene)  4, 9

Parsons, John & Katherine  94,
  270
Pei, I. M.  125, 201
Pendar, Kenneth W.  26
Perry, Ralph Barton  54, 60
Picasso, Pablo  87, 122, 186-7,
  191, 214
Piero della Francesca  198
Pierson, Charles  24
Platt, Charles  17, 22
Platt, Geoffrey  22, 76, 95, 125,
  153, 160
Platt, Helen (Mrs. Geoffrey)  75,
  160, 175
Pollock, Jackson  186, 191,
  193-5, 199-200, 215-6, 274
Pool, Lawrence  274
Poor, Alfred Easton  4
Porter, Isabelle  22
Powell, Reed  221
Pratt, Charles  86
Price, Lucien  56

Pusey, Nathan Marsh  228, 254
Putnam, William E.  16-7, 21

Rembrandt  79, 188, 193, 198-9, 216-7, 274
Renoir, Pierre Auguste  211-2
Richardson, Elliot Lee  146
Robb, James Hampden  28-9, 31, 33-4
Rockefeller, John D.  160, 250
Rockefeller, Happy  162
Rockefeller, Nelson  152-4, 157, 160, 162-3, 236, 238
Rodin, Auguste  277
Roosevelt, Franklin D.  42, 45, 52, 99, 114, 118, 121, 141
Roosevelt, Theodore  67
Ross, Marie  209
Rowlandson, Thomas  272
Rubens, Peter Paul  277
Rusk, Dean  94, 138-9, 164
Ryder, Albert Pinkham  215

Saarinen, Eero  127, 249-50
Saarinen, Lilian Swann  43, 127-8, 152, 203
Sadik, Marvin Sherwood  109, 127-8, 154
Saint-Gaudens, Augustus  151, 250
Saltonstall, Nathaniel  14-5, 21
Sargent, John Singer  146, 199, 209-10, 250
Sassoon, Siegfried  64
Schlesinger, Arthur M., Jr.  53, 113
Schlesinger, Mrs. Arthur M.  180-1, 195
Scott, Dick  23-4
Scott, Sally T.  xi
Scott, Susie  75
Scranton, William Warren  228, 237-8, 264
Scully, Vincent Joseph, Jr.  233

Seale, Bobby  222-4
Sears, Jean  24
Seavey, Warren A.  221
Shay, Fern  8-9
Shay, Frank  4, 8-9
Shurcliff, Margaret Homer (Mrs. Arthur)  16
Sizer, Theodore Ryland  228
Sizer, "Tubby"  228
Stendahl, Krister  147
Stern, Frank  59
Stewart, Potter  145, 148
Stewart, Robert Giffen  23
Stratton, Jay  146

Talbott, Harold Elstner  130, 255-7, 259
Tamayo, Rufino  186
Tarbell, Frank Bigelow  210
Taylor, John  4, 7
Taylor, Robert  xv
Tener, Alexander Campbell  257-60
Thomas, Dylan  142
Thorn, George Widmer  210
Titian  193, 216-7
Toepfer, Louis Adelbert  141, 144
Truman, Harry  99
Turner, J.M.W.  194, 277

Valliant, Marian  180
Vance, Cyrus  222, 228, 264
Van Gogh, Vincent  98, 122,
Velásquez, Diego  188, 198-9
Venturi, Robert  201-4
Von Stade, F. Skiddy, Jr.  223
Vorse, Ellen  7, 10
Vorse, Heaton  7
Vorse, Mary Marvin Heaton  4, 7-10

Warren, Earl  42, 108, 133, 148-51, 171

Wheeler children   13
Wheelwright, Joe   14-5
White, Byron   108
White, Cornelia "Neilly"
   (Mrs. Richardson)   12, 21-3, 75
White, Peter   12-3
White, Richardson   12, 21-3
Whitehead, Alfred North   54-61, 92, 94, 96
Whitehead, North   58
Whitney, Jock   86
Wiesner, Jerome Bert   146
Wilson, Edward Osborne   xvi, 239-42

Winthrop, Angela
   (Mrs. Frederick)   21, 24
Winthrop, Frederick   21
Wister, Bill   24
Worrall, Harry, John & Maisie   77
Wright & Sullivan   202
Wylde, Cecil I.   21
Wyzanski, Charles E., Jr.   52, 146, 174, 214

Zerbe, Karl   185, 213

Typography by Sarah F. Bauhan, Portsmouth, New Hampshire
in Monotype Sabon with titles in Monotype Perpetua.
Sketches reproduced from the originals taken from Gardner Cox's
notebooks, and these and other illustrations photographed in fine-line
and 300-line screen for printing by offset lithography.
Printed at The Stinehour Press, Lunenburg, Vermont
on 70 lb. Mohawk Opaque Text.
Bound by the New Hampshire Bindery, Concord, New Hampshire.
Designed by W. L. Bauhan and Sarah F. Bauhan.
Edited by W. L. Bauhan and W. W. Keen James.